40

12

THEORY CONSTRUCTION AND THE SOCIOLOGY OF THE FAMILY

THEORY CONSTRUCTION AND THE SOCIOLOGY OF THE FAMILY

Wesley R. Burr

A Wiley-Interscience Publication

JOHN WILEY & SONS, NEW YORK · LONDON · SYDNEY · TORONTO

Copyright © 1973, by John Wiley & Sons, Inc.

All rights reserved. Published simultaneously in Canada.

No part of this book may be reproduced by any means, nor transmitted, nor translated into a machine language without the written permission of the publisher.

Library of Congress Cataloging in Publication Data

Burr, Wesley R 1936–
    Theory construction and the sociology of the family.

    "A Wiley-Interscience publication."
    1. Family. 2. Social sciences—Methodology.
I. Title.
HQ728.B87   301.42′01′8   73-1680
ISBN 0-471-12513-X

Printed in the United States of America

10-9 8 7 6 5 4 3 2

To
Ruth Joy

PREFACE

The social sciences have made major progress in the past two decades in the methodology of theorizing. Books such as those by Homans (1951), Simon (1951), and Zetterberg (1954) pioneered in explaining how to have theoretical explanation with social variables, and this work was later systematically built upon by Zetterberg (1963, 1965), Homans (1964, 1964a), Stinchcombe (1968), Dubin (1969), and Blalock (1969). These methodologists have gradually found ways to make the highly abstract ideas in the philosophy of science literature usable by the social scientist.

This progress in the methodology of theorizing has created a unique incongruity in the social science literature. Most of the theoretical ideas were stated before these advances were made, and the field is thus now able to state theories in a more sophisticated way than most of them are formed. The result is that not only has a need been created to reformulate earlier theoretical formulations to clarify, systematize, and integrate them, but we now have the methodological tools to do it. Blalock comments about this process:

> The careful reworking of verbal theories is undoubtedly one of the most challenging tasks confronting us. The major portion of this enterprise will undoubtedly consist of clarifying concepts; eliminating or consolidating variables, translating existing verbal theories into common languages, searching the literature for propositions, and looking for implicit assumptions connecting the major propositions in important theoretical works [1969:27].

This book is the first report of an ongoing project that is attempting to undertake such theoretical reformulation. The project was begun in 1968 at Portland State University and has been continuing since 1969 at Brigham Young University. The long-term goals of this project are (1) to identify theoretical propositions that seem to be useful in understanding processes in the social institution of the family, (2) to analyze the nature of these propositions to determine what is asserted and the circumstances under which they are asserted to occur, (3) if there is no defensible way to improve the original theoretical formulations, an attempt is made to integrate them with other theoretical ideas when this is possible, (4) to improve the propositions if possible by such techniques as clarifying concepts or relationships, relabeling variables when they are the same as other variables but have different labels, identifying clearly those assertions that are made in the formulation and those that are not, and identifying the logical relationship of the propositions with other propositions, (5) to examine the relevant empirical data to determine the amount of proof that exists either for or against various aspects of the theoretical ideas, (6) to identify how the theoretical ideas can be used in applied professions such as teaching, counseling, and community action, and (7) to develop computer simulations with some of the theoretical models.

The present book reports those current theoretical reformulations that are in a sufficiently complete form that they can be shared. *They should not, however, be viewed as completed products. They are tentative statements that are written only to be revised, expanded, and modified by further improvements in theorizing and additional empirical tests.* I hope this work represents progress beyond what has been done in the past in the areas that are covered, but the very nature of scientific theories make them tentative, frequently speculative, and continually subject to revision in the light of still undisclosed data. There are many other theoretical ideas about family processes that are not included in this book. Some of them have been worked with in the project, but the reformulations are too premature to be included here. Numerous other theories have not yet been worked with because of the limited resources in the project. It should also be mentioned that virtually nothing is done in this book with the goals of identifying how the theoretical ideas can be used in applied professions and developing computer simulations. I hope these goals will be addressed in the future.

There are several reasons why this book is being published while the theories are still in the process of being developed. First, it seems important to share the work that has been done. Second, I hope that this book can be used as a vehicle to involve others in the same type of theory building either because they like what I have done and want to become involved in it or because they are so enraged by the poor quality of this work that they think someone ought to do it right. A third reason is that it will hopefully set the stage for a larger group of theorists to publish a more comprehensive statement of family theory in a multivolume work. I was tempted to title this volume *Famology: Theory Building and Testing with Family Variables*, but my colleagues persuaded me that such a presumptuous title was premature. Perhaps it won't be if a large group of theorists can be brought together to develop a relatively comprehensive statement of family theories.

There are two major sections in this book. The first is methodological in that it describes the techniques that are used in this project to rework theories. Chapter 1 identifies the way the term "theory" is used and Chapter 2 discusses the methodology of using empirical data to assess the validity of the ideas in this type of theory. This methodological section seems to be necessary for several reasons. First, there is a great deal of variability in the way the term theory is used in the modern social sciences and since this book is more than anything else a book about theory it is imperative that the nature of theory is explicated in some detail. Moreover, the recent literature on the methodology of theorizing has identified a number of characteristics of theory that are important, but this literature is widely scattered and some of it is highly technical. Chapter 1 is an attempt to correct these deficiencies by providing a comprehensive explanation of the nature of theory that does not demand mathematical or philosophical background. A third reason the methodological section seems useful is that several innovations are made in this project, such as paying attention to the "amount of influence" in a causal relationship. These are not found in other literature, but they are explained in this chapter.

The second section of this book is the substantive part, which analyzes theory. It is highly selective in that only a very limited group of theoretical ideas are examined, but I hope this type of reformulation, integration, and extension of theory will expand in the future. The particular areas that are included were selected because (*a*) they represent a broad spectrum of ideas that are all related to the family, (*b*) there have been theoretical ideas formulated in the past in each of the areas, and (*c*) there is a body of empirical research that can be used to begin assessing the validity of the ideas in these areas. As can be seen in these chapters, the empirical data are meager in most instances, but this will probably be corrected in the future.

If this project is to be viewed in its proper perspective, several comments should also be made about its origin. It grew out of a rather sizable project at the University of Minnesota, which has come to be known as the Inventory of Research on Marriage and Family Behavior. Reuben Hill and his associates began in the early 1950s to systematically collect empirical studies and work toward theory building. The goals of that project were outlined by Hill and Simpson (1957) as follows:

1. The identification of the empirical foci which have been investigated by marriage and family researchers.
2. The classification and summarization of the research findings among these foci.
3. The identification of the competing frames-of-reference which have been used as theoretical approaches by marriage and family researchers.

4. The isolation of the major conceptual apparatus of each of the frameworks that are identified.

5. The theoretical organization, where possible, of research findings into a set of interrelated hypotheses and propositions [1957:89].

My graduate study at the University of Minnesota exposed me to the "Inventory," and this experience provided the initial stimuli that led to the current project. An examination of the goals of this project and the goals of the Inventory will reveal considerable similarity. The major differences between them is that great attention has been given by the Minnesota group to isolating and examining conceptual frameworks and strategies of theorizing to facilitate theory building. In the present project considerable attention has been given to having clearly identified definitions of concepts, and care is exercised to not use concepts that are incompatible in one theoretical formulation. However, little attention is focused on conceptual frameworks themselves, and little attention is given to the identification of different strategies of theorizing. Instead, the emphasis is on identifying theoretical formulations irrespective of whether they are inductively or deductively acquired, and irrespective of any particular conceptual framework, and then (*a*) analyzing the nature of these formulations, (*b*) reworking them if the analysis indicates they can be improved, and (*c*) analyzing the empirical data that are of value in assessing the validity of these ideas.

There are many individuals to whom one becomes indebted while writing a book such as this. Most important are those who provide emotional support and encouragement while the author travails this long in a task so difficult. Ruth Joy and our four children are, I think, aware of my gratitude. I also appreciate the administrative support of J. Joel Moss and Blaine R. Porter for protecting my time, and the Research Division of Brigham Young University for providing some release time during the academic year of 1971–1972 to work on this project. Boyd C. Rollins was a most helpful reactor to several of the chapters and F. Ivan Nye and his students at Washington State University provided a long list of helpful suggestions after using most of the manuscript in graduate seminar. Reuben Hill's thorough critiques of several of the chapters and his advice about such things as the presentation of the material have been most useful. A long list of secretaries were helpful in translating my hieroglyphics into the English language, but Mary Sechrest and Susan Mickelsen both did yeoman duty as each of them typed the entire manuscript.

December 1971
Brigham Young University, Provo, Utah   **Wesley R. Burr**

CONTENTS

xi

Chapter 5
THE EFFECTS OF PREMARITAL FACTORS ON
MARRIAGE

FIGURES

TABLES

THEORY CONSTRUCTION AND THE SOCIOLOGY
OF THE FAMILY

CHAPTER 1

THE NATURE OF
DEDUCTIVE THEORY

There is an interesting paradox in the way the term "theory" is used in the modern social sciences. Although it is almost universally agreed that science can progress only as fast as theories are developed, tested, and revised, social scientists have not agreed on what a theory is. A number of scholars have recognized these differences and attempted to develop typologies of theories. For example, Nagel (1961:25–40) identified four different types of scientific explanation: deductive, mechanical, genetic, and functional or teleological explanation. Zetterberg (1965) identified three ways "theory" has been used in sociological classics, sociological criticism, and theoretical sociology. His theoretical sociology is virtually the same as Nagel's deductive method, but his other two are uniquely different uses of the term. Another approach is seen in the work of symbolic interactionists such as Blumer (1956), Bolton (1963), and Wilson (1970), who argue that when a symbolic interactionist approach is used the theory must be an "interpretive scheme" (Wilson, 1970:707).

These differences in the way the term theory is used are not just substantive differences. They are unique ways of defining what theory is, and not only does the process of theorizing differ, but the end products are very different. This can be illustrated by comparing Parsons' (1951) use of "theory" with what most philosophers of science and methodologists call deductive theory.[1] Parsons views theory as an elaborate set of terms or concepts that are designed to analyze social systems. Each unique analysis of a specific system is viewed as a theoretical analysis, and the lasting scientific contribution of the approach is the set of concepts that are used in understanding the processes within the various systems. In the deductive method that is propounded by such social scientists as Zetterberg (1965) and Homans (1964), the goal of theorizing is to acquire "laws" about nature that can be used to explain and predict more specific phenomena.

The fact that there are so many different ways to define "theory" means that it is necessary to identify its meaning whenever it is used. Since this book is an attempt to synthesize, integrate, and analyze the proof of a number of "theoretical" ideas it seems imperative to explain just how this term is used here. It would be convenient to state that the *deductive* type of theory is used and have this label communicate everything that is denoted and connoted by the term; however, this would not communicate very effectively what is meant by the term theory. There are two major reasons that it is insufficient to merely state that deductive theory is the method of theorizing that is used.

First, there are a number of different ways to use many of the terms that are employed as parts of deductive theory. For example, there are substantial differences of opinion among philosophers of science and research methodologists on how such components of deductive theory as concepts, proposition, causality, and explanation are defined. This means that merely stating that one is using deductive theory leaves a great deal of ambiguity. The other reason it is necessary to do more than just state that deductive theory is being used is that the literature that discusses the nature of deductive theory is highly fragmented. Some parts of deductive theory are discussed in some sources and other parts are discussed only in other references. There is no single reference that discusses all of the major components of deductive theory in a way that social scientists can use. It is likely that many individuals who are interested in the substantive theories that are analyzed in this book will not have been exposed to all of these disjointed discussions, and this argues for a relatively extensive explanation of just what is meant by deductive theory.

Since deductive theory is the type of theory that is used in this book, and since there is a need for a brief yet relatively comprehensive explanation of what deductive theory is, this first chapter is an attempt to analyze the nature of deductive theory. The first section of the chapter is a brief description of what deductive theory is and an illustration of how it is used. The second section expands on the first section with a more thorough analysis of the basic components of deductive theory. This expanded analysis of the components of deductive theory describes in detail many of the terms that are used but not defined or described in the attempt to briefly describe deductive theory. Moreover, there are some differences of opinion among philosophers and methodologists on which terms should be used to describe these components, and an attempt is made in this section to identify which of these terms are used in the subsequent chapters. The last section of Chapter 1 discusses a number of complex issues about deductive theory where there are major differences in point of view among philosophers and methodologists. These issues are not discussed with the objective of resolving them in any final form, but before anyone can use deductive theory it is necessary that some position be taken on these issues. Hence the objective of this section is to identify the issues and to explain which of the various positions are taken in this book.

Deductive Theory

Deductive theory can be described briefly as an attempt to increase human understanding by providing explanations of why certain things occur. It provides this explanation by having a set of propositions and then deducing that, if these propositions are true, and if certain other conditions are met, certain specific and observable events occur. The more specific events are then "explained" by the more general propositions that have been used as premises in deducing that the specific events occur. The explanation is only as valid as the propositions and logic that are used in the deduction, but one of the goals of science is to gradually eliminate invalid propositions and increase the number of useful, valid ones. Braithwaite describes deductive theory as follows:

A deductive system in which observable consequences logically follow from the connection of observed facts with the set of fundamental hypotheses of the system. . . .

Every deductive system consists of a set of propositions (to be called the *initial propositions*) from which all the other propositions (to be called the *deduced propositions*) follow according to logical principles. Some of these propositions follow immediately or mediately from the set of initial propositions. Every deduced proposition in a deductive system occurs at the end of a chain of deductive steps which starts with the set of initial propositions. The chain which leads to any particular proposition may be short or long, but it is always of a finite length, so that the proposition is reached after a limited number of steps of immediate deduction (1953:22).

This phenomenon of deductive explanation can be illustrated with some ideas about one factor that probably influences premarital sexual permissiveness. This example is presented without extensive explanation of the definitions of the variables or the nature of the relationships in the propositions because the objective here is to illustrate deductive explanation rather than develop a fully adequate theoretical model.

From Christensen's (1969) normative theory of sexual permissiveness the following proposition may be stated:

PROPOSITION 1.1: The content of social norms (beliefs about what people should or should not do) influences the behavior in the group where they occur so the behavior tends to conform to the norms.

A second proposition can be deduced if there is variation in the degree to which the social norms in a group proscribe premarital sexual permissiveness, and if proposition 1.1 is true and all other phenomena are invariant.

PROPOSITION 1.2:   The amount that social norms in a group proscribe premarital sexual permissiveness influences the amount of premarital sexual permissiveness, and this is an inverse relationship.

From proposition 1.2 it can be further deduced that if the social norms in the United States proscribe premarital sexual permissiveness more than the norms in Scandinavia, then, assuming proposition 1.2 is true and all other phenomena are invariant, the amount of premarital sexual permissiveness is higher in Scandinavia than it is in the United States.

It would be possible to gather empirical support either for or against the validity of this deduction by measuring the amount of sexual permissiveness in a representative sample of individuals in each of these countries and comparing them. This could be done by selecting a measuring instrument such as Reiss' (1964) Premarital Sexual Permissiveness Scale and testing a hypothesis such as the following one:

HYPOTHESIS 1.3:   Scores on the Reiss Premarital Sexual Permissiveness scale are higher in Scandinavia than in the United States.

The scores obtained in the samples are then compared, and the hypothesis is either accepted or rejected. Acceptance provides some empirical evidence that the propositions are valid, whereas rejection provides some evidence that one or more of the propositions or the logic or assumptions used in the deductions are invalid.

In this example the more specific deductions are "explained" by the more abstract propositions that are used as premises in the deductions. The abstract propositions provide the explanation as to why sexual permissiveness is different in the two countries involved. It is different because there are differences in the norms about sexual permissiveness and norms about premarital sexual permissiveness influence sexual permissiveness.

This example can be diagramed in a way that can economically communicate some very complex theoretical ideas. Figure 1.1 shows each of the three propositions in the example and the testable hypothesis. The variables are named and the propositions are numbered. The arrows with the solid lines indicate the direction of influence and the dotted lines indicate the logical connections between the propositions.

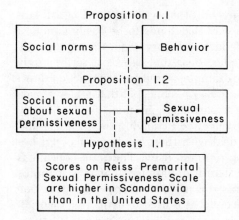

Figure 1.1 A minitheory of sexual permissiveness.

Components of Deductive Theory

The description of the nature of deductive theory in the previous section is nothing more than a brief introduction to deductive theory. Many components of deductive theory that were referred to are highly technical terms, and it is imperative that they be carefully defined. For example, the propositions that are used in deductive theories are intricate statements that make assertions about variables, and these variables are certain types of concepts. This means that it is necessary to understand the meaning of terms such as "concept" and "variable" before it is possible to accurately understand what propositions are. Components of deductive theory defined and discussed in the following sections include concepts, variables, relationships, propositions, logical relationships between propositions, and the principle of ceteris paribus.

Concepts

Concepts are one of the most elementary components of deductive theory. A concept is a term or word. It symbolizes some aspect of reality that can be thought about and communicated. Concepts are linguistic symbols that represent an ideational phenomenon. Dubin (1969: Ch. 3) uses "unit" rather than "concept" to denote what is usually referred to by the term concept. However, there is enough consensus among methodologists (Doby, 1967: Ch.3; Kerlinger, 1964: Ch.3; Kaplan, 1964: Ch.2) on what the term concept means that replacing it with the term unit is more redundant and confusing than helpful.

The term concept is also used several other ways in the English language, and there is one particular way that tends to be easily confused with the way concept is used in deductive theory. Educators frequently use "concept" to refer to very complex ideas that can be described only with a sentence or paragraph. For example, a unit in a marriage adjustment course might try to teach the idea or "concept" that when a married couple, while trying to solve a particular problem, is emotionally upset they can frequently be more effective in solving the problem and have fewer problems later if they deal with their emotional feelings before they attempt to cope with the problem itself. The term concept is used this way so much that it can hardly be argued that it is inappropriate. However, it is imperative that this use of the term concept not be confused with the definition of concept that is used in deductive theories. In deductive theories a concept is one single term—not an abstract, complex idea.

Stinchcombe (1968:38–40) accurately points out that concepts in the social sciences do not remain as static ideas. Rather, as new developments are made, the concepts are revised, redefined, and in some cases discarded. This unfortunately creates some frustrations for the scientist because he must continually assess what the meaning of the concept is at the time it is used. At the present stage of the social sciences, however, this evolutionary nature of scientific concepts seems to be inescapable.

Some methodologists prefer to make a distinction between concepts and constructs. Kerlinger, for example, states that "a construct is a concept. It has the added meaning, however, of having been deliberately and consciously invented or adopted for a special scientific purpose" (Kerlinger, 1964:32). This distinction is not used in the book for two reasons. First, there is not agreement that the distinction just identified is the crucial difference between concepts and constructs. For example, the distinction Kaplan (1964:55) makes is that constructs are those concepts that can be thought of in operational terms. The second and more important reason this distinction is not used here is that the reason for the invention of a concept seems to be a relatively unimportant concern. The utility, clarity, and ease with which a concept can be operationalized are important issues in regard to concepts, but the motives in creating them are not. Thus the term concept is used to refer to all of the scientific terms that are used in this book.

Conceptual Clarity

Since concepts are really symbols for meanings, and meanings are mental processes, the most crucial aspect of concepts when they are used as a part of theory is that they are clear. Conceptual *clarity* (Phillips, 1966:32–34) refers to whether the meanings that concepts have in the minds that use them are lucid in the sense of being free from obscurity, ambiguity, or multiple meanings and whether they are communicable to others. It is much less important that what is referred to in a concept is easily observed or measured empirically than it is that the scientist who uses it have a clear understanding of what he is referring to when he uses the concept, and that he is able to differentiate between the meaning of that particular concept and other concepts. Because of the importance of this aspect of conceptualization, and the relative lack of clarity in many concepts that are used in the social sciences, one of the major goals of this book is to help increase the clarity of the concepts that are used.

Conceptual clarity is acquired by defining concepts, but there are two very different ways of using definitions to attain clarity. One method is to use concepts to define a concept. This strategy is an attempt to explicate in reasonably clear and precise language just what a concept means. The definitions identify what the concept refers to ideationally, and this attempts to provide the scientist with a clear idea of what the concept denotes. This technique is referred to by Guilford (1954) and later by Straus (1964:339) as the *rational approach;* it is called the *constitutive method* by Kerlinger (1964:33). This approach creates a complex set of problems in trying to operationalize certain concepts, but it has the advantage of maximizing the "meaning" a concept has. Because meaning is very valuable in theorizing, this rational method is the technique that is preferred in this book.

The other method of defining concepts is to use operational "definitions." This method of having the meaning of a concept be determined by the technique that is used to measure it or observe it empirically has enjoyed considerable popularity in the social sciences. It has a number of advantages; for example, terms that have operational definitions can be used easily in empirical research, and there is usually high consensus about what the terms denote. Unfortunately, however, this strategy of defining also has a number of disadvantages. The major one is that operationally defined terms have very limited "meaning" to the scientists that use them (Kerlinger, 1964:33–38). This is a most serious limitation because when scientists think with concepts and the concepts they use have very limited "meaning" to them, this justifies wondering about the value of whatever it is that is going on in their minds.

The fact that these two strategies of defining have such contrasting advantages and disadvantages has led to a long-standing debate about which is the more appropriate strategy in science (Marx, 1963:21–24). This debate will undoubtedly continue in the future, but in the meantime theorists have to be either rationalists, operationalists, or some combination of both. In this book, more value is given to the meaning of concepts than to ease of operationalizing them, which means that the rationalist method is generally preferred. Operational definitions are used here only when a rational definition cannot be supplied. *Operationalizations are generally viewed here as attempts to measure concepts* rather than as definitions of the concepts. They are empirical indicators rather than empirical definers.

Variables

Many concepts are not static categories of reality but are phenomena that can vary in some manner. Those concepts that can vary are referred to as *variables* (Stinchcombe, 1968:28–30; Kerlinger, 1965:32–33). This can be illustrated by noting that the term "social norm" is a concept that symbolizes a belief about what people ought to either do or not do. The phenomenon of norm does not, however, vary, and hence it is not a variable. It is only a concept. Norms can, however, vary in their importance. They can vary between being unimportant and highly important. However, when the importance of norms varies, it is not the "normness" that is varying; it is the importance. Thus the *importance of norms* is a concept that is a variable, but norm is a concept that is not a variable. Variables are an important part of deductive theory. In fact, one of the major purposes of theory is to explain the circumstances under which variation in some variables influences variation in other variables.

There is some disagreement among scientists about whether it is possible to have bona fide scientific variables that are not operationalized. Bridgeman, for example, argues that "In general we mean by any concept nothing more than a set of operations; the concept is synonymous with the corresponding set of operations" (1927). Others, however, such as Francis (1967) and Dubin (1969: Ch.9) argue that theoretical ideas can deal with variables that are not operationalized. The position taken in this book is in accord with Kerlinger, who states, "It is important to note that not all constructs in a scientific theory are defined operationally. Indeed, it would be a rather thin theory that has all its constructs operationally defined" (1964:37). In fact, it seems defensible to argue as Willer and Webster (1970) do that most of the variables in contemporary theories in the social sciences are maximally useful when they are rationally defined rather than viewed as synonymous with operationalizations. In this view the scientist thinks with rationally defined concepts, and the theories tend to be built with these variables. Theories are empirically tested by research with variables that can be operationalized; thus science would be impossible if none of the concepts were operationalized. It does not, however, seem defensible to conclude from this that all of the variables *must be* operationalized.

It is important to distinguish between independent and dependent variables. A *dependent variable* is one whose variation is dependent on the variation in some other variable. It is influenced by the other variable, and the one that does the influencing is known as the *independent variable*. In the terms of cause and effect, the variation in the independent variable is the cause and the variation in the dependent variable is the effect.

There are two different ways that variables can vary, and they are sufficiently different that they should be identified. One is categorical and the other is continuous variation.

Categorical Variables

Categorical variables have discrete categories in the way they vary. This means that the values of the variable are separate, distinct parts. An example of this type of variable is sex. Sex has the two categories of male and female, and people fall into one category or the other. There is, of course, some blurring in the case of hermaphrodites, but these are rare exceptions, and for all practical purposes this is a categorical variable in the social sciences. The way sex varies is very different from variables that are not categorical such as masculinity, where there is a gradual gradation between very different extremes and no discrete categories along this gradation.

There is one type of categorical variable that is more extensively used in the social sciences than other types. This is the *dichotomy*, which is merely a categorical variable that has only two categories. It is possible to also identify a certain type of dichotomous variable that differs from other dichotomies. Dubin (1969:34–41) refers to this unique type as *attributes*. They are the type of variable where variation occurs between the quality being either present or absent. This differs from dichotomies where a quality is present, and has two different values. An example of an attribute is parenthood in that it is either present or absent.

Not all categorical variables are dichotomies. There are also trichotomies, and many variables have even more categories. Religious affiliation, for example, is usually viewed in the social sciences as a categorical variable, and there are a large number of categories. Frequently many of them are collapsed in empirical research into the trichotomy of Catholic, Protestant, and Jewish, but this is usually for economical reasons in the research project, and this type of collapsing ignores some of the variation in the variable.

Continuous Variables

Most of the variables that are dealt with in the social sciences are not categorical variables but are rather what are referred to as *continuous* variables. They range continuously from one extreme to another, and if categories are assigned to them, the particular categorical system or set of values that are used is arbitrarily assigned. Height is an example of a continuous variable. It would be possible to be very precise in describing minor variations in height such as changes of one-millionth of a millimeter, but more convenient categories such as distinguishing between inches or feet are usually used. Masculinity is another continuous variable. It is, of course, a different conceptualization from the dichotomous variable of sex that was mentioned in the previous section since it varies continuously between the extremes of masculine and feminine.

It was mentioned earlier that whenever concepts are used in the later chapters attempts will be made to define them clearly. In addition to this conceptual definition, attempts will also be made to *identify the range of variation* in variables and the *categories* that exist in this range if there are categories. This is, of course, easier for dichotomous and categorical variables than it is for many of the continuous variables. It is most difficult when a continuous variable is identified that has been operationalized several different ways in the literature, and the particular operationalizing techniques have been viewed as real, discrete categories rather than merely arbitrarily assigned categories or ideal types. Usually what is done in the later chapters is to identify the extremes in the continuous variables and then specify as many points on the range of variation as feasible. Most of these are merely reference points rather than points that identify equal intervals on the range of variation, but even these reference points are valuable in understanding the nature of the variable. Much more work needs to be done in identifying the way that most of the variables in the social sciences vary.

Relationships between Variables

Relationships are systematic patterns of covariation between variables. They exist whenever variation in one variable tends to be accompanied by a systematic variation in another. There is much more, however, to relationships than just their existence. For example, relationships can differ in direction, shape, and amount of time involved in them. In addition, there is one other characteristic of relationships that is identified in this book that has received very little attention elsewhere. This is variation in the amount of influence that occurs in relationships. These five characteristics of relationships are discussed in the following sections.

The Existence of Relationships

The existence of a relationship is determined by whether the variation in one variable is accompanied in a systematic manner with variation in another variable. This particular aspect of relationships has been a prime concern in the social sciences, but most of this concern has not been with identifying relationships that exist in deductive theories. It has just been an attempt to find empirically demonstrable relationships about socially valued variables. In fact, most of the research that has dealt with identifying relationships in the social sciences has been singularly atheoretical. Most has consisted of attempts to determine the probability of making an error in concluding that relationships do in fact exist in the real world.

This issue of the existence of relationships is one that would be easy to ignore with the erroneous conclusion that it is a simple, uncomplicated issue in deductive theory. There is, however, one aspect that is fairly complex and should be discussed. It would be easy to assume that when a causal relationship is asserted, the proposed relationship should be found in all empirical data, and if it is not found, this is evidence that the proposition is not true. At the present stage of sophistication of the social sciences we cannot conclude either that relationships should always be found in empirical data or that if they are not found this should necessarily be interpreted as evidence of the invalidity of the propositions that assert the relationships. This would be the case only if there were a complete specification of the circumstances under which the causal processes in the proposition operate, and if these circumstances were taken into account in analyzing the data. In fact, very few of these circumstances are known in the social sciences, and, even where some of them are specified, they are only some of the circumstances that influence when the causal processes operate.

Direction of Relationships

Another important aspect of relationships is their direction. If a relationship does exist, then when movement from one value to another occurs in the independent variable there will be some type of variation in the dependent variable. If this variation in the dependent variable occurs in the same direction as the independent variable, it is a *positive* relationship; if it occurs in the opposite direction, it is an *inverse* or *negative* relationship.

The Shape of Relationships

The shape of a relationship refers to the particular pattern of the covariation of the variables, and relationships can assume a number of different shapes. One of the most common and easily understood shapes is the *linear* relationship. This is where variation in different places in the range of variation in the independent variable is accompanied by the same amount of concomitant variation in the dependent variable, and the variation in the dependent variable is in only one direction. If the pattern of covariation does not have this linear shape, it is referred to as a *curvilinear* relationship.

Being able to designate a relationship as linear provides a great deal of information about the shape of the relationship, but designating one as curvilinear provides very little. All that it really designates is that a relationship is not a linear covariation. There can be so many unique shapes of curvilinear relationships that labeling them as such generally is insufficient in identifying their shape. They could be expressed in mathematical terms if all of the variables were rigorously quantified, but this rarely occurs when dealing with social variables. There is, however, another method of communicating the type of relationship that occurs in propositions, which communicates subtleties in the patterns of covariation and does not demand highly rigorous operationalization procedures. This is to use a figure that plots the variables on different axes, and to then insert a scatter plot of how cases fall on the two variables. This is done in Figure 1.2 for a proposition that has a linear, inverse relationship.

Although scatter plots like Figure 1.2 are a highly informing way to communicate the shape of relationships, they are time consuming and bothersome. It is much easier to simplify the data, and one way to do this is to calculate the mean score of the dependent variable in each of the values of the independent variable and draw a line between these points. When this is done for the relationship diagramed in Figure 1.2, the relationship is summarized with the line in Figure 1.3.

This method of diagraming the pattern of covariation is much easier than making a scatter plot, and it communicates a great deal about the nature of the relationship. There is, however, some information that is

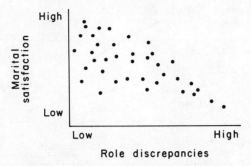

Figure 1.2 A scatterplot of the relationship between role discrepancies and marital satisfaction. This is an inverse linear relationship.

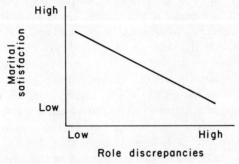

Figure 1.3 The relationship between role discrepancies and marital satisfaction summarized with a line plotting the means of marital satisfaction for each value of role discrepancy.

lost when a relationship is diagramed in this manner. For example, in the proposition that is diagramed in Figure 1.3, the fact is not communicated that the variation of scores on the dependent variable is greater in the low range of the independent variable than in the higher ranges. Because of this, a slightly different technique is occasionally used in this book for diagraming relationships. It is used whenever there is a unique relationship that cannot be communicated easily with a verbal label or a figure such as Figure 1.3. The technique is to draw three lines that represent the values of the dependent variable at the tenth, fiftieth, and ninetieth percentile of a population (Figure 1.4). This type of graph is only slightly more complicated to construct than Figure 1.3, but it conveys a great deal more information.

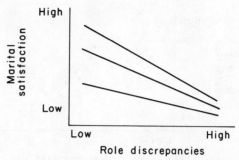

Figure 1.4   The relationship between role discrepancy and marital satisfaction, showing the tenth, fiftieth, and ninetieth percentiles.

There are several labels other than linear and curvilinear that can be used to identify the shape of relationships. *Monotonic* relationships (Hayes, 1963:642) are those relationships where variation in one direction in the independent variable is always accompanied by either an increase or decrease in the dependent variable. In other words, the relationship never changes direction. This is a less demanding assertion to make about a relationship than is linearity, because in a linear relationship the *amount* of variation in the dependent variable is the same in all parts of the range of variation in the independent variable. In a monotonic relationship no assertion is made about the amount of variation in the dependent variable; it is only asserted that there is some variation.

Another group of terms identify a number of different shapes of relationships. If a relationship has two directions such as lines *A* and *B* in Figure 1.5 this is referred to as a *second-order* or *quadratic* relationship. If it has three directions such as line *C* in Figure 1.5 it is referred to as a

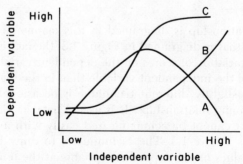

Figure 1.5   Various types of relationships.

third-order or *cubic* relationship. Very few theoretical propositions have been identified with familial variables that have cubic relationships. It is likely, however, that this is because of the elementary level of the theorizing rather than because they do not exist. It is very possible that as theoretical and methodological sophistication increases these may become common.

The Amount of Influence in Relationships

One concept that seems to be useful in describing the shape of relationships is the *amount of influence.* This refers to the amount of variation in a dependent variable that is caused by a certain amount of variation in an independent variable. In some situations, a given amount of variation in an independent variable causes great variation in a dependent variable, and in other situations the same amount of variation in an independent variable brings about only minor variation in a dependent variable. This concept can be illustrated with the relationships diagramed with B and C in Figure 1.5. Line C describes a relationship where variation in the independent variable at either of its extremes has virtually no influence on the dependent variable. However, variation in the middle part of the range of this independent variable has a great deal of influence. Line B describes a relationship where the amount of influence is greater in the upper part of the independent variable than in the lower part.

There can also be differences in the amount of influence in linear relationships. In linear relationships independent variables that cause major variation in a dependent variable have more influence than independent variables that cause only minor variation. Those with relatively little influence may frequently be theoretically important because of the influence they have, but they make less difference than the more influential variables.

A number of statistical procedures have been developed to measure variation in the amount of influence in certain types of relationships. Correlational techniques such as the Pearsonian, which measure the strength of relationships, estimate the amount of influence when it can be assumed that the distributions of the variables are normal and that the relationships are linear. Curvilinear regression analysis can also frequently be used to describe and analyze variation in the amount of influence when there are curvilinear relationships.

Time Involved in Relationships

Zetterberg (1965) makes a distinction between what he calls coextensive and sequential propositions. In the coextensive propositions there is no assertion of any time differences in when the variation occurs in the variables, whereas in the sequential propositions there is a time differential between when the independent and dependent variables vary. This distinction between these two types of propositions seems useful, but Blalock (1969) later pointed out that this issue is more complicated than Zetterberg's typology indicates. Blalock demonstrates that in the type of propositions that Zetterberg labels sequential there are differences in the amount of time involved, and he suggests that attention should be paid to these time differences. It seems reasonable to expect that as social theories become more sophisticated this issue of time will become important, but at the present stage of development of social theories very little is said about temporal characteristics of relationships.

In Sum

Since the nature of relationships is a crucial part of theories, it is imperative that as much of this information as possible be identified in a book such as this. Therefore every attempt is made in subsequent chapters to specify the characteristics of relationships. This is done by identifying whenever possible (*a*) the definitions of variables, (*b*) how the variables vary, (*c*) if an assertion is made that a relationship exists, (*d*) if the relationship is asserted only as a covariational relationship or as an influential (causal) relationship, (*e*) the direction of the relationship that is proposed, (*f*) the shape of the relationship, (*g*) the amount of influence in the relationship, and (*h*) the length of time involved in the relationship.

Propositions

Propositions can be defined in a general way as statements that assert, or at least attempt to assert, a truth. They are different from concepts and variables because concepts and variables are just terms that symbolize some aspect of reality. Propositions are declarative sentences that assert something about these terms.

This general statement about propositions needs to be refined, however, because there are some important differences in the way this term is used. There has been a tendency in some recent sociological literature to use the term in a slightly more restricted way than it is used in philosophy of science literature. Philosophers such as Braithwaite (1953) view propositions as any declarative statement that attempts to assert a truth. They view propositions as statements about the characteristics of a concept, predictions, assertions that a relationship exists, and so on. Sociologists such as Homans (1964:811), Zetterberg (1965:64), and Blalock (1969:2), however, seem to prefer to restrict the meaning of the term propositions to those statements that identify relationships between variables. Dubin (1969) is still more restrictive in the way he uses the term because he defines propositions as those statements that make predictions about the values variables will have in different circumstances. Dubin refers to statements that identify relationships between variables as "laws of interaction" (1969: Ch. 4).

Obviously, it would be irrational to use all definitions of the term proposition here; a choice must be made among the definitions. Dubin's system is his own and is not widely used in the literature, hence it is not used here. Since there seems to be some value in differentiating between several different types of declarative statements that are used in theorizing, the definition selected here is the one that views propositions as those statements that identify relationships between variables.

When propositions are viewed as only being those statements that relate variables, it is necessary to use different labels to refer to several other types of declarative statements that are used in theorizing. One convention that is extensively used in the methodological literature is to use the term *definition* (Zetterberg, 1965: Ch. 3) to refer to those declarative statements that define concepts. Another widely used convention is the use of the term *prediction* (Simon, 1969:435; Dubin, 1969:170–171) or *estimation* (Blalock, 1969:3) to refer to those statements that make predictions about the values that specific variables will assume in various circumstances. The terms definition and prediction are used in this book to refer to these types of declarative statements.

It would be convenient if this set of terms were the only ones that had to be defined to communicate what propositions are and what they are not. Unfortunately, however, there is ambiguity in the literature on whether propositions are different from or synonymous with other terms such as hypotheses, theorems, axioms, postulates, and invariances. Thus it also seems necessary to examine the meaning of these other terms and explain how the term proposition is being used in relationship to them.

The term hypothesis is used by some writers such as Braithwaite (1953) as a synonym for the term proposition, whereas others such as Zetterberg (1965:101) view hypotheses as only one type of proposition. Others, including Marx (1963: Ch. 1), use "hypothesis" in lieu of "proposition." This variability in the way hypothesis is defined illustrates that at the present time the only way to be sure what the term hypothesis means is to find how it is defined in each context. In this book, the distinction that is made by Simon (1969:37) and Dubin (1969: Ch. 9) between hypotheses and propositions is used. They view hypotheses as predictions about the relationships between variables that are sufficiently concrete that they are empirically testable. Dubin states:

An hypothesis may be defined as the predictions about values of units (concepts) of a theory in which empirical indicators are employed for the named units in each proposition. This is a simple definition. It says that every time the name of a unit appears in a proposition, there must be substituted for it an empirical indicator that measures values on this unit. Thus, for example, if one proposition of a two-person interaction system is "Friendliness of interaction is directly related to frequency of interaction," then one hypothesis testing this proposition could be "Expressed liking between two people as measured by the Dubin Interaction Love and Liking Yardstick (DILLY) is directly proportional to the number of hours spent in contact" (Dubin, 1969:212).

This distinction is very similar to Zetterberg's (1965:79–85) distinction between ordinary and theoretical propositions. Zetterberg's low informative or ordinary propositions seem to be the specific, testable assertions that are referred to here as hypotheses. His theoretical propositions have more of what he calls "informative value." He explains this difference as follows:

In general, the larger the number of different ways in which a proposition can conceivably be proved incorrect, the higher its informative value. Put differently, the higher the informative value of a proposition, the greater is the variety of events for which it can account (1965:79).

Thus Zetterberg's theoretical propositions are comparable to what are conceptualized in this book as propositions, and his ordinary propositions are what are here termed hypotheses.

The distinction being made here between propositions and hypotheses is also very similar to Blalock's distinction between axioms and theorems:

A deductive theory must contain both axioms and theorems. Axioms are propositions that are assumed to be true. Theorems, on the other hand, are derived by reasoning, or deduced from the axioms . . . our axioms should be causal assertions that strictly speaking will be untestable because of the fact that it will never be possible to control for all "relevant" variables. For example, if we assume that a change in Y, even if we observe covariations and temporal sequences we can never be sure that these have not been produced by some extraneous factor. But if our axioms contain such causal assertions, and if we make certain additional assumptions concerning the operation of extraneous factors, we shall then be in a position to derive from our axioms testable theorems about covariances and temporal sequences (1969:10–11).

The distinction made in this book is not exactly the same as Blalock's because it is contended here that the abstract theoretical propositions need not always be causal statements. They *could* be assertions that only propose that covariation occurs. If this minor difference is ignored, Blalock's distinction between axioms and theorems seems to be the same as the difference here between propositions and hypotheses.

The Logical Relationships
Between Propositions

Deductive Explanation

The components of deductive theory that have been discussed in the last several sections are necessary parts of deductive theory, but there is one additional component that is absolutely essential before deductive theory exists. It would be possible to have a large conceptual framework (list of concepts or taxonomy) and to have a large number of propositions, but if this additional component of deductive theory is not present there is no theory. There is no explanation and the concepts and propositions are scientifically useless without this additional component, which is thus an extremely valuable part of deductive theories. Unfortunately, it is also the part that social scientists tend to have the most difficulty understanding and using. This component is the particular type of logical relationship between propositions that provides explanation or understanding, referred to as *deduction*—the process of using certain propositions and other identifiable conditions as a basis for explaining why other propositions or conditions exist. Braithwaite explains this logical process in the following manner:

> The propositions in a deductive system may be considered as being arranged in an order of levels, the hypotheses at the highest level being those which occur only as premises in the system, those at the lowest level being those which occur only as conclusions in the system, and those at intermediate levels being those which occur as conclusions of deductions from higher level hypotheses and which serve as premises for deductions to lower level hypotheses (1953:12).

This analysis of how the logical relationship between propositions provides explanation would be inadequate unless this particular type of explanation is contrasted with a second type of explanation that also exists in deductive theory. The type of explanation that has just been identified is acquired by deducing either relatively specific propositions or empirically observable hypotheses from other propositions that serve as premises. This is generally known as *deductive explanation* (Braithwaite, 1953; Nagel, 1961), and it explains why the relationships exist in the more specific propositions. It is important to realize here that his type of explanation does not provide certain other explanation. For example, it does not explain why some propositions are more useful than others or why a given dependent variable varies at a certain time. It merely explains why there is a relationship between certain variables.

The other type of explanation that exists in deductive theories, labeled *causal explanation* by Braithwaite (1953: Ch. 10), explains why variation occurs in a dependent variable, and it is present whenever there is a causal assertion in a proposition. A causal proposition explains that variation occurs in a dependent variable because there is variation in a certain independent variable. In other words, causal explanation is explanation of *why there is variation* in a particular variable, and deductive explanation is explanation of *why there is a relationship between certain variables.* Causal explanation occurs within a proposition, and deductive explanation occurs by deducing between propositions of different levels of generality.

The use of the deductive process is valuable for other reasons in addition to the fact that it provides explanations of why relationships in specific propositions exist. One additional reason is that it permits deducing similar more specific propositions that have not been known before. Thus deduction from highly general theoretical propositions is a useful tool in helping to extend scientific theories. In addition to these two points, the use of both highly general propositions and more specific deductions is a parsimonious way of summarizing knowledge. Hence the use of multiple levels of generality is not only informing in that it provides explanations of more specific phenomena, but it extends and is an efficient way of summarizing knowledge.

Induction

Induction is another type of logical relationship between propositions that is important in deductive theory. It is logical movement from the specific to the general, and it is indispensable in theory building. It is used by having one or more specific propositions, or even somewhat general propositions, and then inducing that there is a more general proposition (or propositions) that explain why the relationships in the more specific propositions occur. This process does more than just increase the level of generality of the theoretical formulations because the new, more general propositions will also usually explain a wider range of more specific propositions (through deduction) than the theorist started with.

The processes of using deduction and induction are vital to theory building and theory testing. One way to illustrate their importance is to explain how both deduction and induction can be used together to expand theoretical knowledge. This particular use of both deduction and induction has been called *retroduction* (Hanson, 1958, 1958a, 1960). If a theorist has one or more theoretical propositions, and is able to either find an existing more general proposition that has not been integrated with his proposition or to induce a new proposition that explains the relationship in the first propositions, this is the use of induction and the theory is thereby extended. It is then possible to deduce other propositions from the general proposition, and new testable hypotheses can then be tested. The findings of these tests are not only useful as evidence for or against the validity of the specific theoretical ideas closest to the data, but, since the data deal with the entire theoretical system, they are useful in assessing the validity of the whole theory.

Ceteris Paribus

Ceteris paribus is Latin for "other things being equal," and it is an indispensible part of theorizing. It would be impossible to take into account all of the circumstances and conditions that influence the relationships studied in the social sciences. Because of this, whenever a proposition is asserted there is an assumption that all other variables are invariant or held constant. As Marshall says:

We reduce to inaction all other forces by the phrase "other things being equal"; we do not suppose that they are inert, but for the time we ignore their activity. This scientific device is a great deal older than science: it is the method by which, consciously or unconsciously, sensible men have dealt from time immemorial with every difficult problem of ordinary life (1961:xiv).

One of the major goals of science is to gradually acquire knowledge about how variables that are temporarily ignored influence the operation of the relationship in a proposition. This type of knowledge, however, is acquired very slowly, and it can be attained only by using the principle of ceteris paribus to ignore the effects of most variables in theorizing and research and then gradually take them increasingly into account.

Most of the theoretical propositions that are stated in the social sciences are sufficiently simple that nothing is known about the circumstances under which they operate. Thus most of them can be stated only as assertions that a certain variable influences another variable when all other variables are invariant. Future theorizing may gradually identify the ways that other variables influence the operation of these relationships.

Fortunately, the social sciences do have a few theoretical assertions that identify how variables influence the operation of relationships. Some identify how a third variable influences something about the relationship between an independent and dependent variable. Lazarsfeld (1955:122) refers to these third variables as *conditions* if they are pre-existing conditions and as *contingencies* if they occur temporally between the independent and dependent variable. These third variables can influence relationships in several ways. They can influence the direction, shape, amount of time involved, strength, or amount of influence in a relationship. Zetterberg (1965:71) refers to these third variables as contingent variables and this is the term that is used in this book.

There are also some theoretical ideas that identify how several independent variables "interact" in influencing a dependent variable. The variables can interact in an *additive* manner in that a combination of variables has more influence than any of them have individually. They can also interact in such a way that any of several variables is a *sufficient* but not necessary cause of variation in a certain dependent variable, and having more than one of the independent variables does not have any more influence on the dependent variable than any one of them would have individually.

Theory

The basic ingredients that have been identified—*variables, propositions* that identify *relationships, explanation* that is provided by logically *deducing* and the principle of *ceteris paribus*—are the basic components of deductive theory. When they are present, there is enough explanation that theory genuinely exists.

Theories can become highly complex by adding a number of additional characteristics to the propositional structure, but this is an expansion of the theory as theoretical explanation is ipso facto the type of explanation that is made with these basic components. Homans summarized some of these ideas in his statement on the nature of theory:

> One may define properties and categories, and one still has no theory. One may state that there are relations between the properties, and one still has no theory. One may state that a change in one property will produce a definite change in another property, and one still has no theory. Not until one has properties, and propositions stating the relations between them, and the propositions from a deductive system—not until one has all three does one have a theory (Homans, 1964a:812).

Theorizing is a mental process. It is the process of scientists acquiring explanations about why certain variations occur and why they do not. It is not merely a matter of finding empirical relationships that happen to occur in the real world, but rather of learning the circumstances under which variation in variables brings about variation in other variables in a way that acquires multiple levels of generality. It is usually not appropriate to label one isolated simple proposition a theory. One proposition may provide causal explanation, and, as such, it is the beginning of a theory. In order, however, to have an explanation that can be dignified with the title of theory, it should usually be a group of interrelated propositions with multiple levels of generality.

It should also be noted that theory is useful for more than just understanding. It can be used for predicting when variation will occur in certain dependent variables. Prediction, however, should not be confused with explanation. It is possible to predict, and to predict very accurately, and not have a theory. As Dubin (1961:10) and others have pointed out, however, it is also possible to have extensive theoretical understanding and not be able to predict well at all. Theoretical development should facilitate at least some types of prediction, but it is erroneous to conclude that because theory exists it will then be possible to predict efficiently, or that it is prediction rather than explanation that is the end of science. Prediction may occur or it may not occur when theory exists, but the crucial matter is that the end of science is not prediction but understanding through the use of theory.

Issues about Deductive Theory

Causality

There are widely different points of view in the literature about whether the assertions that are made in propositions can include assertions about causality, and even among those who believe they can, there are differences of opinion about whether they should. In Dubin's (1969:89–103) system of theory building he states that the term causality can be used, but if it is, it should only be used because it is psychologically comfortable to use that term in describing sequences of events. He uses a deductive type of theory but contends that assertions about causality are inappropriate. Dubin argues that propositions should only state patterns of covariation between variables and there should be no contention that any phenomenon is either a cause or effect. He further states (1969:102–103) that Nagel (1961: Ch. 10, 14), Kaplan (1964), and

Popper (1959) also support his point of view. Other methodologists such as Blalock (1964, 1969) seem to believe that causality not only can be included, but that important theoretical ideas should include assertions about causality. It is also important to note that this issue of whether causality should be included in theories is not just a problem in the social sciences. It is a concern in several disciplines and, as volumes such as Lerner's (1965) *Cause and Effect* illustrate, it is hotly debated.

Braithwaite (1953:308 ff) argues for the relevance of causality. He discusses several criteria for identifying certain types of propositions as causal and then differentiates between causal and teleological explanation. In addition, contrary to Dubin's claim that Nagel (1961) argues against causality, Nagel seems very clearly to argue for its relevance. In his analysis of causality in *The Structure of Science* (1961) and in his later chapter in Lerner's (1965) monograph, Nagel identifies several different types of what he terms "causal" explanation. He points out that the term causality is used in many different ways, but he does not exclude causal propositions from being a part of deductive theory. In fact, Nagel states: "Nevertheless, though the *term* may be absent, the *idea* for which it stands continues to have wide currency in scientific processes" (1965:12; italics his).

The position that is taken in this book is that many of the propositions in deductive theory need only identify what Braithwaite refers to as "regular sequences, regular simultaneities and regular precedences" (1953:309), and these types of statements do not make any assertions of causality. They only state that there are regularities that occur in the variation of variables. In other words, they merely identify patterns of covariation between variables. These could appropriately be labeled *covariational* propositions. Even though this is the case, however, it is argued here that it is also possible to state propositions that assert more than just covariational relationships. It is possible to also identify causal processes. The term causality, however, has many different meanings and implications in the literature, and because of this it seems necessary to define rather precisely how the term is being used here.

The idea of causality as it is used here follows quite closely Braithwaite's (1953:320–322) use of the term in his analysis of causal explanation. Causality means that variation in some variables is the effect of or result of either the occurrence of certain values in other variables or certain types of variation in other variables. It is the idea that the occurrence of a certain value in one variable or the variation in that variable either directly or indirectly *influences* the other variable so it varies or at least tends to vary in a certain way. This use of the term causality does not imply in any sense that the variation in the influential or causal variable is the only variable that can influence variation in a dependent variable unless this is specifically stated in the proposition. In fact, most social phenomena are influenced by more than one variable, and because of this any given proposition should not be expected to explain all of the variation that can or does occur in a dependent variable. All that it should be expected to explain is why some of the variation in it, under certain circumstances, does occur.

It should also not be assumed that variation in any particular variable is necessary for variation to occur in a dependent variable unless that too is specifically stated in a proposition. *All that is implied when a causal or influential proposition is asserted is that if a certain value of a variable occurs, or if a certain type of variation occurs in the causal or influential variable, this condition creates some type of influence that will, under certain conditions, tend to bring about a certain type of variation in the dependent variable.* It is also not crucial that all of the details of "how" the variation in the causal variable brings about the effects in the dependent variable be understood; it can just be accepted that it does. The variation in the causal variable could create a force that could exert pressure on the dependent variable, or if an assumption is made that a rational process is operating, it could create a situation that makes certain responses more rational than other responses. All that is implied is that an influence is exerted. The causal variable that is identified in a proposition can, of course, also be any one of the prior events in a chain where there are a series of causal relationships.

This particular use of the term causality is difficult for some social scientists to grasp. This may be at least partly because certain methodological traditions in the social sciences have made scholars ask a certain type of question: How much of the variation in a dependent variable can be accounted for by variation in a particular independent variable? Concern with this type question tends to prevent an appreciation of this view of causality. The scholar who asks this problematic question then attempts to account for as much variation as possible. When causality is viewed as variation in one variable *influencing* variation in another variable, the independent variable may cause only slight variation in any given dependent variable, and concern with accounting for as much of the variation in the dependent variable as possible diverts the scholar's attention from the important issue. The concern should be with whether the variation in the independent variable brings about *any* variation in the dependent variable, and if it does, the object should be to specify the circumstances under which it does. If social scientists were to think in terms of the consequences of variation rather than accounting for variation, they would probably find deductive theory more useful than they do at present.

In this book there is not only an acceptance of the position that causal propositions are admissible in theories, but there is also a value judgment that they are usually more valuable in the scientific enterprise than the type of propositions that just assert covariation. The covariational propositions provide insight into regularities in nature, but the causal propositions provide understanding of more than just these regularities. They provide understanding of how some parts of nature are influenced by other parts. The covariational propositions are valued in this book only to the extent that they facilitate the process of gradually acquiring the causal propositions, and they are seen as having relatively less value in and of themselves. They are, of course, more valuable than isolated empirical findings, but they are less valuable than theoretical assertions about how variation in certain variables influences other variables.

Concern with Effects of Variation in Independent Variables Rather Than Explaining Variance in Dependent Variables

There are many different strategies of developing theoretical ideas, but the reasons for choosing among them and the consequences of their use are not well analyzed. One of these strategies that has acquired considerable prominence in recent years is the view that the best way to engage in scientific inquiry is to attempt to account for variance in dependent variables by finding covariance with independent variables (Kerlinger, 1964). This particular technique has become highly popular with scholars who are primarily concerned with quantification procedures and statistical testing of data; elaborate statistical tests have been devised to identify, at various levels of significance, the amount of variance that is accounted for.

The strategy that is used in this book is very different from this process of accounting for variance in dependent variables. The main difference is that the strategy used here emphasizes the identification, clear explication, and evaluation of the consequences of variation in independent variables, and the concern with explaining a certain proportion of the variance in dependent variables is deemphasized. The focus here is on the *consequences* of variation rather than *antecedents* of variation.

It seems to the author that the strategy of accounting for variance in dependent variables has several undesirable consequences that should be identified. First, it is very probable that this technique is sufficiently limiting that it will focus scientists' concern on epistemological details and emphasize so much the means of the scientific process that it will prevent maintaining a proper perspective on the more bona fide end of developing and testing theory. The field may hence become highly developed in techniques that matter relatively little and have inadequate development in attaining the more weighty goal of providing theoretical explanation. Second (although in the practice of science this makes more difference), it is likely that there is such an infinitely large number of interactional patterns that can bring about the same type of variation in highly valued dependent variables that it is an impossible task to ferret these relationships out by focusing only on the proportion of variance in the independent variable that different variables tend to account for. Instead, this strategy may lead to an endless list of conflicting findings and wasteful arguments between various groups on what it is that is really causing the variation, and which of the independent variables is having the greatest impact. The field of psychology has already experienced this squirrel-cage problem in the nature-nurture controversy.

The point of view taken here is that a more efficient strategy in accomplishing the major ultimate goals of the sciences is to strive toward analyses of the effects of variation of independent variables rather than accounting for the variance in the way that important dependent variables vary. It is hoped that this system of focusing on the independent variables and trying to discern their consequences will provide a gradually accumulating body of theoretical relationships that can be used in understanding progressively better the factors that influence highly valued dependent variables.

In actual fact both of these approaches are useful, but they are useful at different stages of theoretical development. The concern with the correlates of variation in the dependent variables is useful in identifying potentially meaningful independent variables, and as such this strategy is useful in the initial stages of theoretical formulation. In the more advanced stages, however, it is useful to shift the emphasis to the consequences of variation in the independent variables if very profound theories are to be developed. Even after considerable theoretical sophistication has been acquired, there is some value in using the first technique to identify additional independent variables that might be useful. However, when these are identified, the focus should then shift to the consequences of their variation.

One of the important effects of focusing on the consequences of variation rather than maximizing the amount of variance that can be accounted for in a given circumstance is that the theorist is concerned with finding any and all influencing variables, and he is not greatly concerned in an early stage of the development of the theory that the theoretical ideas only account for some of the variation in dependent variables. Whenever any source of variation is identified it is valued for the influence it has. This more precise identification of all influential variables would probably not occur if the goal of theoretical formulation were merely to maximize the amount of variation that could be accounted for in specific situations.

Directness of Explanations

Another aspect of theoretical explanation that must be understood if theories are to be adequately appreciated is that the directness of explanations in a theory can vary. The *directness* of an explanation refers to whether there are intermediate relationships that occur between the variation in an independent variable and a dependent variable. The directness of explanation does not refer to the type of explanation called "deductive explanation" earlier, but only to the type labeled "causal explanation." It refers to whether there are intermediate causal relationships that occur between the variation in an independent variable and the resulting variation in the dependent variable.

This can best be illustrated by referring to a chain sequence of influence where variation in one variable (*A*) causes variation in another variable (*B*) and this variation in the first dependent variable (*B*) acts in an influential manner resulting in variation in a third variable (*C*). In this causal sequence the cause of the variation in variable *B* is reasonably direct, and so is the relationship between *B* and *C*. However, it would be legitimate to speak of variation in variable *A* influencing variation in variable *C*, and thus there is a meaningful theoretical relationship between variables *A* and *C* when *B* is ignored. This influential relationship is, however, "less direct" than the other two relationships identified between *A* and *B* and between *B* and *C*.

The main point here is that highly indirect theoretical explanations may be very valuable. As Braithwaite points out, this type of causal explanation gives "great intellectual satisfaction to those who have been educated in the contemporary natural sciences" (1953:321) as long as the explicans or explanatory independent variable is "the first member of a *causal chain* of events ending with the explicandum," which is the variable explained. There is, of course, little reason to try to find highly indirect theoretical relationships in the social sciences, but there is good reason to be concerned about directness. This is the case because the most comprehensive theoretical formulations will certainly explicate sequential events and will hence contain a number of indirect relationships. Moreover, many times a theoretical proposition will be identified, and then subsequent research will discover more direct theoretical relationships that ought to be taken into account. This process should be viewed as adding to the comprehensiveness of the theory rather than as correcting the theory by eliminating an unnecessary factor.

Indirect relationships should not be confused with spurious relationships. Spurious relationships are those where there is in fact no causal relationship between two variables when there previously seemed to be some basis for asserting there is a causal relationship. Indirect relationships are bona fide theoretical relationships. They just do not identify the most direct antecedent of the variation in the dependent variables.

Summary

Deductive theory is a group of propositions that identify relationships between variables. It has multiple levels of generality that permit deductive explanation, the expansion of the theory through the use of induction and deduction, and the testing of the theory through deduction and empirical testing. The process of empirically testing theoretical ideas is itself a complex procedure, and much of the scientific method is a specification of how this is done. Chapter 2 examines in some detail the procedures for testing the ideas in deductive theory.

Note

1. Zetterberg's (1954, 1965) work has led to the term "axiomatic theory" also being used in sociology to refer to this same type of theory. The label "deductive theory" is used here because it is also used by sociologists (see Blau, 1970), and it is more extensively used in the philosophy literature.

ASSESSING THE VALIDITY
OF DEDUCTIVE THEORIES

One of the goals of this book is to evaluate empirical data that test the validity of the theoretical ideas that are identified. This is done to determine which aspects of the propositions have been tested, and the amount of evidence that exists either for or against these aspects. Since there is considerable evaluation of empirical data in the following chapters, it is important that the methodology of this assessment is made explicit. This chapter thus attempts to explain how inferences are made from empirical data about the validity of theoretical ideas.

The process of using empirical data to test the validity of theoretical ideas is not a simple matter of proving or disproving the ideas. It is a highly complex procedure, and, as Cohen and Nagel (1934:231) point out, the validity of theories can never be proved in an absolute sense. Validity can only be inferred from empirical data. In addition, the logic that is used in this inferential process is fairly complicated, and there are a number of other factors that influence not only the type of inferences that can be made but the confidence that can be placed in these inferences. The first section of this chapter explains the logic used in relating theoretical ideas and empirical data. The second section examines the many factors that influence the type of inferences that can be made from data and the confidence that can be placed in these inferences.

The Logic of Inference from Data to Theory

For a statement to be a theoretical proposition it has to be sufficiently abstract and general that it is possible to explain more specific phenomena through the process of deduction. This means that propositions are by their very nature relatively abstract. This is valuable to science because it permits explaining complex phenomena in an orderly way, but it also means that the variables in propositions are frequently so abstract that they cannot be observed directly with empirical indicators. Thus their validity cannot be directly tested with empirical processes but can only be inferred on the basis of a logical connection between these abstract propositions and the less abstract ideas that can be empirically observed. This logical connection is that when an abstract theoretical proposition is to be tested it is necessary to deduce from that proposition more specific propositions that specify how the relationship is expected to occur in certain given circumstances. This deductive process is then repeated until a sufficiently concrete and specific deduction is made that it is possible to test it with empirical data. These, it will be recalled, are defined in this book as hypotheses.

It is possible with this distinction between propositions and hypotheses that a proposition could, under some circumstances, also be a hypothesis in that it might be possible to deduce from it and also directly test it. Usually this is not the case, however, because seldom in the social sciences is a testable statement sufficiently abstract that deductions can be made from it. This would probably never be the case with highly abstract propositions.

The crucial aspect of this logical relationship between propositions and hypotheses is that when a hypothesis has been tested with empirical data and categorically either accepted or rejected, this provides evidence that can serve as at least part of the basis for making inferences about the validity of the more abstract propositions from which the hypotheses can be deduced (Stinchcombe, 1968:15–24). If the hypothesis is proved untrue, this adds weight to the inference that at least one of three things is also invalid: (1) some aspect of the theoretical proposition itself may be invalid; (2) some aspect of the logical process of deducing the hypothesis may be indefensible; or (3) the circumstances under which the hypothesis is assumed to be deducible from the proposition may be inappropriate.

In making these inferences it should also be kept in mind that a hypothesis may deal with any of the characteristics of a relationship, but it is probably impossible for any single hypothesis to deal with *all* of the aspects of a theoretical relationship. A hypothesis that tests for the existence of a relationship is very different from one that tests the direction or shape of the relationship. The inferences that can be made from the test of a hypthesis can only deal with those aspects of the proposition that are specifically tested by the hypothesis.

The same logical relationship exists between the relatively specific theoretical propositions and the more general propositions from which they are deduced. The more general propositions are tested indirectly by the gradual accumulation of evidence for or against the more specific propositions that are deduced from them. In fact, this is the only method of testing highly general propositions other than with evidence for or against increasingly general propositions.

Since the propositions in deductive theories can be tested only in this indirect method, it is very seldom that a particular test of one hypothesis provides what Pratt (1965) and Stinchcombe (1968:24–28) call a "crucial experiment" that will justify by itself accepting or rejecting the theoretical formulation from which it was deduced. Rather, what the test does is add weight to the evidence either for or against the proposition or propositions. It is also important that excessive confidence is not placed in one or two empirical studies when they are used to assess the validity of theoretical propositions. It is much more defensible to have an accumulation of evidence from the tests of a number of different hypotheses that can be deduced from a proposition before the proposition is viewed as highly verified. Selltiz et al. (1961) emphasize the point that a great deal of tentativeness should be used when empirical data are used to assess the validity of theories:

> It must be stressed that such evidence merely provides a reasonable basis for inferring that X is or is not a cause of Y; it does not provide absolute certainty. On the one hand, if the evidence does not support the hypothesis of a causal relationship, it may be that we have neglected some condition under which X is a determinant of Y, and thus that we have been wrong in completely rejecting the possibility that X is a determining condition of Y. On the other hand, if the evidence supports the hypothesis, it may still be that we have neglected some other factor associated with X which is, in fact, the determining condition of Y. In short, we may conclude that it is reasonable to believe that X is or is not a cause of Y, but we can never be certain that the relationship has been conclusively demonstrated. The cumulation of studies that point to one or the other conclusion helps to increase our confidence in its probable correctness, but still does not constitute absolute proof (Selltiz et al., 1961:88).

In assessing the level of proof of a theory it is also important to make a distinction between the acceptance or rejection of a proposition as opposed to accepting or rejecting a theory. If a substantial amount of evidence indicates a proposition is not valid, this does not necessarily indicate that the rest of a theory is also invalid. Each theoretical proposition has to be assessed separately as well as in relation to related propositions. Evidence against a relatively specific proposition provides a basis for increasing doubt about the validity of the more general propositions in a theoretical formulation from which it is deducible, but it may be that it is only the specific proposition that is invalid.

When there is evidence of the invalidity or validity of a specific proposition in a theory this can frequently be valuable in several ways other than just as a test of that proposition. For example, as Merton (1968: Ch. 4, 5) has pointed out, this type of data can be useful in revising theories or in extending them. When this is done, however, the evidence that leads to these revisions in most circumstances should be viewed only as a low level of proof of these revisions, since subsequent verification with additional data usually is needed.

Factors Influencing the Evidence That Data Provide for or against Propositions

It is very difficult to identify a list of criteria that can be used as a basis for accepting data as evidence for or against theoretical propositions or for deciding just how much evidence they provide. If one were to be a purist and require that the data for these inferences be free from limitations and provide an unquestionable basis for making inferences, he would at the present time find very few if any usable data in the social sciences. Because of this scarcity of perfect data and the importance of using empirical data to assess the validity of our theoretical ideas, it seems defensible to be slightly less pure at the present time and to try to find any ways that our highly limited data provide evidence for or against various propositions.

There are numerous factors that influence the particular type of inferences that can be made from empirical data and the amount of confidence that can be placed in these inferences. Some of these factors are identified in the following sections of the chapter; and then at the end of the chapter there is an explanation of how these factors are taken into account in the present book in using empirical data to assess the validity of theoretical ideas.

Concomitant Variation

Selltiz et al. (1961:80–88) identified three factors that are crucial in making inferences about the validity of propositions. One is the evidence of concomitant variation between the variables. This means that the two variables covary in some manner, and evidence of concomitant variation is the major concern in making inferences about the existence of relationships.

It seems important to point out that evidence of concomitant variation only provides a basis for making inferences about the existence of relationships, and propositions frequently specify much more than the existence of covariation between variables. For example, they frequently specify such things as the amount of influence, the shape of the relationship that occurs, or directionality. If empirical data are to provide a basis for making inferences about these other assertions it is necessary that these phenomena be present in the empirical data in addition to just having concomitant variation. It is, of course, very possible to have concomitant variation in data and not have information about these other characteristics. When this occurs it is possible to make inferences about the existence of covariation, but no inferences should be made about other characteristics of the relationship.

Thus it is not possible to make one monolithic inference about the nature of relationships. Instead, inferences are made about a number of different characteristics of relationships and each inference is made independently of other inferences. Each inference is made on the basis of (*a*) whether a particular characteristic of a relationship in the data is similar to what is asserted in the proposition, and (*b*) the probability of making an error in concluding that the characteristic found in the data is not due to chance. These inferences can be made about the following five characteristics of relationships:

1. The existence of a relationship. (This is the aspect of relationships that Selltiz et al. were discussing in their analysis of concomitant variation.)
2. The direction of the relationship.
3. The shape of a relationship.
4. The amount of influence in a relationship.
5. The amount of time that occurs between the variation in the independent variable and the variation in the dependent variable.

Statisticians have developed an impressive array of techniques that can be used to identify the probability of making errors when conclusions are made about the first and second of these factors, and these are very common in the literature. Regression analysis can also be used in regard to the third point. It identifies the "best" line to summarize the pattern of covariation in a relationship. It is, however, limited in providing estimates of the probability of making errors in making conclusions about how much the line in the population may differ from this line, but it is still a highly valuable technique. Any inferences about the other two aspects of relationships are at present highly dependent on the judgment of the scholars making them.

Temporal Sequence

Selltiz et al. (1961) also mention that the temporal sequence in the variation of the variables is important. It is impossible for variation in one variable to influence variation in another before the variation in the independent variable occurs. As has been pointed out in the social psychological literature, however, it is possible for the expected variation in a variable to have considerable influence before that variable itself varies. In this situation, however, the independent variable that is varying is a subjective *expectation,* not the variable that is expected to vary. The crucial point here is that evidence that the variation in a dependent variable does not vary before the variation occurs in the independent variable increases the ability to infer that an influential or causal relationship genuinely exists.

Evidence Ruling Out the Effects of Other Independent Variables

The third factor Selltiz et al. (1961:95–98) mentioned is the elimination of other possible causal factors. Their point is that the more evidence there is ruling out other factors as possible influential factors, the greater is the basis for inferring that the factor specified in the proposition is the influential variable. These extraneous variables can be controlled better in some research designs than others, and this is the biggest advantage of experimental designs since the experimenter can randomize or systematically control potentially confounding variables. Just as in some of the physical sciences such as astronomy, however, many of the theoretical concerns in the social sciences cannot be subjected to experimentation, and other methods (e.g., Blalock, 1964) are necessary.

There is an apparent contradiction between the point being made here and an idea made in Chapter 1. It was stated in the preceding chapter that it is possible for many independent variables to influence certain dependent variables, yet here it is contended that it is important to rule out the possibility that there are other influential factors in order to increase the justification of inferring that a proposition is true or false. The reconciliation of this apparent contradiction is that it is theoretically possible for many independent variables to influence certain dependent variables, and here the issue is *testing* the theory. When theories are being tested the consequences of the other variables must be separated from the effects of the independent variable being tested so the consequences of the variation in the independent variable can be detected. The more the covariation between the theoretically relevant independent variable and the dependent variable can be isolated from covariation between the dependent variable and the other possible independent variables, the greater is the basis for inferring that the theorized variable genuinely influences the dependent variable. Occasionally, of course, propositions suggest that independent variables exert an influence only when interacting with specific other variables. When this is the case, if there is to be a test of the validity of these propositions, a research design is necessary that will isolate this particular type of inter-action.

Explicit Hypotheses
Deducible from Propositions

It is impossible to test a proposition unless there is a testable hypothesis that is explicitly stated. It is not, however, necessary that the hypothesis be stated in the original publication of a research study. It could be that a research study has data that are highly relevant for a particular proposition, but the hypotheses were either not stated in the previous publication of the data or they were stated so poorly that they have to be restated. It seems proper for a reviewer who is attempting to assess the validity of a proposition to state a hypothesis for the first time or to restate one in an improved manner. In fact, only then can he assess how the data are relevant as evidence for or against the propositions from which the hypothesis can be deduced.

If empirical data are to be relevant as evidence for or against theoretical propositions, it is also necessary that the hypotheses that are tested by the data are deducible from the theoretical propositions. It is not necessary that this particular deductive process be spelled out in the original publication of a study. This too can be identified later by a reviewer who is attempting to assess the validity of a theoretical proposition. It is, however, necessary that the various circumstances under which the hypothesis can be deduced from the proposition be identified before data can be meaningfully used as evidence for or against a proposition.

Categorical Tests of Hypotheses

Although it is implicit in what has been said about hypotheses, it should be made explicit that useful hypotheses are statements which can be categorically accepted or rejected. This acceptance or rejection is valuable in making judgments about the validity of the theoretical propositions from which they were deduced. In actual fact, however, many hypotheses that are labeled hypotheses in the literature cannot really be categorically answered with acceptance or rejection, and hence in the way they are phrased they have little if any relevance for theoretical ideas. This means that evaluating the empirical literature to test theoretical ideas is a highly selective process, and many statements that are identified as hypotheses are not useful in assessing the validity of theories.

Measurement Error

Measurement error exists whenever there are differences between what an empirical indicator measures and what is conceptualized by the variable being measured. This is an important factor whenever attempts are made to use empirical data to assess the validity of theories because the errors in measurement detract from the inferences that can be made from the data to the theoretical ideas. The greater the error, the less defensible are the inferences that can be made.

There are unfortunately a large number of different sources of measurement error, and these are examined in great detail in methodological literature such as Straus' (1964) analysis of the measurement of family variables, Campbell's (1967) analysis of sources of invalidity, and Blalock's (1971) analysis of causal models. It is not the intent of this discussion to review the numerous sources of measurement error. It is merely to point out that it exists and that it must be taken into account in trying to ascertain how useful empirical data are in testing the validity of theoretical propositions.

One of the consequences of the existence of measurement error is that it is almost always sufficient reason to not view one or two empirical studies as necessary to either prove or disprove a theoretical proposition. Instead, the data that are used to test hypotheses are evaluated in terms of the amount of evidence they provide. When there are several studies that investigate a particular relationship and they use several different operationalization techniques, this increases the evidence that can be brought to bear on a proposition, and this increases the confidence scientists can have in their conclusions about the validity or invalidity of that proposition.

Sampling

Most of the empirical research in the literature does not provide a complete or sufficient basis for accepting or rejecting specific propositions in part because an empirical researcher attempting to test the validity of the propositions has to work within some very practical limitations. For example, research is limited by such factors as economic resources, temporal pressures, and the number of trained personnel that can be used in the project. Thus an entire population is almost never measured. Rather, the researcher selects a sample of subjects hoping it is representative of a meaningful universe. Usually these are small and in several ways not representative of populations; or they may be representative of certain types of populations but not of others. The result is that the type of sample that is used in research has to be evaluated in trying to ascertain just what evidence a study provides for the validity or invalidity of various theoretical propositions.

It should also be noted, however, that scientists can be and frequently are too concerned about sampling procedures. Sampling procedures are highly crucial in *descriptive* research, but they are relatively less important in verificational research. Probably because so much of the social research that has been done in recent decades has been merely descriptive rather than testing relationships that have a theoretical basis, a belief has developed in the social sciences that researchers should be highly concerned about the sample that is used. However, in the type of research that tests theoretical ideas it is possible to move the priority of the sampling issues down considerably in the list of issues that must be satisfactorily coped with. Verificational research is interested in testing theoretical relationships, and it is not very impairing if the particular sample that is used in a study is taken from a very restricted universe. This is especially true in the beginning stages of testing the validity of a theory because one or even several separate studies do not provide a high order of proof. Eventually it is necessary to test theoretical ideas in systematically different universes not only to determine the circumstances under which the influence operates but also to compensate for other problems such as measurement errors; however, in the slow process of revising and testing theories a great deal of meaningful research can be done with economical, biased, and small samples.

Post Facto Data

Another factor that should be taken into account in assessing the level of proof that empirical data provide is whether the data were used to originally formulate the theoretical ideas or whether they were acquired independently of the formulation of the proposition. A proposition is initially formulated when there is a basis either in some empirical research or other theoretical ideas for thinking it is valid. The evidence that is used to generate this new theoretical idea, however, is almost never enough to conclude it is valid. The data do provide some evidence of the validity of the propositions, but it is usually considered a reasonably low level of proof. The theoretical insights that emerge while examining data should always be held as tentative until additional data have been examined to see if the relationships occur elsewhere.

Subjective Distortion

Whenever data are used to evaluate the validity of theories it is also important to recognize the possibility that the data might have been distorted in the process of being gathered and analyzed. It is not impossible that some researchers might engage in such practices as selectively publishing only those data that fit their ideas, changing the way data are presented so they will appear more favorable to their ideas than they are, and even fabricating data. It is, of course, very difficult for a reviewer to determine when this has occurred, but it is important that they be aware of the possibility that some of the published findings are erroneous.

Rosenthall (1967) has demonstrated that subjective distortion can also occur in another way. His data indicate that personal biases can influence observations and interpretations even when researchers are specifically trying to be as honorable as possible. Merton (1963) discusses some of the reasons for this, but in the present context the main concern is not with the causes of it as much as its consequences. One consequence is that multiple studies are needed to provide conclusive evidence either for or against theoretical propositions. Subjective distortion also may justify the practice of slightly underweighing the supporting evidence that comes from scholars who are obviously advocates of various theoretical ideas and overweighing the supporting evidence of opponents of theories. Certainly these differences in the weight of evidence should not be major differences, but there seems to be some basis for making this type of distinction.

Assessing the Validity of Theories in This Book

One of the major goals of the subsequent chapters of this book is to identify a large number of theoretical propositions that are useful in understanding family processes. This goal is accomplished by attempting to systematize, integrate, and extend theoretical ideas that exist in the literature. This goal is, however, only one of the two major goals of this book. The other is to systematically assess the level of proof that is presently available for or against these propositions. Chapter 2 has examined this process, but little has been said about just how these factors are taken into account in the subsequent chapters.

The system that is used here to assess the validity of the propositions is to first explicate a proposition or coherent group of propositions and then examine the data that are relevant for those propositions. The relevant data are examined by the following process:

1. Identifying the nature of data that seem to be relevant by briefly summarizing the source of the data, the hypotheses tested, and the findings.

2. Specifying the logical relationship between the hypotheses and the theoretical propositions. This includes identifying the assumptions that have to be made if the data are to be viewed as logically related to the propositions and the particular inferences that can be made from the data.

3. Evaluating how the unique limitations in the data influence the amount of confidence that can be placed on the inferences that are made.

It is important to point out that this process of evaluating when a particular inference is possible and how much confidence should be placed in it is a highly subjective process. Numerous factors influence the type of inferences that can be made, but the conclusions about which inferences are defensible are very much a matter of judgment. In addition, there are so many subtle ways that these factors influence the amount of confidence that should be placed in these inferences that any conclusions that emerge in an analysis of data are subject to question. The view that the scientific process is a highly impersonal, mechanical process that follows strict rules is a view that underappreciates the subjective elements in the acquisition of scientific knowledge. The subjective judgments that permit making some inferences and not others —especially at the frontiers of knowledge—are frequently highly tentative and debatable.

The kind of analysis that is undertaken in this book in evaluating the proof for and against theoretical ideas, in addition to being viewed as subjective, should be viewed as a process that occurs at one particular period in the history of a science, and much if not all that is in it will subsequently be revised. It will be revised by new theoretical and empirical developments as well as by corrections of misinterpretations of existing formulations or misapplication of the process of assessing the validity of theoretical ideas. It is thus a continual process, and the assessments made in this book are made only to be improved at a later time.

CHAPTER 3

MARITAL SATISFACTION

The main objective in this chapter is to examine propositions that explain variation in marital satisfaction. Before these propositions can be identified, however, it is necessary to explain what the term marital satisfaction refers to and how it is different from terms such as marital adjustment, happiness, or success. There is a great deal of ambiguity and confusion in the way these terms are used and this means that the usual pattern of merely providing definitions of terms is probably not the best solution. Instead, there needs to be a substantial reformulation of the conceptualization, and the first priority in this reformulation should be to maximize the clarity of the concepts. The first section of this chapter suggests an integrated conceptual scheme that will hopefully be useful. A number of theoretical ideas are then examined in the later sections.

A Conceptual Reformulation

There has been extensive criticism (Waller and Hill, 1951; Burr, 1967; Lively, 1969) of the very obscure conceptualization of the dependent variables that have been labeled with such terms as marital adjustment, happiness, integration, success, satisfaction, or effectiveness. The main points of criticism are that (1) most of these terms have never been carefully defined, (2) frequently, several different investigators use identical terms for what seem to be very different conceptual ideas, (3) different terms are frequently used by different investigators for what seems to be exactly the same idea, although in regard to this and the former point, the lack of definitions prevent scholars from being sure just what is being denoted, (4) most of the terms are highly value laden, (5) the multidimensional term and operationalizing procedure introduced by Burgess and Cottrell (1936) that has been used more extensively than any other approach is (a) conceptually so multidimensional and obscure that it is relatively meaningless, and (b) so limited by the idealistic, preselected criteria of success that it is probably misinforming when theorizing about many groups. Because of these characteristics of the earlier conceptualizations, the following conceptual revisions are suggested and then used in this chapter.

41

In Winch's (1963:663) attempt to clarify the conceptualization in this area and in the conceptual reformulation suggested by Burr (1967: Ch. 1) the term *success* is defined as the attainment of an end or goal. With this definition it is a nonspecific term that does not refer to any particular goal. When it is preceded with the adjective "marital" it refers to some type of marital goal, and this is different from theorizing about other types of success such as occupational success or educational success. The various marital goals that are of concern when theorizing about marital success have to be conceptualized separately, and there are a number of them that have been of concern in the literature. Some of these refer to the goals of the individuals, others to the goals of a couple, and others to the goals of a large social unit such as a society.

Stability is one marital goal that has been conceptualized frequently (Bernard, 1966). It is defined as the continued existence versus the termination of a marriage. When dealing with sociological variables, the theorist is concerned with variation in rates, and these are continuous variables such as rates of divorce, desertion, legal separation. When theorizing on a less macroscopic level by dealing with individuals, the concern is with the dichotomous variables of the occurrence versus nonoccurrence of these same phenomena.

Satisfaction is another marital goal that is highly valued in a number of contemporary cultures. It is defined as the degree to which the desires of individuals are fulfilled. This can be conceptualized either as satisfaction with the marriage situation as a whole, which would be *marital satisfaction,* or as satisfaction with specific aspects of the marriage situation such as satisfaction with sex or satisfaction with companionship. Apparently in all of these different ways of conceptualizing this phenomenon it is viewed as a continuous variable varying in degrees from low to high satisfaction. Whereas marital stability is an overt process that can be objectively detected, satisfaction is a subjective phenomenon that occurs within individuals.

Winch (1963:33 ff; 748–749) has conceptualized the term functionality, which can also be viewed as a marital goal. *Functionality* is the degree to which the family rather than other organizations carry out basic functions for a society. If there were agreement in the literature on the basic functions of a society, this would be a categorical variable, but at present it is apparently a relatively continuous variable that is best viewed as varying in such categories as high, moderate, and low degrees of functionality.

Hill (Waller and Hill, 1951:361–364) has conceptualized a phenomenon that is apparently best labeled as *personal development,* which can also be viewed as a marital goal. It is apparently a continuous variable that denotes the degree to which the individuals involved in a marriage are able to experience continuing development or growth rather than a lack of it in their personalities.

Another term that has been widely used is *marital adjustment*. It is proposed in this reformulation that this term be used to label the idea that was initially formulated by Burgess and Cottrell (1936) that gives an overall, general assessment of the marital experience. The present author finds it difficult to identify just what is denoted by this term and because of this meaninglessness finds the term difficult to use in theoretical formulations. Hence the best definition that is possible is an operational one stating that, whatever it is that the Burgess and Cottrell (1939) and later Locke and Wallace (1959) instruments measure—that is what is labeled as marital adjustment. It is a general, multidimensional concept that should not be confused with the more specific variables that have rational definitions.

Another conceptual development is the attempt by Farber (1957) to develop an index of *integration*. In his formulation, he viewed integration as being composed of two separate factors. One of these is the amount of *consensus* in a couple. Consensus is defined as the amount of agreement of opinion within a couple. In Farber's formulation he is concerned specifically with agreement on the importance of family goals. He labeled the other aspect of integration as role tension. *Role tension* is the degree to which the individuals perceive the presence of undesirable personality traits in their spouse's behavior. The more undesirable traits there are, the greater the role tension. This indicates failure to meet what is assumed to be the goal of avoiding tension. Since both of these two factors that Farber deals with as the components of integration are conceptually unique phenomena compared to the other goals that have been identified in this conceptual scheme, and since each could be viewed as being a marital goal, they could be included as separate types of marital success rather than as components of integration.

There are several other terms that have been used in the literature such as the term *love*. Blood and Wolfe (1960) identify this as a separate marital goal. It is apparently the subjectively experienced sentiment for the other person in the marital relationship and a continuous variable that is experienced in degrees of intensity from a low to a high level of love. It is to be differentiated from *romanticism* such as that dealt with by Dean (1961, 1964) and others. Apparently the term romanticism is a continuous variable that conceptualizes the degree to which the love that is experienced is spontaneous and irrational as opposed to being rationally controlled and calculated. The term *happiness* has also been widely used. Terman (1938) used it for what has here been labeled adjustment, and Landis (1963) used it as a relatively specific dimension. The part of reality Landis was dealing with closely approximates what has in the present formulation been defined as marital satisfaction. Because of this redundancy no unique use can be found for this term in the present formulation. There are also other conceptual terms that have been used in this type of research that have not been dealt with here because of limitations of space. These include family interests, effectiveness, and disorganization. Their inclusion will need to wait for an extension of this conceptual systematization.

Theoretical Propositions about Marital Satisfaction

Nye and Bayer (1963) point out that family scholars have conducted more research on marital success variables than in any other area of inquiry. It is lamentable to observe, however, that most of this research has consisted of very atheoretical inquiries into the mere existence of relationships between variables. Very little of it has been guided by systematic theoretical ideas. Some of it has been guided by conceptual developments in some of the conceptual frameworks that have been evolving in recent decades, but seldom have these conceptual abstractions been used to develop bona fide theory. There are, however, scattered beginnings of theoretical formulations, and some of these will be integrated here so they can then be expanded and additional tests can be made. Most of the theoretical propositions in this section deal with factors that influence marital satisfaction, but occasionally an influential relationship is identified that has one of the other marital goals as the dependent variable.

Propositions from Symbolic Interaction

Hill and Hansen (1960) and Stryker (1959, 1964) have pointed out that the conceptualization in the symbolic interaction literature has provided the basis for a great deal of research on family processes. Stryker also commented, however, as follows:

> Those who view the family from the framework of symbolic interaction presumably aspire to the development of theory which fits the data of the family as a social unit; by and large, as will be suggested, this task remains to be done (Stryker, 1964:125).

This unfortunate condition of having a great deal of empirical data and very little systematic theorizing is gradually being remedied because there have been several attempts in recent years to use the concepts in the interactionist perspective to generate bona fide theoretical propositions. Mangus (1957) was the first to identify a group of propositions that assert how variables influence the marital relationship. Others such as Cottrell (1933) had earlier argued that the concept of role is useful in understanding marital dynamics, but they had not made any relationships explicit. One of Mangus' assertions was that "the integrative quality of a marriage is reflected in the degree of congruence between what a spouse expects in a mate and what he actually perceives in the one he married" (1957:208). This initial statement of the idea leaves much to be desired in conceptual clarity, but it can be stated more clearly if several of the concepts in the interactionist conceptual framework are defined.

The term *norm* is usually defined (e.g., Biddle and Thomas, 1966:26–27) as prescriptions or proscriptions that identify the behavior that "should" or "ought" to be either performed or not performed. Prescriptions define what should be done and proscriptions identify what should not be done. Norms seldom state that a behavior is either appropriate or inappropriate in an absolute sense, but rather define what should or should not be done in various situations. The term *role behavior* (Biddle and Thomas 1966:26; Hill and Rodgers, 1964:182) is the action of a person when occupying a social role. When the role behavior does not conform to norms this creates a certain type of discrepancy, and these have been conceptualized by Mangus (1957) and Burr (1967, 1971) as *role discrepancies*. This variable of role discrepancies varies continuously from a low number to a high number of discrepancies, and it seems to be the independent variable in the propositional assertion made by Mangus.

The dependent variable in Mangus' formulation is also ambiguous, since he merely identifies it as the "integrative quality of marriages." The context of his proposition indicates, however, that he was apparently primarily concerned with what has been called marital satisfaction in the conceptual reformulation in this volume. If this is the case, his idea can be stated as a proposition.

PROPOSITION 3.1:   The number of role discrepancies in the marital relationship influence marital satisfaction and this is an inverse, linear relationship.[1]

Mangus seemed to imply that this relationship is inverse and monotonic, but Ort's (1950) and Burr's (1967) data both had linear relationships. Burr speculated that if the extremes of the ranges of variation in these variables were to be taken into account, it would be likely that the re-

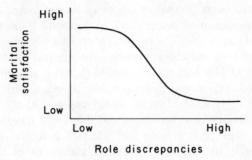

Figure 3.1 Theorized relationship between role discrepancies and marital satisfaction.

lationship would be a third-order or cubic relationship as diagramed in Figure 3.1, but no data have supported this speculation.

There have been several empirical studies that have tested this relationship. Ort (1950), Kotlar (1961), Burr (1967, 1971), and Hawkins and Johnsen (1969) tested hypotheses deduced from this proposition and found correlation coefficients ranging from .60 to .85 between the variables. There is thus considerable evidence that this relationship exists, that it is linear, and that there is considerable covariation between the variables. This provides some evidence that this is a relatively influential relationship. This evidence should be viewed cautiously, however, since similarities in the way the two variables were measured in each study may have introduced measurement error that would inflate the covariation. Moreover, since no variables were controlled in any of these studies, there is a possibility that much of the covariation is spurious. Additional research is thus needed to measure the variables in different ways and control other variables.

Extension of Proposition 3.1: There have been two attempts to extend the simple, two-variable proposition 3.1 beyond the elementary statement that an influential, linear relationship exists. One of these is Orden and Bradburn's (1968) attempt to demonstrate that there are two independent dimensions that influence marital satisfaction:

> Marriage happiness may be viewed as a resultant of two independent dimensions, a dimension of satisfactions and a dimension of tensions. Both dimensions are related to marriage happiness, yet they appear to operate independently in specifying levels of happiness. Tensions and satisfactions are, however, virtually independent of each other (1968:715).

The two independent variables in this formulation are fairly clear. Both are apparently continuous variables, and they vary in number. Satisfactions vary between having nothing in the marital situation that has a positive effect to having a large number of aspects that have a positive effect. Tensions vary between having none and having a large number of aspects of marital situation that have negative effect. These authors use the label "happiness" for their dependent variable, but conceptually they seem to be concerned with individual's subjective rating of the satisfactoriness of their overall marital situation. This was labeled in the conceptual reformulation as marital satisfaction, and hence this term will be used in this analysis of their ideas. The assertions in the Orden and Bradburn formulation can be summarized in the following three propositions.

PROPOSITION 3.2: The number of satisfactions in the marital relationship influences the overall marital satisfaction and this is a positive, linear relationship.

PROPOSITION 3.3: The number of tensions in the marital relationship influences the overall marital satisfaction and this is a negative, linear relationship.

PROPOSITION 3.4: The number of satisfactions in the marital relationship is not related to the number of tensions.

Orden and Bradburn do not explicitly state that they are postulating linear relationships in propositions 3.2 and 3.3, but the context of their paper seems to indicate this is the intent.

This formulation can be integrated with proposition 3.1 if variation in role discrepancies is viewed as one type of "tension" in the marital relationship. When this is done, proposition 3.1 can be deduced from the more general proposition 3.3. The logic is that if role discrepancies are one type of tension in the marital relationship, and if proposition 3.3 is true in asserting there is an influential relationship between the number of tensions and marital satisfaction, it follows that the relationship in proposition 3.1 can be expected to occur. With these two propositions being logically related in this manner the empirical data that support assertions made in proposition 3.1 can also be viewed as indirectly supporting these same aspects of proposition 3.3. Thus it is likely that the relationship in proposition 3.3 is inverse, linear, and probably very influential.

Orden and Bradburn also analyze some data as a test of their ideas. Their data are from a NORC study of psychological well-being conducted in 1965 on 781 husbands and 957 wives drawn from probability samples in several major metropolitan centers. They analyzed a relatively small number of aspects of marital relationships since data were gathered on only 18 recent experiences of the individuals, but the data are consistent with the propositions. The positive and negative dimensions have coefficients of association beween −.01 and −.15 while two dimensions correlate with overall "happiness" ratings between .20 and .44. This thus provides some data in support of their formulation.

Another attempt to extend the ideas in proposition 3.1 was by Burr (1967). In this formulation the objective was to theorize about the circumstances under which role discrepancies differ in their influence on marital satisfaction. This was done by using value as a contingent variable and theorizing that the value of role discrepancies influences the impact that role discrepancies have on marital satisfaction. *Value* was defined as the subjective definition of the relative worth or importance of a particular phenomenon, and its variation was viewed as continuous between the extremes of being highly negatively valued through neutrality to a high degree of positive value. This definition is very similar to Nye's (1967), but it differs in that Nye restricts values to a "high level abstraction which encompasses a whole category of objects, feelings, and/or experiences" (1967:241). In the definition used in Burr's formulation an evaluation can be made of a wide range of things from a piece of property to a type of behavior or an emotional feeling. It is merely an assessment of the relative worth or importance of something, and this can be made about virtually anything.

After the valuing process was defined, a very general proposition (3.5) was then identified from which a more specific proposition was deduced.

PROPOSITION 3.5:   The value of a phenomenon influences the amount of effect this phenomenon has in social processes and this is a positive, monotonic relationship.

This relationship was suggested as a positive relationship that probably operates in a logarithmic manner as diagramed in Figure 3.2. Burr argued that it was difficult to know how influential it is but intuitively suggested it should be highly influential.

This proposition was initially proposed as a result of two very different pieces of literature. One was Sumner's (1906) analysis of the difference between folkways and mores, and the other was Christensen and Carpenter's (1962) analysis of the effects that variation in values has on the consequences of premarital sexual behavior.

Sumner (1906) argues that mores are different from folkways in that the "welfare" of the group is more at stake when mores are violated. He then contends that the mores influence behavior more than folkways. Burr (1967) added the value dimension to this reasoning by arguing that

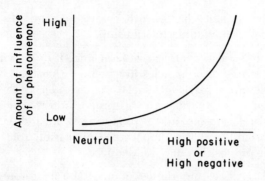

The value of the phenomenon

Figure 3.2 The proposed relationship between values and the amount of influence in social processes.

the fact that mores are more valued may cause them to influence behavior more than folkways. He reasoned, for example, that if a cultural belief were valued less, even though nonconformity may in unknown ways jeopardize the welfare of the group, it would probably influence behavior less than if the belief were more highly valued.

Christensen and Carpenter's (1962) research was viewed as relevant because they found that the guilt that was experienced with premarital coitus was associated with the culturally defined importance of the sexual behavior rather than the behavior itself. This seemed to justify the rather specific proposition that variation in the value of the sexual behavior influences the effect this behavior has on guilt. This idea was then used as part of the basis for inducing the idea in proposition 3.5.

The idea in proposition 3.5 was used to try to explain why role discrepancies vary in their influence on marital satisfaction by deducing that if evaluative distinctions are made about how important it is that behavior conform to norms, and if proposition 3.5 is true, then variation in this type of value judgment probably influences the impact the conformity or nonconformity has on such things as marital satisfaction. This rather specific type of value judgment was conceptualized by Burr (1967, 1971) as the *importance* of role discrepancies, and it was defined as the relative value placed on behavior conforming to norms. It was suggested that, being a particular type of valuing, it is a continuous variable varying in degree from a high negative value to a high positive value. Proposition 3.6 emerges from this reasoning.

PROPOSITION 3.6: The importance of role discrepancies is related to the amount of influence that variation in role discrepancies has on other variables and this is a positive, monotonic relationship.

This proposition is also relatively general since it deals with variation in the influence of role discrepancies in general rather than with why their influence varies in a particular social system such as the marital relationship. If, however, the idea in this proposition is specifically applied to the marital relationship, and if propositions 3.1 and 3.6 are true, and if there is variability in the importance of marital role discrepancies, then a further proposition may be deduced.

PROPOSITION 3.7:   The importance of marital role discrepancies is related to the amount of influence in proposition 3.1 which asserts that marital role discrepancies influence marital satisfaction; and this is a positive, monotonic relationship.

This relationship is probably similar to the curve in Figure 3.2, but the amount of influence is difficult to assess.

When the theoretical ideas in proposition 3.1 and proposition 3.7 are combined into one proposition, this results in what Zetterberg (1965:71) refers to as a contingent proposition.

PROPOSITION 3.8:   The number of role discrepancies influences marital satisfaction; and this is an inverse, linear relationship, but the amount of variation in marital satisfaction varies according to the amount of importance that is attributed to the role discrepancies.

This contingent proposition is concerned with a more complicated issue than the earlier simple proposition about the influence of role discrepancies since it attempts to specify some of the circumstances under which role discrepancies differ in their influence on marital satisfaction.

The only research that has been found that is related to these propositions about the importance of role discrepancies is Burr's (1967, 1971) study of a sample of middle-class married couples. He measured the importance variable and found that those role discrepancies rated low in importance had a lower correlation with marital satisfaction than those higher in importance. The study provided more new questions than conclusive findings, however, because the importance variable seemed to make more difference for the husbands than the wives, and it did not operate in exactly the way expected. The role discrepancies that correlated highest with marital satisfaction were those that were rated moderately high in importance. Those that were rated as most important, especially for the wives, had an intermediate amount of covariation. The study thus provides some supporting evidence for the assertions in these propositions that a relationship exists, but it provides some evidence that the nature of the relationship in propositions 3.5, 3.6, and 3.7 may be curvilinear with the moderately high levels of importance having the greatest effect.

Compensation: Wallin and Clark (1964) introduced a new theoretical insight in their attempt to investigate whether certain aspects of the marital situation tend to compensate for dissatisfaction with other areas in the marital relationship. It is possible to integrate their work into the theoretical ideas that have been identified thus far. They found that for the wives in their sample their religiosity tended to mitigate the detrimental effect that sexual maladjustment has on marital satisfaction. They did not, however, find the same compensatory effect for husbands. The variables that Wallin and Clark studied are relatively specific and it is not possible to generalize very much with them. It is, however, possible to ignore these particular variables and to focus on the social processes that are involved; and when this is done it is possible to inductively generate several more abstract theoretical propositions. In a very broad sense, what these authors are proposing is that some aspects of a relationship can, under certain circumstances, compensate for the detrimental effects of role discrepancies in other areas of interaction. Since some aspects of marital relationships are apparently compensatory and some are not, the *compensatoriness* of these phenomena can be viewed as a variable. If this variable is defined as the degree to which something counterbalances or offsets the disruptive influences of role discrepancies, it is likely that this can be a useful variable. It is suggested that compensatoriness is a continuous variable ranging from having no compensatoriness to having a high degree of compensatoriness.

The main theoretical idea that can be gleaned from the Wallin and Clark study is that they suggest that it is the "value" of something that influences whether or not it will be compensatory. Value in this context is being used as it was defined on page 48. In the case of the particular variables they were studying, Wallin and Clark suggest that variation in the value of religiosity made it compensate for the wives and not compensate for the husbands. If the specific variables dealt with in their study are ignored while concern is focused on the valuing process itself, and if the idea in proposition 3.5 is applied to this situation, it is then possible to state proposition 3.9.

PROPOSITION 3.9:   The value of a phenomenon influences its compensatoriness and this is a positive, monotonic relationship.

Wallin and Clark also argue that one of the reasons that religiosity was not compensatory for the husbands was because of the high value of the sexual aspect of marriage. If this valuing process is also generalized beyond just this one specific area, it is possible to also induce a new proposition.

PROPOSITION 3.10:   The value of a phenomenon influences the degree to which other phenomena are compensatory for it and this is an inverse, monotonic relationship.

The last two propositions are fairly general in that they deal with valuing in general rather than valuing any specific, identifiable phenomenon. It is now possible, however, to deduce to additional aspects of marital relationships other than religiosity and sexual satisfaction to see if these general propositions are defensible. It is hoped that this will be done in future research.

Homans' Propositions

A sizable literature has accumulated in recent years on how variation in interaction influences human processes. Some of this has focused specifically on how certain aspects of interaction influence marital processes, but a great deal of it has dealt with these variables at a general level only and has never applied them to the marital relationship. This section of Chapter 3 is an attempt to integrate some of these general propositions and explicitly identify their relevance for the marital relationship.

Interaction and Sentiment: Homans' (1950) classic monograph on *The Human Group* identifies several general propositions that deal with such variables as activity, interaction, and sentiment. Interaction can be defined as action reciprocating between humans "when and insofar as the acting individual attaches a subjective meaning to it" (Weber, 1947:88). As Homans pointed out in his later monograph (1961:35), however, this type of definition of the concept of interaction does not identify it as a variable. It is just a concept. He then proceeded to identify two ways that interaction varies—in amount of interaction and in the value of interaction.

The *amount of interaction* conceptualizes variation in the volume or quantity of interaction or the frequency of it within a given period of time. It is a continuous variable varying from none to a high amount. The other variable of the *value of interaction* is quite different from the amount. The concept value was defined earlier as a differentiation or variation in the worth or importance of something. Homans' (1961:40) definition is essentially the same, and he also views it as varying from a highly positive to a highly negative degree. Thus the *value of interaction* is a variable that conceptualizes variation in the worth or importance of interaction, and it varies continuously between the two poles of highly negative to highly positive.

One of Homans' other main variables is sentiment. This is defined as the affective feeling a person experiences, and Homans (1961) argues that this can also vary in quantity and in value. The quantity of sentiment, however, varies in a slightly different way from the quantity of interaction. The quantity of interaction varies from being absent to having a large amount of it, but the quantity of sentiment varies in two directions from its point of absence. It varies continuously in degree from a high amount of negative sentiment through a point of neutrality or absence of sentiment to a high amount of positive sentiment. The value of sentiment also varies in this same manner between the sentiment having a high amount of negative value to a high amount of positive value. These four variables were not identified with this same degree of clarity in Homans' initial formulation (1950) where apparently he was theorizing only about the quantity of interaction and the quantity of sentiment. The nature of the variation of each of these variables, however, is made explicit in his later (1961) monograph.

The main theoretical idea that Homans proposes that is useful in understanding the marital interaction processes and marital satisfaction lies in a proposition that Zetterberg (1965:72) refers to as an interdependent proposition. It relates the amount of interaction and amount of sentiment. Homans proposed that if either of these two variables vary, it influences the other. This assertion is restated here not as one interdependent proposition but as two separate, simple propositions.

PROPOSITION 3.11:   The amount of interaction influences the amount of sentiment and this is a positive, monotonic relationship.

PROPOSITION 3.12:   The amount of sentiment influences the amount of interaction.

It is difficult to discern just what type of relationship Homans was proposing in his formulation. He apparently views the relationship in proposition 3.11 as a monotonically positive relationship, but he does not attempt to identify the pattern of covariation in more specific terms than this. The relationship in proposition 3.12 is apparently more complex than that in 3.11. Apparently variation in positive sentiment is positively related to interaction and variation in negative sentiment is inversely related to interaction.

Homans' (1950) extensive analysis of data that are related to these two propositions has been regarded as one of the classics in the social science literature. The variety of data he brings to bear in evaluating these propositions is sufficiently impressive that the reaction to them has since been one of refining them to determine the factors that influence how and when they operate and to study the variety of social situations where deductions can be made. Newcomb comments about these propositions as follows:

> So widespread and so compelling is the evidence for the relationship between frequency of interaction and positive attraction that Homans has ventured to hypothesize that "If the frequency of interaction between two or more persons increases, the degree of their liking for one another will increase." Actually speaking, the evidence is altogether overwhelming that, *ignoring other variables,* the proposition is correct in a wide range of circumstances (1956:576).

Exchange Proposition

Several years after Homans published his monograph on *The Human Group* (1950) he published a paper (1958) in which he viewed human behavior as an exchange relationship. This paper was one of the earliest of a large number of publications by students of human behavior that have attempted to use what has come to be known as "exchange theory" as a method of explaining social processes. This literature includes such work as Homans' (1961) monograph on *Elementary Forms of Social Behavior,* Thibaut and Kelley's (1959) analysis of *The Social Psychology of Groups,* and Goode's (1960) "Theory of Role Strain."

Exchange theory is not a different strategy of theorizing from the type of formulation that occurs in deductive theory. Each of the publications mentioned in the last paragraph uses a deductive type of explanation in its analyses. Exchange theory can be differentiated from other deductive theories only in that the theorists using it have concentrated on a unique set of variables that have been relatively ignored by other theorists. The value of the exchange theory literature in the present context is that it extends the ideas in the two interactional propositions that were just mentioned, and the expanded formulation seems to be potentially very

useful in explaining variation in marital satisfaction. Before this formulation can be related to marital satisfaction, however, it is necessary to
identify several additional concepts and several relatively general propositions.

Profit: Homans (1961:61–64) identifies a concept that he labels *profit*.
Others refer to this same conceptual phenomenon with other terms. For
example, Thibaut and Kelley (1959: Ch.13) use the term outcomes. The
particular label that is used is not important but the phenomenon denoted by these terms is. *Profit* here denotes the particular balance of rewards and costs that individuals experience from something. A reward is
apparently defined by these authors as a desirable consequence, and a
cost as an undesirable consequence. As Thibaut and Kelley state:

> For some purposes it is desirable to treat rewards and costs separately; for
> other purposes it is assumed that they can be combined into a single scale of
> "goodness" of outcome, with states of high reward and low cost being given
> high-scale values and states of low reward and high cost, low-scale values
> (1959:13).

None of these theorists are very specific in identifying just what it is
that is varying when this profit variable varies. It is difficult to know
whether it is the number of rewards or costs or whether it is some sort
of psychological intensity of them. Thibaut and Kelley, however, note:

> The cost is high when great physical or mental effort is required, when em-
> barrassment or anxiety accompany the action, or when there are conflicting
> forces or competing response tendencies of any sort. Costs derived from these
> different factors are also assumed to be measurable on a common psychologi-
> cal scale, and costs of different sorts, to be additive in their effect (1959:13).

What both they and Homans seem to be saying is that rewards and
costs vary continuously, and that they vary in amount. The variation in
amount is probably not the same as variation in number, since some
things that are rewarding or costly provide a greater "amount" than others. It is apparently a psychological assessment of the overall amount of
cost and/or reward.

Profit from Interaction: Profit is very relevant for Homans' propositions
about interaction and sentiment. As he points out (1961:186–187), the
profit received from interaction seems to influence the type of sentiment
that is produced in proposition 3.11, which asserts that variation in interaction influences sentiment. Homans argues that variation in interaction influences the amount of sentiment whether the interaction is rewarding or costly. If, however, it is rewarding, it produces positive sentiment; if it is costly, it produces negative sentiment. The independent

variable in this formulation is profit from interaction, and in this idea Homans is concerned with it only as a dichotomy that varies between being a cost or reward. The dependent variable is the type of sentiment, and this too is only a dichotomy that varies between being positive or negative. Proposition 3.13 identifies this idea.

PROPOSITION 3.13:   If the profit from interaction is rewarding, the sentiment produced by interaction tends to be positive, whereas if the profit is costly, the sentiment tends to be negative.

This proposition deals with these variables as dichotomies only, and hence it does not take into account any of the additional variation that can apparently occur in the amount of profit or the amount of sentiment. It is possible, however, to expand these ideas and theorize about how the variation in the amount of profit has an important influence.

Homans is not explicit in stating a proposition about how the amount of profit influences other variables, but he does state (1961:55) that the value of the activity each person receives influences the frequency of interaction, and he further states that "no exchange continues unless both parties are making profit" (1961:61). What he seems to be identifying is a chain sequence of events with the value of interaction influencing the profit from it and the profit influencing the amount of interaction. These assertions can be summarized in the two following propositions.

PROPOSITION 3.14:   The value of interaction influences the amount of profit from the interaction and this is a positive, monotonic relationship.

PROPOSITION 3.15:   The profit from interaction influences the amount of interaction and this is a positive, monotonic relationship.

There is little basis for asserting anything about the nature of these relationships other than that they are probably positive and monotonic. It is likely, however, that in proposition 3.15 the influence of the profit variable increases as it reaches its extremes. If this is the case, the relationship is summarized with line A in Figure 3.3. It may be, however, that this is not the shape of this relationship. Homans' point that interaction will not continue when the profit variable decreases to costs may mean that the variation in the profit variable has its greatest influence at the marginal point where the profit variable moves between cost and reward. If this is the case, line B in Figure 3.3 summarizes the relationship in this proposition. There are at present no data that demonstrate that

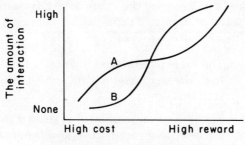

Figure 3.3 The relationship between the profit of interaction and the amount of interaction.

either of these shapes is the accurate description of this relationship. Perhaps future research will provide data from which inferences can be made about the shape of this relationship.

Thus far no literature has been found that suggests how the variation in the profit from interaction has any other influence, but it seems likely that there is another relationship. It is possible that when the profit from interaction varies, this positively influences the amount of sentiment that results from interaction. Homans' proposition identified here as 3.11 states that variation in interaction positively influences sentiment, and what is being proposed here is that the profit from the interaction operates as a contingent variable and positively influences the amount of influence that the interaction has on sentiment.

PROPOSITION 3.16:   The amount of profit from interaction is related to the amount of influence interaction has on sentiment and this is a positive relationship.

There is no empirical basis for knowing the nature of this relationship. It could correspond to either of the curves in Figure 3.3, or it may be linear. This can be learned only through future research.

Profit from Sentiment: Two other propositions closely related to the last propositions should be identified before this formulation is tied to marital satisfaction. These have to do with the profit from sentiment and the value of sentiment. Homans (1961: Ch.3) explicitly identifies the variable of the value of sentiment, but he then only makes casual reference to it in his substantive chapters. It seems reasonable, however, that the value of sentiment and the profit received from sentiment would operate in much the same way that the value of interaction and the profit from interaction operate in influencing the relationships Homans proposes between interaction and sentiment. The ideas that are being suggested can be stated in the two following propositions.

PROPOSITION 3.17: The value of sentiment influences the amount of profit from the sentiment and this is a positive, monotonic relationship.

PROPOSITION 3.18: The profit from sentiment is related to the amount of influence that variation in the amount of sentiment has on the quantity of interaction.

These propositions are both highly speculative, so there is only an intuitive basis for suggesting the nature of the relationships in them. No additional assertions are made about the relationship in 3.17 other than that it is positive and probably monotonic. In proposition 3.18, however, it seems reasonable that a different relationship exists. When positive sentiment occurs the variation in the profit from the sentiment is probably positively associated with the influence the sentiment has on interaction. However, when negative sentiment exists, it is likely that the relationship is uniquely different. It is very possible that variation in the profit from the negative sentiment would be inversely related to the amount of influence the negative sentiment would have on interaction. In other words, in a situation where there is high profit from a negative sentiment, the negative sentiment would not decrease interaction as much as if there were low profit from the sentiment. If this is the case, variation in profit would exert a positive influence on the impact of positive sentiment and a negative influence on the influence that negative sentiment has on interaction. These speculations are, of course, nothing more than speculations, and empirical data are needed to test their validity.

Exchange Propositions and Marital Satisfaction: Thus far in the present formulation, this rather complex set of exchange propositions has not been specifically tied to the marital relationship. They are all sufficiently general that they could be applied to a wide range of interpersonal situations ranging from relationships in business to religious cloisters. They can, however, be specifically related to the marital institution by identifying a proposition that seems so obvious and commonplace that this author has not even found it explicitly stated in the scientific literature. This is that sentiment is related to marital satisfaction.

It is probably the case that variation in sentiment is not related to many types of satisfaction such as satisfaction with an inanimate object

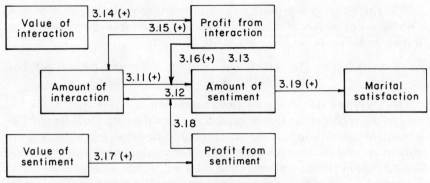

Figure 3.4 The relationships in propositions 3.11 to 3.19.

or satisfaction with a person occupying a political office. In the institution of marriage, however, the sentimental feelings toward the other person are usually defined as one of the important components of the relationship, which leads to proposition 3.19.

PROPOSITION 3.19:   The amount of sentiment influences marital satisfaction and this is a positive, monotonic relationship.

The relationship in this proposition is undoubtedly positive, but it is likely that it is not linear. Probably variation at the extremes of sentiment has significantly greater influence than variation at the neutral part of the independent variable.

These interactional and exchange propositions form such a complex model that it is probably desirable to summarize the entire formulation. This is done in Figure 3.4, which shows the relationships between the variables in propositions 3.11 to 3.19. The boxes in this figure identify the variables, and the lines identify the relationships between the variables. An arrow this indicates that causality or influence is asserted, and the number by each line is the proposition number. Whenever there is a clear-cut direction to the relationship a (+) or (−) is added to indicate the direction.

Altruism

Buerkle and his associates (Buerkle and Badgley, 1959; Buerkle and Anderson, 1961) have investigated the possibility that altruism is a general factor in marital satisfaction. They view altruism as a tendency for individuals to respond in ways that favor the other person when there is a conflict of interest. It is apparently a tendency to combine sympathy and adaptability as a typical way of interacting with the other person. This seems to be a continuous variable that varies in degree from no altruistic behavior to all behavior being altruistic.

PROPOSITION 3.20:   The amount of altruism influences marital satisfaction and this is a positive relationship.

The literature that discusses this proposition does not specify the nature of the relationship that is expected, other than that it is asserted as a positive relationship. This was probably because the authors were only interested in determining whether the relationship existed. Buerkle and Anderson (1961) gathered data from a group in a clinical setting to determine whether they differed in their altruistic behavior. They found no relationship between the variables and conclude that if altruism is an important variable in marital interaction, it is within specific contexts rather than as a general trait. Their data were not detailed enough to provide information about the contexts within which altruism operates and hence can only be viewed as evidence against the existence of the relationship as it is identified in proposition 3.20. There is thus no evidence that the trait of altruism is related to marital satisfaction, and some evidence of the absence of a relationship.

Empathy

There is a large body of literature that suggests that empathic behavior is conducive to the type of interpersonal relationships that are satisfying in marriage (Foote and Cottrell, 1955). This phenomenon of empathy is defined in several different ways, so it is important that its definition in this context is explicit. In the social sciences, empathy is the intellectual understanding of an aspect of another person such as their attitudes, intentions, emotions, or behavior (Dymond, 1953). It is the accurate, intellectual awareness of the aspect of the other rather than a vicarious experience similar to the other person's. This latter meaning is an accurate use of the term in the English language, but it is not included in what is denoted when the term is used as a scientific concept. Empathy as a variable is a continuous variable that varies from being absent when there is no understanding to the logical possibility of complete understanding.

The relationship between empathy and marital satisfaction has been proposed as a positive relationship. Burgess and Wallin state, for example, "A moderately high degree of empathy markedly facilitates marital adjustments" (1953:625). It is interesting that this statement does not seem to imply a linear relationship. It seems that they are rather asserting that inadequate levels of empathy hinder adjustment and moderate levels facilitate it, but no statement is made about high levels of empathy. The relationship that is suggested here conforms to this with the additional expectation that increases in empathy beyond moderately high levels do not continue to facilitate marital adjustment. This is diagramed in Figure 3.5.

PROPOSITION 3.21: The amount of empathy influences marital satisfaction and this is a positive, curvilinear relationship with the influence occuring in the low range of empathy.

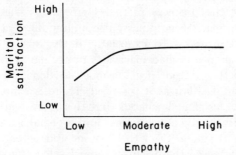

Figure 3.5   The theorized relationship between empathy and marital satisfaction.

Although there has been considerable research concerning this proposition, it is relatively inconclusive since some studies have found no relationship between empathy and marital satisfaction and others have found the relationship as theorized. Dymond (1953) had 15 couples predict their mate's responses to 115 items from the Minnesota Multiphasic Personality Inventory. She found significant differences between the "happy" and "unhappy" groups in their ability to correctly predict the other person's responses. Corsini (1956), on the other hand, investigated 20 university students' marriages using a 50-item Q sort of adjectives describing personality and found no evidence indicating happiness in marriage was related to understanding the mate. Wallen (1957) found no relationship in his study of the ability to predict the mate's child-rearing goals. He concluded that prediction was more a function of the predictor's own self-preferences and group stereotypes than it was of an empathetic ability. Hobart and Klausner (1959) found that predicting the spouse's responses to a personality inventory and a list of personal characteristics was correlated with marital adjustment, but predicting the spouse's conception of marital roles was not.

One interesting empirical finding in regard to this proposition is that some data indicate the relationship in this proposition may operate for wives but not for husbands. Luckey (1961) found that the accuracy of the wife's perceptions of her husband's self views was related to the husband's satisfaction, whereas there was no relationship between the accuracy of the husband's perceptions and the wife's satisfaction. Stukert (1963) also found the accuracy of wife's perceptions to be related to the wife's satisfaction with the marriage and the accuracy of the husband's empathy to be unrelated. He also further analyzed his data and found that when the husbands' opinions about marital roles were different from their wives, the accuracy of their perceptions was *negatively* related to their own marital happiness. The highly different husbands who were poor empathizers were especially likely to be happy if they thought most other people had marriages pretty much like theirs.

These findings thus do not provide much evidence in support of the validity of this proposition as it is stated. There is some evidence it is more valid for wives than husbands, but this is meager evidence. The fact that the findings are contradictory, and especially Stuckert's finding that such things as similarity of the spouses and perceptions of other's marriages are related to these issues, indicate that the relationship between empathy and marital satisfaction is influenced by other variables. It hence may be that if this proposition is true, it will be of little value until additional theorizing is undertaken to specify how some of these other variables interact with empathic abilities in influencing such things as marital satisfaction.

There is one additional point that is relevant in assessing the usefulness of this empirical research as a test of the validity of the proposition. Since this research deals with mature adults who are able to function relatively well in society, and since several of the samples came from university populations, it seems likely that the lower ranges of the empathy variables were never included in the samples. It may be that when the empathy variable is genuinely low it makes considerable difference, and none of the studies detected this extreme type of variation.

Marital Satisfaction and Balance Theory

There has been a great deal of research on the relationship between marital satisfaction and such variables as similarity, congruence, consensus, and homogamy. Most of this research has never been integrated into a theoretical model, but it is possible that it can be integrated in a meaningful way with what has come to be known as balance theory (Heider, 1958; Newcomb, 1961). Newcomb has published one of the most extensively developed and systematic formulations using balance theory in his analysis of the acquaintance process, and the present section of this chapter is an attempt to integrate his model with the research that has investigated the relationship between marital satisfaction and the previously mentioned similarity-type variables. The first objective of this process is an explication of the nature of balance theory.

Balance Theory: Several of the main ideas in Newcomb's formulation are summarized in his assertion that "Our system-like formulations include not only the assumption that attitude change is influenced by attraction but also the converse—that change in attraction is influenced by existing attitudes" (1961:20). This rather general statement introduces his ideas, and it is now necessary to identify the variables, define them, determine how they vary, and clearly state the relationships that are asserted by Newcomb to exist between them.

The term *attitudes* is used by Newcomb to refer to a very broad, inclusive phenomenon. He defines attitudes as an orientation "toward a non-person object" (1961:7). Orientations are apparently persisting cognitive and emotional reactions that can vary in that they can be either positive or negative or favorable or unfavorable reactions. Newcomb refers to this variation in orientation as variation in sign. Attitudes themselves are not variables. It is the sign of an attitude—whether the reaction is positive or negative—that is the variable since it can vary.

One of the other major concepts in Newcomb's statement just cited is attraction. He defines attraction as orientations toward other persons:

> Such phrases as "I'm rather fond of her," or "I refuse to have anything to do with him," suggest both sign and intensity of direct interpersonal orientations. It is doubtless natural to equate attraction with "liking," but we prefer to conceptualize attraction in somewhat broader terms. Thus respect, admiration, and dependent all refer to positive person-to-person orientations, and yet any of these may be associated with either positive or negative liking. In its most general form, therefore, attraction refers to any direct orientation (on the part of one person toward another) which may be described in terms of sign and intensity (1961:6).

It seems that what Newcomb thus defines as attraction is for all practical purposes the same conceptual phenomenon that Homans (1950) defines as sentiment (as noted earlier in this chapter) except that Homans does not limit this sentiment to just being a feeling toward a person. Both sentiment and attraction are continuous variables that vary in degree from strongly negative through a neutral point to strongly positive emotional reactions to other persons. Since Homans' terminology has already been used in this book, it is selected as the label that is used for this phenomenon. It can be easily seen that this particular type of orientation can vary in what Newcomb refers to as intensity and Homans refers to as amount.

The heart of Newcomb's formulation is that individuals have a tendency to maintain a balance "between perceived similarity of attitudes and sentiment." *Balance* is a condition in which the degree of sentiment toward another person is congruent with the degree of similarity of their attitudes. If, for example, a person perceives another person's attitudes as very different from his own attitudes, this relationship would be in balance if he has considerable negative sentiment for this person. If he were to like this person, however, there would then be a condition of imbalance. Apparently the variable of balance is a dichotomous variable varying between the two discrete categories of balance and imbalance. What Newcomb suggests is the following:

(If a relationship) is in fact imbalance(d), then one or more of the members of the collectivity will discover the fact; this discovery will be followed by individual strain-instigated changes on that member's part (and, assuming that they are observed by others, on their parts also) that tend to reduce the collective imbalance (1961:19).

This statement introduces another variable that Newcomb refers to as *strain*. This variable seems to denote personally experienced stress or discomfort. It can apparently vary from a point of absence to relatively high degrees, and Newcomb seems to view it as a continuous variable. The theoretical ideas that have thus far been introduced in this formulation are that changes in perceived similarity cause imbalance, imbalance causes strain, and when individuals experience strain they attempt to change something to reduce their strain.

There are two other variables that have to be defined before these rather complex ideas can be stated in propositions and then related to marital satisfaction. One is the importance or *value of the attitude*, and the other is the *relevance of the attitude* for the individuals in the relationship. The valuational variable was initially defined earlier in this book as variation in the worth or importance of something, and, as was pointed out, it varies continuously between positive and negative extremes. The value of attitudes varies in that some attitudes are highly valued, some are highly devalued, and many range in value between these two extremes. The other variable is the relevance of attitudes. Newcomb defines this as the joint dependence of two persons upon an object. He says that "*A* considers an object of high common relevance to himself and *B*, then he perceives that their relationship to it is that of 'common fate': the object is seen as having common consequences for both of them" and is relevant (1961:13).

Newcomb's comment about how these two variables fit into the theoretical formulation is, "Thus the intensity of strain hypothetically varies, other things being equal, not only with the strength of *A*'s attraction toward *B*, but also with the importance and the common relevance that" is attributed to the object (1961:13). Newcomb integrates all of these concepts in his model by proposing that when an individual experiences strain as a result of imbalance in a relationship, he will attempt to eliminate the strain. He presents five alternatives for reducing this type of strain. The strain hence positively influences variation in one of five variables or some combination of them in an attempt to try to reestablish balance. These five alternatives are (1) variation in the amount of sentiment, (2) change in one's own attitude, (3) change in one's perception of another's attitude, (4) change in the perception that the attitude is relevant for one or both members of the relationship, or (5) change in the importance of the attitude.

It is now possible to state these rather complex formulations in a series of propositions as follows and to diagram the causal sequences that occur (Figure 3.6).

PROPOSITION 3.22: If, in an ongoing balanced relationship, the perceived similarity of attitudes varies in either direction, this results in an imbalance in a relationship.

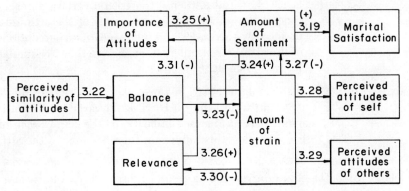

Figure 3.6 The relationships in Newcomb's balance theory integrated with variation in marital satisfaction.

PROPOSITION 3.23:   The perception of balance influences the perceiver's subjectively experienced strain and this is an inverse relationship.

PROPOSITION 3.24:   The amount of sentiment influences the amount of strain experienced as a result of dissimilarity of attitudes and this is a positive relationship.

PROPOSITION 3.25:   The importance of attitudes influences the amount of strain experienced as a result of dissimilarity of these attitudes and this is a positive relationship.

PROPOSITION 3.26:   The relevance of attitudes influences the amount of strain experienced as a result of dissimilarity of these attitudes and this is a positive relationship.

PROPOSITION 3.27:   If the amount of strain varies as a result of dissimilarity of attitudes, then if there is no variation in perceptions of similarity of attitudes or the relevance or importance of the attitudes, this influences the amount of sentiment and this is an inverse relationship.

PROPOSITION 3.28:   If the amount of strain varies as a result of dissimilarity of attitudes, then if there is no variation in sentiment, the importance or relevance of the attitudes, or the perceptions of the attitudes of others, this influences one's attitudes to change toward the attitude of others.

PROPOSITION 3.29:   If the amount of strain varies as a result of dissimilarity of attitudes, then if there is no variation in sentiment, the importance or relevance of the attitudes, or one's own attitudes, this influences one's perceptions of the attitudes of others to change so they are similar to one's own attitudes.

PROPOSITION 3.30:   If the amount of strain varies as a result of dissimilarity of attitudes, then if there is no variation in sentiment, perceptions of similarity, or the importance of the attitudes, this influences the relevance of the attitudes; this is an inverse relationship.

PROPOSITION 3.31:   If strain varies as a result of dissimilarity of attitudes, then if there is no variation in sentiment, perceptions of similarity of attitudes, or the relevance of attitudes,

this influences the importance of the attitudes; this
is an inverse relationship.

This rather complex formulation can be integrated with marital satisfaction by tying in proposition 3.19, which asserts there is a positive relationship between the amount of sentiment and marital satisfaction.
When this is done the integrated theoretical model uses balance theory
to explain some of the variation in marital satisfaction. These propositions are summarized in chart form in Figure 3.6, and the key ideas in
this integration are that propositions 3.22, 3.23, 3.24, and 3.19 identify an
indirect, influential relationship between the similarity of attitudes and
marital satisfaction.

This theoretical model is abstract because it conceptualizes attitudes
at a highly general level. It deals with attitudes as they are defined by
Newcomb, and this is as an orientation toward any nonpersonal object.
It seems meaningful to deduce from this proposition additional propositions that deal with more specific types of attitudes, and when this is
done this balance theory provides the basis for integrating a substantial
body of empirical research. All of the research that investigates the relationship between marital satisfaction and "similarity" variables can be
integrated into this model, and this includes research with numerous
variables. The process of integrating this empirical research with this
model has another advantage in addition to just integrating the rather
varied findings: it provides a theoretical explanation of findings that previously have been empirically demonstrable but very atheoretical.

Both Terman (1938) and Burgess and Cottrell (1939) in their classical
studies of marital relationships found a positive correlation between the
amount of consensus between couples and their marital adjustment. In
fact, the relationship was consistent and high enough that it was not
only incorporated into the larger measures of marital success that Terman and Burgess and Cottrell used, but it was included in Locke's
(1958) reduction of the size of the instrument.

Smaller studies have found the same conclusion. For example, Jacobson (1952) compared the similarity of attitudes of 100 divorced and 100
married couples. He found greater conflict among his divorced group
than married group. Pineo's (1961) longitudinal analysis of marriage
found that the couples who were the most disenchanted with marriage
also tended to be those who lost the most consensus over the years.
Using more recent data, Stuckert (1963) compared relative similarity
and dissimilarity with marital satisfaction and found more evidence for
similarity being related than for dissimilarity.

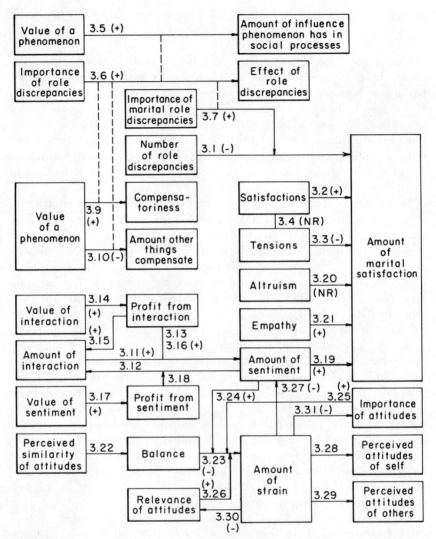

Figure 3.7   Propositions about marital satisfaction.

In spite of the rather massive empirical literature that demonstrates that similarity is positively related with marital satisfaction, there is also some literature that argues that even if this proposition is generally true, the relationship does not hold in regard to all types of attitudes. Benson's (1955) analysis of the Burgess and Wallin (1953) data indicated that commonality of interests as he operationalized them was not related to marital adjustment. Moreover, the theory of complementary needs in mate selection (Winch, 1958, 1967) argues that contrasting "orientations" toward certain phenomena may produce the type of attraction that is sought in the marital relationship. The research testing this theory is thus overwhelming that this proposition is generally valid, but future research is necessary to determine the circumstances under which it may not be and the nature of the relationships in the propositions.

Summary

This chapter has identified a number of propositions about factors that influence marital satisfaction. These propositions have been gleaned from a wide variety of theoretical perspectives such as symbolic interaction, exchange theory, and balance theory, but an attempt has been made to integrate them into one fairly complex model. This model is summarized in Figure 3.7, and it is hoped that the explication of this model will stimulate additional theoretical reformulation and empirical research to test the validity of the ideas in the model and to extend it to include more variables and relationships.

Note

1. There are many different ways that propositions can be stated. One common way is to use the "if, then" method by stating that if one variable varies, then the other variable will vary. Another common way is to state that the greater one variable, the greater the other (or for an inverse relationship—the greater one variable, the less the other variable). Both of these styles of stating propositions have the limitation that all they do is identify the existence of a relationship. They do not permit making any additional assertions about the nature of the relationship such as the shape of the relationship and existence of causality. Therefore a more complex method of stating propositions is used for most of the propositions in this book. This method is to state propositions in sentences that have three different phrases. The first phrase is used to identify the conditions under which the relationship occurs. The kind of assertions it makes are such things as "when role strain is high . . . ," or "when marital satisfaction is low. . . ." This phrase need not always assert that "when all

other variables are invariant . . . ," but this idea is always assumed whenever a proposition is stated. Very frequently this first phrase is not used because there is no basis for making any assertions about the circumstances under which the relationship occurs. The second phrase in a proposition identifies the existence of the relationship and states whether the relationship is merely a covariational relationship or one in which causality is asserted. In this phrase, the independent or causal variable is identified first and then it is stated that this variable either "influences" or "is related to" the dependent variable. When the term "influences" is used this asserts that there is a causal relationship (refer to Chapter 1 for an explanation of how causality is used in this book), and when the words "is related to" are used this identifies that only a covariational relationship is asserted. A third phrase is then added to identify any additional characteristics of the relationship that have been asserted in the literature or that seem to be defensible. In this phrase characteristics of the relationship such as the direction, shape, amount of influence, and amount of time involved are identified.

CHAPTER 4

MATE SELECTION AS
A DEPENDENT VARIABLE

There have been two very different concerns in the theorizing and research on mate selection. One deals with the factors that influence the choice of the spouse. In this literature the mate selection is the dependent variable, and the objective is to theorize about how a variety of other factors influence mate selection. The other major concern is with the consequences of the particular selection that is made. In the latter theoretical issue the independent variables are different aspects of mate selection such as age or similarity and the concern is with how they influence other variables such as marital stability, socialization practices, and kinship structures. Since these two theoretical foci are so different they will be dealt with in two separate chapters. Chapter 4 deals with the factors influencing mate selection; Chapter 5 analyzes the consequences of various aspects of mate selection.

General Normative Propositions

Katz and Hill (1958) published a classic analysis of the residential propinquity research in which they synthesized a theoretical formulation from a group of empirical studies that individually had very little theory. They identified several different theoretical ideas and then summarized them with what they termed a "norm-interaction" theory of mate selection. This analysis was a major contribution at the time it was made, but the rather dramatic advances in the methodology of theorizing made since that time should permit a more sophisticated statement to be made now. The first section of this chapter is an attempt to rework this norm-interaction theory of mate selection to improve its clarity, comprehensiveness, and testability. The changes that are made in the present reformulation are (1) an increase in the precision with which the theoretical ideas are identified because more of the ideas are stated in propositions, (2) a clarification of the different levels of generality that were implicit but not explicit in the earlier formulation, and (3) the ideas in the norm-interaction theory are integrated with several other propositions. This section of the present chapter deals only with the normative part of the norm-interaction formulation, and the interaction part of the theory is analyzed in a later section, "Interactional Propositions."

Katz and Hill state that "marriage is normative," and they view this statement as an assumption from which they then begin their theorizing. In the present reformulation the influence that normative definitions have on mate selection is viewed as an important theoretical concern itself, and several propositions are identified that deal with this process. A highly general proposition that deals with much more than just mate selection is identified first, and this is then used as a basis for deducing more specific propositions about how normative factors influence the choices that are made in selecting a spouse.

This highly general proposition is an idea that is so central to sociological thinking, so extensively documented and universal that it is virtually a social law. We do not yet know all of the circumstances under which this relationship operates or very much about how different variables influence the nature of this relationship, but even with these limitations the proposition is highly valuable. This theoretical idea is that the normative definitions in a culture influence behavior, so behavior tends to be consistent with the normative definitions. Normative definitions or *norms* were defined earlier as beliefs or definitions that proscribe or prescribe specific behaviors. They proscribe by defining what should not occur, and they prescribe by defining what should occur. They seldom make absolute definitions about behavior but rather define what ought or ought not to be done in certain specific situations. Homans defines a norm as "an idea in the minds of the members of a group, an idea that can be put in the form of a statement specifying what the members or other men should do, ought to do, are expected to do under given circumstances" (1950:1212).

There are a number of different aspects of norms that can vary, and some of these are discussed by such authors as Morris (1956) and Jackson (1966). In the present context, however, the only aspect of norms that is of concern as a variable is whether or not they exist. Thus the *existence* of norms is a dichotomous variable that varies between a normative definition not occurring and occurring.

The dependent variable in this highly general idea is the behavior of people. This is also a dichotomous variable in that behavior can either occur or not occur.

PROPOSITION 4.1: The existence of norms in a social group influences the behavior in that group so the bahavior tends to conform to the normative definitions.

This proposition was stated in less formal terms over two decades ago by Davis:

> A strong element in the culturally acquired patterns is the normative element—the feeling that the culturally acquired patterns *ought* to be followed. The factual order is what it is, therefore, partly because the normative order is what it is. This becomes plainer when we realize that the norms often (though not always) conflict with biological inclination. They are controls. It is through them that human society regulates the behavior of its members (1949:52).

There is a massive amount of evidence supporting the validity of this proposition. The idea is a central idea in a number of classic analyses of human behavior such as Linton's (1936) *The Study of Man,* Sumner's (1906) *Folkways,* and Weber's (1947) *The Theory of Social and Economic Organization.* For those who prefer highly systematic, empirical studies to test the proposition, this type of research too is voluminous. In studying the family there is excellent evidence in such research as Christensen's (1969) analysis of how cultural norms influence premarital sexual behavior and Hollingshead's (1950) analysis of how cultural norms influence mate selection. Much more, of course, needs to be learned about how other variables influence the relationship in this proposition, but some progress is even being made in this direction (Biddle and Thomas, 1966).

This highly general proposition is useful in theorizing about mate selection because more specific propositions can be deduced from it that help explain the ways that normative factors influence marital choices. It can, for example, be deduced that when societies have norms about mate selection, then, if proposition 4.1 is true, proposition 4.2 follows.

PROPOSITION 4.2:   The existence of norms about mate selection influences the mate selection so it tends to conform to these normative definitions.

This proposition is still relatively general, and additional deductions are necessary if this theoretical model is to be useful in understanding mate selection. Before making any additional deductions, however, it seems useful to first integrate another highly general theoretical proposition with these normative propositions. It will then be possible to deduce from both of the general formulations, and this should result in a more comprehensive theory than would exist if deductions were to be made with only the two normative propositions that have been thus far identified. This other general proposition deals with the effects of variation in the importance of conformity to norms.

The Importance of Conformity to Norms

A relatively general formulation was made in Chapter 3 about how evaluative processes influence other variables. It was theorized in proposition 3.5 that the value of a phenomenon influences the amount of impact this phenomenon has on other social variables, and that this is a positive relationship.

It is possible to integrate this earlier theoretical formulation about values with the normative propositions being identified in this chapter by making a deduction from proposition 3.5. This deduction is that if proposition 3.5 is true, and if proposition 4.1 is true in asserting that variation in the existence of norms influences behavior so it tends to conform to these normative definitions, and if evaluative distinctions are made about the importance of conformity to norms.

PROPOSITION 4.3:　The importance of behavior conforming to norms is related to the amount of influence the norms have on behavior and this is a positive, monotonic relationship.

This proposition can be specifically applied to mate selection by deducing from it to the mate selection situation. It can be deduced that if proposition 4.3 is true, and if proposition 4.2 is true in asserting that norms about mate selection influence mate selection so it tends to conform to the norms, and if it is true that evaluative distinctions are made about the importance of conformity to norms about mate selection, this provides a basis for proposition 4.4.

PROPOSITION 4.4:　The importance of conformity to norms about mate selection is related to the amount of influence in proposition 4.2 which asserts these norms influence selection, and this is a positive, monotonic relationship.

There is little basis for identifying the precise nature of these two relationships. They are undoubtedly positive and monotonic, and are probably also similar to the relationship in proposition 3.5, but the shape of the relationship is open to question. However, even though little is known about the nature of these relationships, they seem to be useful. They identify how one contingent variable probably mediates the influence that norms have on behavior.

This formulation needs to be tested with empirical data, but it is sufficiently general and abstract that it is impossible to directly test it. It is, however, possible to use these propositions to make additional deductions about mate selection processes, and the empirical data that are available to test these more specific deductions are useful as indirect tests of the more general formulation. The next section is an attempt to make a number of these more specific deductions and assess any empirical data that are related to them.

One additional aspect of these four propositions should be made explicit before the more specific deductions are made about mate selection. Each of the variables in these propositions seems to be able to vary in several different ways. They can be either characteristics of groups or characteristics of individuals, and the variation can be either between groups or individuals, or it can vary over time. For example, in regard to the independent variable in proposition 4.4, the definition of the importance of conforming to norms about mate selection can be a group characteristic, and the definition of how important a norm is can vary between two or more groups or it can vary over time within a group. This same phenomenon of the importance of conformity can vary at an individual level. Two different individuals can differ in their definitions of how important something is, or definitions of importance can vary over time within one individual. At the present stage of the development of these theoretical ideas, there is no basis for speculating about how the relationships would differ in any of these four different ways that these variables can vary. Thus it is suggested that the propositions probably operate the same way in each of these situations.

More Specific Normative Propositions

A number of relatively specific propositions can be deduced from the very general theoretical ideas identified in propositions 4.1 to 4.4. Several of the more specific propositions that are acquired in this process are uniquely valuable because they can then serve as the basis for deducing several empirical relationships that have been found repeatedly in the contemporary culture of the United States, and this incorporates these previously atheoretical findings into a bona fide theory. For example, deductions can be made from general, normative propositions about how specific types of normative definitions such as norms about interracial, interreligious, and interethnic marriages influence mate selection. These more specific propositions then provide one basis for explaining why racial, religious, and ethnic homogamy tends to occur.

The next sections of this chapter identify deductions about how several specific types of normative constraints influence mate selection. Deductions are made about how racial, religious, age, ethnic, socioeconomic status, and education norms influence the choices of mates. It would be possible to deduce a large number of other propositions, but only these eight are identified here. They were chosen because (*a*) they effectively illustrate the type of deductions that can be made from the more general normative propositions, and (*b*) there is considerable research about several of them, which is useful in assessing the validity of the entire formulation. Future theorizing may identify additional deductions and also identify how different types of normative definitions interact in their influence on mate selection.

Race

If proposition 4.2 is true in asserting that norms about mate selection influence marital choices so these choices tend to conform to the norms, it follows that if norms about interracial marriage are a specific type of these norms about mate selection, then proposition 4.5 holds.

PROPOSITION 4.5:   The existence of norms about interracial marriage influences the amount of interracial marriage and this is a positive, monotonic relationship.

The independent variable in this proposition can be defined as cultural prescriptions and proscriptions about what are defined in a culture as interracial marriages. It can be viewed as a trichotomy with the three categories of normatively proscribing interracial marriage, having no norms about interracial marriage, and normatively prescribing interracial marriage. It is important to note that these normative definitions have nothing to do with actual differences between racially different categories of people, and hence we do not have the conceptual problems that occur in physical anthropology and biology where attempts are made to identify differences between races. In these two fields, the technical characteristics that permit differentiating between races have so many complex problems that they are highly controversial. In the present formulation, however, the racial differences are cultural definitions that racial differences occur, and these cultural definitions may have little to do with characteristics that would be admissible in physical anthropology or biology. They are only definitions that individuals are sufficiently different in their physical characteristics that they are defined in the culture as being different in race.

The dependent variable in this proposition is the amount of interracial marriage. When this is viewed as a sociological variable it denotes variation in the number of interracial marriages in a social category or in the rate of interracial marriage.

It can be deduced that if proposition 4.4 is true, and if proposition 4.5 is true, then proposition 4.6 follows.

PROPOSITION 4.6:   The importance of conformity to norms about racial heterogamy is related to the amount of influence in proposition 4.5 which asserts that these norms influence the amount of interracial marriage, and this is a positive, monotonic relationship.

These propositions thus provide one explanation of variation in intermarriage rates. They argue that proscriptive norms about racial heterogamy decrease intermarriage and the more important the norms are, the more they decrease it. There are undoubtedly other variables that also influence interracial marriage rates such as those asserted by Thomas (1951), but this set of propositions does not take these into account.

There is some research that is useful in assessing the validity of these propositions. Burma's (1952, 1963) studies of changes over time in the rates of interracial marriages are relevant for proposition 4.5. He studied changes in intermarriage rates in Los Angeles County from 1948 to 1959 and found an increasing rate of interracial marriages during this period. Until 1948 intermarriage of whites with persons of other races was prohibited by law, and in 1959 the legislature forbade asking race as part of the application for marriage. If these changes indicate this was a period of variation in the content of normative proscriptions toward less proscription of racial heterogamy, then the marked increases Burma found in the intermarriage rates can be interpreted as supporting the relationship asserted in proposition 4.5.

This study is a meager test of the idea in this proposition, but it is some evidence of concomitant variation if the assumptions are valid. It is, however, impossible to know just how much of the covariation in this study is due to variation in the content of cultural norms. It is likely that some of it is, but it is also likely that several other factors are involved. Heer (1966), for example, has shown that differences in status, differences in residential segregation, and variation in the size of racial groups within populations are related to interracial marriage rates. It is important that these factors eventually be taken into account in propositional form, and that the ways these various factors interact is investigated.

There is another hypothesis that has been deduced from the idea in proposition 4.5 that could be used to test its validity. If groups were to differ in the degree to which they normatively proscribe racial heterogamy, then if the proposition is true, the groups would probably differ in their rates of interracial marriage. Burchinal speculates that this would be the case in stating that among "the intellectually oriented university students and younger professionals, racial equalitarianism and integration are leading causes with which youth can identify and to which they can lend support. Interracial dating and, consequently, the possibility of interracial marriage may occur more frequently among these students" (1964:648). No studies, however, have yet been found that systematically test this particular deduction either among the youth groups Burchinal speculates about or any other groups, but his reasoning identifies a potential avenue of research.

Some additional data are relevant for proposition 4.6. There is some consensus among scholars that the norms regarding interracial heterogamy are relatively more important than norms dealing with other types of heterogamy such as age, religion, or social class. For example, Leslie (1967:433) says, "Nowhere are the homogamy norms more widely held to, or more rigorously enforced, than in the area of race." Hollingshead (1950:621) states, "Our data show that the racial norms place the strongest, most explicit, and most precise limits on an individual as to whom he may or may not marry," and Burchinal (1964:646) concludes, "Race is still the most rigidly enforced endogamous norm and reflects almost 100 percent homogamy."

Hollingshead's statement is the only one of these three assertions that is based on an examination of empirical data. His data consisted of interviews with 523 couples that were randomly selected from census tracts in New Haven, Connecticut, in 1948. He found no interracial marriages in his data, and he then refers to Kennedy's (1944) analysis of New Haven marriages from 1870 to 1940 to conclude that interracial marriages are extremely rare. He uses these findings as a basis for concluding that racial norms have great control on interracial marriage. The other two assertions were based on reviews of research and personal interpretations of what is occurring in the contemporary United States culture. If these statements are acceptable as scientific observations, they provide evidence of the validity of the relationship asserted in proposition 4.6. The observations that the norms regarding race are more important and hence are more widely adhered to is exactly what is stated in this proposition. If these analyses can be viewed as supporting evidence, they also suggest that the relationship in proposition 4.6 may be highly influential. They provide no information, however, about other aspects of the relationship such as where in the range of variation in the independent variable the amount of influence varies.

Religion

A deduction can also be made from proposition 4.2 about the influence norms about religious heterogamy have on mate selection. This logic is that, if proposition 4.2 is true in asserting that norms about mate selection influence mate selection so it tends to conform to the norms, proposition 4.7 can be expected.

PROPOSITION 4.7:   The existence of norms about interreligious marriage influences the amount of interreligious marriage and this is a positive, monotonic relationship.

The independent variable in this deduction is similar to the existence of norms about interracial marriage. Both are cultural definitions, and both apparently can be viewed best as trichotomies that vary between being proscriptive, having an absence of norms, and being prescriptive. The dependent variable is also the same except it deals with the amount of interreligious marriage. The only characteristics of this relationship that can be identified are that it is probably positive and monotonic.

The amount of influence in this proposition is probably also influenced by the process that was identified in proposition 4.4 which asserts that the importance of conformity to norms about mate selection influences the degree to which behavior conforms to norms. If this is the case, a further conclusion is possible.

PROPOSITION 4.8:   The importance of conformity to norms about religious heterogamy is related to the amount of influence in proposition 4.7 which asserts that these norms influence the amount of interracial marriage, and this is a positive, monotonic relationship.

It is likely that the positive relationship in this proposition is monotonic and, like proposition 4.4, relatively influential. It is also, of course, expected that other factors influence the probability of interreligious marriage (Thomas, 1951), but they are ignored in the present theoretical formulation.

A considerable amount of empirical research is related to these two propositions. One study is Heiss' (1960) analysis of data from the Midtown Mental Health Project. His study is relevant if it is true that norms about religious heterogamy are less important to people who are less involved with religious phenomena than those who are more involved with religion. This is probably a safe assumption for several reasons. The people who are not involved with religion would probably experience less socialization within religious organizations, and these organizations are probably the major institutions that perpetuate the proscriptive norms. Further, since religion in general is less relevant for them, they would probably not expect violation of these particular norms to have serious consequences for them, and hence the norms would be less "important." In addition, since it could be expected that they would tend to associate in groups that are similar to themselves, the groups in which they are involved would probably not support the norms as strongly as more religious groups. Heiss found that interreligiously married couples, when compared to intrareligiously married couples, had less involvement in religion. Religion was also unimportant to more of their parents, a higher proportion of their parents never attended church, and fewer of the subjects attended parochial schools. These findings all argue for the validity of proposition 4.8.

Heiss' analysis also has other data that are relevant for these propositions. He found, for example, that those with interreligious marriages more frequently had dissatisfying early relationships with their parents, more strifeful lives, more tenuous ties to their families, and were emancipated earlier from their families. These findings could be interpreted as also indicating that these relationships are the type where the individuals would *internalize* fewer of the traditional norms of the society, and, if this were the case, the fact that they intermarried would be consistent with what would be expected if proposition 4.7 is true.

Coombs' (1962) study of the social circumstances related to mate selection in college students is also related to these propositions. He administered a questionnaire to 121 randomly selected married couples at the University of Utah. He found that students living at home during courtship tended to have greater homogamy in regard to religion than students not living at home. The logic behind his analysis was that students living at home would be influenced by parents more than students living away from home, and that "the influence exerted by parents in the choice of a mate would most likely be that of encouraging homogamy" (1962:155). If his assumptions are true that the parents encouraged homogamy more than the peers, and if the residential pattern is a valid measure of differences in the salience of the reference relationships, the finding of greater homogamy among those that live at home is consistent with what would be expected if the propositions were true. There was no attempt in this study to control other possible explanatory variables, but the study does provide some evidence of the particular form of covariation that is asserted in these propositions.

Hollingshead's (1950) data are also relevant for these two propositions. He found that "Next to race, religion is the most decisive factor in the segregation of males and females into categories that are approved or disapproved with respect to nuptiality" (1950:622). He does not gather data demonstrating that religious norms systematically differ from other norms, but he interprets the data that way. He notes that there are differences between Catholic, Jewish, and Protestant rates of intermarriage and then states that "The differences in percentage, we believe, are a reflection of the relative intensity of in-group sanctions on the individual in the three religious groups" (1950:622). This interpretation of the data is, of course, exactly what can be deduced from these two propositions.

Age Difference

It is possible that normative constraints on homogamy in age also influence the mate selection process. There are considerable data indicating that marriages tend to be homogamous in regard to age, but it is difficult to know if this is because of normative pressures or if it is because of other factors such as commonality of interests of age groups or merely the fact that most interaction during the ages at which marriage occurs tends to occur with people of similar ages. It is likely that, even though these other factors may be influential, normative constraints also make a difference. Burchinal in his review of this literature contends that it does. He states, "Norms seem to limit marriage choices of men and women of a particular age and marital status to individuals of the opposite sex in the same approximate age range" (Burchinal, 1964:648).

Logically, if there are normative constraints about homogamy in age, a proposition can be deduced from proposition 4.2, which asserts that norms about mate selection influence mate selection so it tends to conform to these norms.

PROPOSITION 4.9:   The existence of norms about age heterogamy influences the amount of age heterogamy and this is a positive, monotonic relationship.

Proposition 4.4 can also be used with this deduction just as it was in regard to racial and religious norms to explain at least some of the variation in the amount of influence these norms have on mate selection. If proposition 4.4 is true in asserting that the importance of conformity to norms influences the impact norms have, then, when there is variation in the importance of norms defining what is appropriate in age differences, proposition 4.10 can be deduced.

PROPOSITION 4.10:   The importance of conforming to norms about age is related to the amount of influence in proposition 4.9 which asserts that these norms influence the amount of age heterogamy, and this is a positive, monotonic relationship.

There are two sets of data that are related to these propositions. One is a study by Bowerman (1956) in which he analyzed a 50 percent sample of marriage-license applications in the early 1940s in King County, Washington, to study age differences in marriages. He found that the variability in age differences was greater for males than for females. Hollingshead's (1950) study of New Haven couples also found the same relationship, and he states that "In short, differences in the customs relative to age and marital partners place greater restriction on a woman's marital opportunities than a man's." Hollingshead thus uses the idea in proposition 4.9 as an interpretation of the finding in his empirical data that there is a sex difference in the rates of interage marriages, and the same explanations can be used for Bowerman's data.

Another finding from Bowerman's (1956) study that is useful in assessing the validity of these propositions is that there are differences in the rates of interage marriages according to the age and previous marital experience of the spouses. He found that age-endogamy is less in remarriages than first marriages, and is less for older persons regardless of previous marital status. If it is true, as Burchinal (1964:649) suggests, that the saliency of norms that govern age differences decreases for previously married and older persons, then this finding can be viewed as supporting the assertion in proposition 4.10 that variation in the importance of norms about age differences influence the amount of impact they have.

Ethnicity

Empirical research has repeatedly found that marriages tend to be ethnically homogamous, and scholars have assumed this is at least partly because of normative constraints. Kennedy (1944) and Hollingshead (1950) found greater homogamy in the three religious categories of Catholic, Protestant, and Jewish than with ethnic differences, but most marriages were still ethnically homogamous. They hence conclude that "ethnicity within a religious group has been a very potent factor in influencing the mate selection process (Hollingshead, 1950). It is possible to use proposition 4.2 as one explanation of why ethnic homogamy tends to occur. When there are norms about ethnic heterogamy then, if proposition 4.2 is true in asserting that norms about mate selection influence that behavior, proposition 4.11 can be deduced.

PROPOSITION 4.11: The existence of norms about ethnic heterogamy influences the amount of ethnic heterogamy and this is a positive, monotonic relationship.

The amount of influence in this proposition is probably influenced by the same evaluative processes that influence the impact of other normative definitions such as those dealing with race or religion. This process is identified in proposition 4.4, and if it is true, then when there is variation in the importance of norms about ethnic homogamy, proposition 4.12 follows.

PROPOSITION 4.12: The importance of norms proscribing ethnic heterogamy is related to the amount of influence in proposition 4.11 which asserts these norms influence ethnic heterogamy, and this is a positive, monotonic relationship.

Part of Hollingshead's (1950) data provide an interesting test of these propositions. He found, for example, that the ethnic variable made more difference in the generation represented by the parents of the couples in their sample than it did in the generation represented by the subjects in their sample. When the assimilation process (Cavan, 1969: Ch. 8) is taken into account, it would be expected that after immigrant groups have been in a new society for several generations they tend to become assimilated into the larger society and lose their ethnic identity. This is a gradual process and proceeds more rapidly for some ethnic characteristics than others, but it seems reasonable that as this assimilation process occurs the normative definitions proscribing ethnic heterogamy would become less salient. Because of this, on the basis of proposition 4.12, these norms would be expected to exert less influence, and this is exactly what Hollingshead found. This finding thus provides some empirical data in support of these propositions. It is very limited evidence, but it is a beginning.

Socioeconomic Status

Socioeconomic status is one of the ubiquitously important factors in social phenomena, and apparently it is also important in mate selection. It may be that it exerts an influence in other ways than just normative proscriptions against status heterogamy, but it can be deduced that if proposition 4.2 is true, then when there are normative definitions about status heterogamy, proposition 4.13 follows.

PROPOSITION 4.13:   The existence of norms about socioeconomic status heterogamy influences the amount of socioeconomic status heterogamy and this is a positive, monotonic relationship.

The earlier proposition on how the importance of conformity to norms influences the impact of the norms is probably also relevant in regard to this proposition. Thus a further proposition is deduced from proposition 4:4.

PROPOSITION 4.14:   The importance of normative definitions about socio-economic heterogamy is related to the amount of influence in proposition 4.13 which asserts that these norms influence the amount of socioeconomic status heterogamy, and this is a positive, monotonic relationship.

A study by Leslie and Richardson (1956) is related to the ideas in these two propositions. They recognize that most studies tend to find status homogamy operating in the mate selection process. They then propose, however, that the norms that proscribe status heterogamy are more important in the larger society than they are on college campuses where less discriminatory norms operate, and because of this there is more heterogamy among marriages occurring on college campuses. They subsequently failed to find the amount of status endogamy among marriages of a sample of Purdue University students that would be expected on the basis of previous research. They did find a slight tendency toward homogamy among those who met before attending college and in their total sample, but among those who met each other and were married while on campus they found no tendency for status endogamy. The differences between these three groups would be expected if Leslie and Richardson's argument is true that engodamy norms are less important on campuses and if propositions 4.13 and 4.14 are true. The study thus provides some data indicating that the relationships in these two propositions do exist.

Coombs' (1962) study of the factors related to homogamy among a group of college student marriages is also related to these propositions. The methodology of this particular study was described earlier in the discussion of the data related to propositions 4.7 and 4.8. Coombs found in addition to the data on interreligious homogamy that the extent of socioeconomic homogamy was also related to the residence of the partners at the time of the marriage. He found that living at home tended to be associated with greater homogamy. Coombs contends that parents tend to encourage homogamy, and that peers stress it less than the parents, and that the difference in the rates of homogamy occur because individuals are influenced more by their immediate associates. The logic in Coombs argument is exactly the same as in propositions 4.13 and 4.14 if the differences between the two reference groups of parents and peers represent variation in the importance of the heterogamy norms. It seems defensible to argue that it does, and hence to view the findings of this study as evidence supporting these propositions.

Education

One additional deduction will be made from the general ideas that were identified in proposition 4.2. This has to do with norms about educational differences. There seems to be a widely held belief that a number of proscriptive norms have developed in contemporary United States culture about marrying someone with a substantially different education. These seem to be based on beliefs that the interests and values of the couple will be substantially different if one has more education than the other and it frequently leads to drifting apart and divorce. If these norms do exist in the contemporary culture, then if proposition 4.2 is true, it is possible to deduce that norms about educational differences influence the probability of marriage. It is also expected that the ideas in proposition 4.4 operate in influencing how much difference the importance of these norms make. These two specific ideas—(1) if norms exist proscribing educational heterogamy and (2) if they vary in importance —lead to two new propositions.

PROPOSITION 4.15: The existence of norms about educational heterogamy influences the amount of educational heterogamy and this is a positive, monotonic relationship.

PROPOSITION 4.16: The importance of conforming to norms about educational heterogamy is related to the amount of influence in proposition 4.15 which asserts that these norms influence the amount of educational heterogamy, and this is a positive, monotonic relationship.

No studies have been found that systematically test the ideas in these two propositions. It is important to note, however, that propositions are verified or refuted as parts of a theoretical model, and that data that are relevant for the other deductions from propositions 4.2 and 4.4 are not only indirectly useful in assessing the validity of these two general propositions, but they provide some basis for expecting that new deductions from these two general propositions are also true. This type of evidence must be viewed as highly tentative, but it is of value and it does provide some basis for believing that propositions such as 4.15 and 4.16 are probably valid.

An attempt is made in Figure 4.1 to integrate these 16 propositions into one schematic model. The relatively general propositions are identified at the top, and the 12 relatively specific propositions that are deduced from them are shown at the bottom. The solid lines identify the relationships between the variables, and the dotted lines identify the logical connections between the propositions. The relatively specific propositions that are deduced from the first four are only examples of the type of deductions that could be made from the more general idea, since it would be possible to make a great number of other specific deductions about how other normative definitions influence the mate selection process. If this type of systematic formalization of theoretical ideas proves fruitful, it will be possible to make this model considerably more complex in the future.

Interactional Propositions

A sizable literature has accumulated in recent years on how various types of interaction influence human attraction. Some of this literature has focused specifically on how certain aspects of interaction influence mate selection, but a great deal of it has dealt only with the general phenomenon of attraction and it has never been specifically applied to the mate selection process. This section of Chapter 4 is an attempt to integrate a number of these propositions and explicitly identify their relevance for the mate selection process.

Integrating Homans' Interactional Propositions with Katz and Hill's Formulation

Homans (1950) identified several very general propositions about the relationship between interaction and sentiment. Two of these were identified earlier as propositions 3.11 and 3.12.

PROPOSITION 3.11:   The quantity of interaction influences the amount of sentiment and this is a positive, monotonic relationship.

PROPOSITION 3.12:   The amount of sentiment influences the amount of interaction.

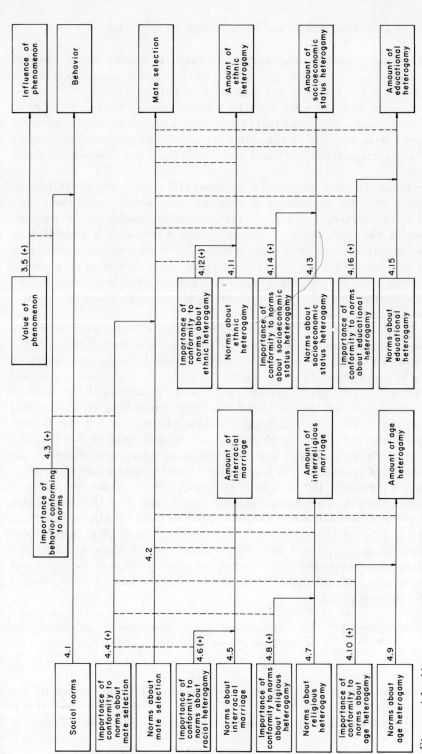

Figure 4.1 Normative propositions about mate selection.

These two propositions about the relationship between interaction and sentiment can be specifically applied to the mate selection process in a number of ways. One is to integrate them with the assertions about interactions made in Katz and Hill's (1958) norm-interaction theory of mate selection. Katz and Hill's ideas regarding the normative aspect of theory were analyzed in the earlier sections of this chapter, but the part of their formulation that dealt with interaction was deferred until this point.

One of the main ideas in the Katz and Hill formulation about interaction is that "the probability of marriage varies directly with the probability of interaction" (1958:33). The dependent variable in this proposition is the probability of marriage, and since it is a statement of probability it varies continuously between the extremes of impossibility to certainty. The way this variable varies is, of course, much easier to identify than the empirical indicators that are used to measure it. The independent variable is the probability of interaction, and this too is a continuous variable.

It seems highly unlikely that the probability of interaction has a very *direct* influence on the probability of marriage. However, if the idea that these two factors are related is integrated with Homans' proposition on the effect of interaction on sentiment, a more comprehensive theoretical formulation emerges. It seems reasonable to argue that the probability of interaction and the amount of interaction are sufficiently similar that they are really conceptualizing the same phenomenon. If this is true, and if the term "amount of interaction" is used to label this variable, what probably occurs is that the amount of interaction influences the amount of sentiment, and among those social groups where mate selection is occurring, the amount of sentiment influences the probability of mate selection. This means that the idea in the Katz-Hill formulation that the amount of interaction is related to mate selection is accurate, but it is a relatively "indirect" relationship. The more comprehensive formulation introduced here views these two variables as parts of a chain sequence in which interaction influences sentiment and sentiment influences mate selection. Proposition 4.17 is the second proposition in this sequence.

PROPOSITION 4.17:   The amount of positive sentiment influences the probability of mate selection and this is a positive relationship.

There is little basis for stating the nature of the relationship in this proposition other than to assert it is positive. It is likely, however, that it is at least a monotonic relationship, and it may be that the influence is greatest in the upper ranges of the independent variable.

Propositions 3.11 and 4.17 form a meaningful chain sequence, but it is possible to integrate several other aspects of the Katz-Hill formulation by adding additional variables to this sequence. This is possible because the main purpose of the Katz-Hill article was to integrate the earlier empirical studies on the relationship between residential propinquity and mate selection in such a way as to synthesize a coherent theoretical statement. Their analysis hence also includes the residential propinquity variable. In addition, they discuss other concepts that they label "opportunities for interaction" and "organizational points." The main ideas that seem to emerge from this part of the Katz-Hill formulation are that organization points and residential propinquity influence the opportunities for interaction and the opportunities for interaction influence the amount of interaction.

Before these ideas can be stated in formal propositions, however, a careful analysis needs to be made of the nature of these additional variables. For example, the concept of organizational points was not defined by Katz and Hill, and, if it is a variable, its particular method of variation has also not been identified. Katz and Hill (1958:33) merely identify organizational points as those places in geographic space where the interaction occurs. This conceptualization does not seem to identify a variable, but identifying the fact that organizational points exist and that they are a different phenomenon from residential propinquity seems to be very close to identifying a variable that may be important. A variable can be identified that can be labeled the *amount of activity* people have in close proximity in social organizations. This seems to be very similar conceptually to what Katz and Hill were labeling as "organizational points," but it has the advantage that the amount of activity people have in close proximity can be viewed as a variable. This variable probably varies continuously from none to the logical possibility of all of two people's activity being in close proximity in common organizations. Probably the most practical way to view its variation is in the proportion of an individual's total activity that is in close proximity to others. It is likely that the variable that it influences is what Katz and Hill identify as the *opportunities for interaction*. This variable apparently varies continuously from none to a large number of opportunities for interaction. Then, to complete the sequence in what seems to be the idea in the Katz-Hill formulation, these opportunities for interaction influence the amount of interaction.

PROPOSITION 4.18:   The amount of activity in close proximity influences the opportunities for interaction and this is a positive relationship.

PROPOSITION 4.19:   The opportunities for interaction influence the amount of interaction and this is a positive relationship.

Again, there is at present very little basis for identifying the nature of these relationships. They are probably positive relationships, and it is likely that they are monotonic, but other than this little can be speculated.

The variable that originally gave rise to the Katz-Hill formulation is *residential propinquity*, and its role in this model has not yet been identified. This variable is defined as variation in the spatial distance of residences. It is usually thought of as varying continuously in units of blocks or miles. It is somewhat difficult to know just how this variable fits into the model that emerges in the present reformulation. There is little question that there is a relationship between propinquity and opportunities for interaction, but there is some question about whether there is any direct influence. It may be that the only way the propinquity variable influences opportunities for interaction is that it influences the amount of activity people have in close proximity in organizations. This is an empirical question, however, and cannot be resolved until data are accumulated that will test it. For the present time, it seems reasonable to present two propositions relating residential propinquity to both the amount of close activity and opportunities for interaction.

PROPOSITION 4.20:   Residential propinquity influences the amount of activity individuals have in close proximity in social organizations and this is a positive relationship.

PROPOSITION 4.21:   Residential propinquity influences opportunities for interaction and this is a positive relationship.

This group of propositions forms a rather complex chain sequence, and the connections between the variables are illustrated by the flow chart in Figure 4.2. As can be seen in this figure, what is being proposed in this reformulation is that residential propinquity influences the amount of activity in common organizations, and it perhaps also directly influences opportunities for interaction. Opportunities for interaction influence the amount of interaction, and the latter variable positively influences sentiment. Finally, sentiment influences the probability of mate selection. Subsequent reformulations of this model should identify ways that some of these variables influence other variables and/or are influenced by variables that are not identified in this formulation, but at the present time these possibilities are ignored.

There is a great deal of evidence that the two phenomena of residen-

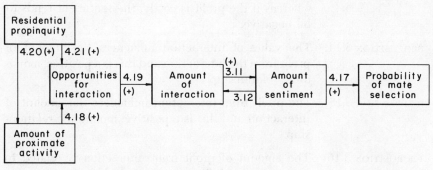

Figure 4.2 Chain sequence of interactional propositions from Homans' and Katz and Hill's formulation.

tial propinquity and mate selection are related. This particular relationship is asserted to be a highly indirect relationship in the formulation suggested in this book, but the fact that covariation does exist between these two variables is relevant in assessing the proof of the model. In addition to the 14 separate studies examined by Katz and Hill (1958) in their theoretical paper, there have been a number of subsequent studies that document the existence of this relationship. Catton and Smirich (1964) and Ramsøy (1966), for example, both document that it exists in recent samples.

A number of investigators have studied ways that the relationship between propinquity and mate selection is related to other factors. For example, Koller (1948) and Sundal and McCormick (1951) both found that the lower the socioeconomic status, the less the distance involved in the mate selection. Koller (1948) found the relationship to occur with no differences during war, depression, and periods when there were neither. Ramsøy (1966) found that the relationship existed independently of homogamy in occupational status. Eventually these findings will need to be integrated into this theoretical model.

Propositions from Exchange Theory

A number of theoretical propositions initially defined in exchange theory were stated in Chapter 3. These propositions are repeated here for convenience.

PROPOSITION 3.13: If the profit from interaction is rewarding, the sentiment produced by interaction tends to be positive, whereas if the profit is costly, the sentiment tends to be negative.

PROPOSITION 3.14:   The value of interaction influences the amount of profit from the interaction and this is a positive, monotonic relationship.

PROPOSITION 3.15:   The profit from interaction influences the amount of interaction and this is a positive, monotonic relationship.

PROPOSITION 3.16:   The amount of profit from interaction is related to the amount of influence interaction has on sentiment and this is a positive relationship.

PROPOSITION 3.17:   The value of sentiment influences the amount of profit from the sentiment and this is a positive, monotonic relationship.

PROPOSITION 3.18:   The profit from sentiment is related to the amount of influence that variation in the amount of sentiment has on the quantity of interaction.

These propositions are closely related to the interactional propositions identified in the previous section, and they seem to be valuable in understanding the mate selection process. They speculate about how additional variables can influence the sentiment that occurs in relationships, and since sentiment is such an important requisite for mate selection, they help explain variation in mate selection. The entire interactional and exchange formulation is summarized in Figure 4.3.

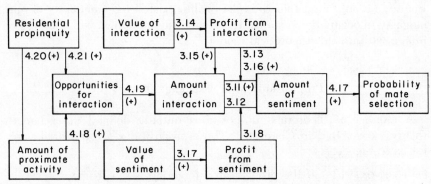

Figure 4.3   The interactional and exchange propositions and mate selection.

Propositions about Mate Selection
from Balance Theory

The balance theory that was explicated in Chapter 3 is also relevant in understanding variation in mate selection. The proposition in this balance theory model (3.22 to 3.31) explain how sentiment is influenced by several different phenomena.

PROPOSITION 3.22:   If in an ongoing relationship, the perceived similarity of attitudes varies in either direction, this results in an imbalance in a relationship.

PROPOSITION 3.23:   The perception of balance influences the perceiver's subjectively experienced strain and this is an inverse relationship.

PROPOSITION 3.24:   The amount of sentiment influences the amount of strain experienced as a result of dissimilarity of attitudes and this is a positive relationship.

PROPOSITION 3.25:   The importance of attitudes influences the amount of strain experienced as a result of dissimilarity of these attitudes and this is a positive relationship.

PROPOSITION 3.26:   The relevance of attitudes influences the amount of strain experienced as a result of dissimilarity of these attitudes and this is a positive relationship.

PROPOSITION 3.27:   If the amount of strain varies as a result of dissimilarity of attitudes, then if there is no variation in perceptions of similarity of attitudes or the relevance or importance of the attitudes, this influences the amount of sentiment, and this is an inverse relationship.

PROPOSITION 3.28:   If the amount of strain varies as a result of dissimilarity of attitudes, then if there is no variation in sentiment, the importance or relevance of the attitudes, or the perceptions of the attitudes of others, this influences one's attitudes to change toward the attitude of others.

PROPOSITION 3.29:   If the amount of strain varies as a result of dissimilarity of attitudes, then if there is no variation in sentiment, the importance or relevance of the attitudes, or one's own attitudes, this influences one's perceptions of the attitudes of others to change so they are similar to one's own attitudes.

PROPOSITION 3.30:   If the amount of strain varies as a result of dissimilarity of attitudes, then if there is no variation in sentiment, perceptions of similarity, or the importance of the attitudes, this influences the relevance of the attitudes, and this is an inverse relationship.

PROPOSITION 3.31:   If strain varies as a result of dissimilarity of attitudes, then if there is no variation in sentiment, perceptions of similarity of attitudes, or the relevance of attitudes, this influences the importance of the attitudes, and this is an inverse relationship.

These are discussed in some detail in Chapter 3 so they will not be individually analyzed here. The discussion in Chapter 3 does not, however, state how these variables are related to the probability of mate selection occurring. These propositions can be integrated with the earlier formulation stated in proposition 4.17 to specifically tie the balance theory propositions to mate selection. Proposition 4.17 states that if sentiment varies, this influences the probability of mate selection, and since Newcomb's balance theory identifies variables that influence sentiment, it is likely that integrating it with mate selection will help understand some of the sources of variation in the choices that are made in mates. Figure 4.4 identifies all of the variables involved in this balance theory, the relationships asserted in the propositions, and the number of the propositions in the entire formulation.

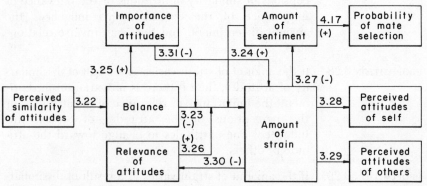

Figure 4.4   Balance theory and mate selection.

Variation in Information

There is another variable in Newcomb's formulation that is informative when these propositions are viewed as explanations of part of the variation in mate selection. Variation can occur in the amount of *information* that people have about each other, and Newcomb uses this information variable in a number of ways in his theory. For example, he theorizes that as the acquaintance process progresses there is an increase in information about the individuals in the relationships, and the initial random sentiments are replaced by more orderly differentiation that occurs in balance-promoting ways. He further proposes that as more information is gathered in groups, the high-attraction groups get larger and the low-attraction groups get smaller. His writings do not specifically state a third proposition, but there is another one that seems to follow: As the amount of information about others varies, there is a certain type of variation in the amount of sentiment that is felt toward them. It seems reasonable that when very little information is present, perceptions of similarity do not result in high degrees of sentiment. They result in some increase in sentiment, but high amounts of sentiment probably tend to occur only when there is a high amount of information. It is further likely that this can be integrated with several other propositions in that the amount of information present is influenced by the amount of interaction. Thus the amount of interaction probably influences the amount of information, and this variation in information then probably influences the amount of sentiment that is indirectly produced by perceptions of similarity of attitudes. There are thus two new propositions that can be included in this formation.

PROPOSITION 4.22: The amount of interaction influences the amount of information the individuals involved in the relationship have about each other and this is a positive relationship.

PROPOSITION 4.23: The amount of information that individuals have about each other in a relationship is related to the amount of sentiment that is caused by the similarity of attitudes and this is a positive relationship.

It is difficult to identify the type of relationship that exists in these two propositions. They are both proposed as being positive relationships, and it is likely that they are monotonic; but beyond these characteristics there is so little basis for asserting other characteristics that nothing more is speculated.

Deductions from Balance Theory

It would be possible to make a number of deductions from this balance theory of mate selection about how variation in similarity of attitudes toward various specific things can be expected to influence marital choices. For example, it could be deduced that similarity of attitudes toward education, race, religion, social status, children, divorce, life after death, and so on, probably indirectly influence mate selection. It is hoped that future theorizing will develop formulations that will (*a*) identify which types of similarity do and do not influence mate selection, and (*b*) identify the factors that influence whether these types of similarity have an influence. This has not yet been worked at very exhaustively in the theoretical project being reported here but may be in the future.

Tentative Integration of the Balance, Interactional, and Exchange Theories

It is possible that the theoretical model identified in the balance theory can also be integrated with the propositions identified earlier in the chapter. This is highly tentative, but it seems reasonable that variation in what Newcomb refers to as "strain" influences the profit that a person experiences from the interaction. This idea can be stated in a proposition.

PROPOSITION 4.24:   The psychological strain experienced in a relationship influences the profit of interaction in this relationship and this is an inverse relationship.

The last three propositions about the influence of interaction on information, the influence of information on the relationship between similarity and sentiment, and the influence of strain on the profit from interaction integrate the three models. The result is a very complex model, and much of it presently has very little empirical support. It seems reasonable, however, to expect that the more clearly these relationships are identified, the more quickly data will be acquired that will test their validity. This formulation is diagramed in the complex flow chart in Figure 4.5.

A Note on Homogamy Theories

It is interesting that the normative theory, the interactional propositions, and the balance theory identified in the preceding section all tend

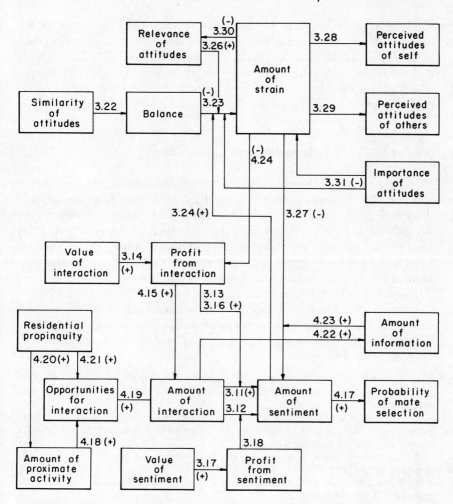

Figure 4.5 Integrating the entire balance theory and exchange theory models.

to fall under the general label of "homogamy" theories. It is possible that some theorists may have a tendency to react to these formulations by attempting to find which one is the "best" or "most adequate" explanation of homogamy. There is even a precedent in the literature for this type of research about these theories (Catton, 1964). This type of research will hopefully not be continued. It may be that some of these variables operate in some situations and others operate in other situations, but all are valid. In addition, even if all three of these theories are valid, there may be other factors that influence the occurrence of homogamy in important ways. Thus the emphasis should be on testing each of these theoretical formulations to determine their validity or invalidity and to refine and extend them rather than attempting to determine which of them tends to be the one that provides the "best" single explanation.

Complementary Need Theory

There is another theoretical formulation about mate selection that is conceptually different from the theoretical ideas that have so far been discussed in this chapter. This is a theoretical position developed by Winch (1954, 1958) that has come to be known as the complementary need theory of mate selection. It has stimulated considerable research, and there have been a number of provocative reactions to it in the literature. Thus it is important that it be included here.

The ideas in Winch's formulation are not communicated in the type of statements that identify variation in variables or relationships between variables. They are instead a series of declarative statements that are designed to identify unvarying aspects of reality. He summarizes his main ideas as follows:

1. In mate selection each individual seeks within his or her field of eligibles for that person who gives the greatest promise of providing him or her with maximum need-gratification.
2. There is a set of needs such that if person A behaves in a manner determined by a high degree of need X, A's behavior will prove gratifying to the need Y in a second person, B.
3. These two needs, X and Y, in the two persons, A and B, are said to be complementary if:
a. Type I complementariness: X and Y are the same need, and the need is present to a low degree in B.
b. Type II complementariness: X and Y are different needs. In this case specific predictions are made about selected pairs of needs. That is, taking account of the particular X, with respect to some Y's, it is predicted that B will have a high degree and with respect to others that B will have a low degree (1963:585–586).

There are a number of new concepts in this formulation that must be defined. It is probably first necessary to define the term *need*. Winch uses Murray's definition of this term:

A construct . . . which stands for a force . . . in the brain region, a force which organizes perception, apperception, intellection, conation and action in such a way as to transform in a certain direction an existing, unsatisfying situation. . . . But usually it persists and gives rise to a certain course of overt behavior (or fantasy), which . . . changes the initiating circumstances in such a way as to bring about an end situation which stills (appeases or satisfies) the organism (Murray, 1938:123–124).

Part of this rather formal definition is quoted by Winch (1963:570) in his statement of the theory. It is important to note that there are several crucial parts to this definition, and the fact that *all* of these parts are there results in the term need being a very complex term. There is some "unsatisfying condition" either inside or outside the organism, and there is also some "force" within the organism that is the need. This force tends to "do" something to eliminate the unsatisfying condition. The word that is probably the closest to being a synonym of the term need is *force*, and it is imperative that when the term need is used in the Winch formulation it is realized that there is a *force* within individuals that has some overt behavioral consequence. This means the term is not synonymous with terms such as perception, wish, desire, or want unless these are sufficiently strong to impel action. This definition is particularly important in understanding Winch's (1967) later reworking of his own theory because in his later paper he seems to include more than just these "forces" in his use of the term.

The other major term in the theory is need complementarity. Winch states in his monograph *Mate Selection* (1958) that needs are "complementary when A's behavior in acting out A's need X is gratifying to B's need and B's behavior in acting out B's need Y is gratifying to A's need X" (1958:93). What he is stating here is that complementarity is synonymous with need gratification. It is apparently a condition in a relationship in which one or both individual's needs are gratified by interaction with the other person. He then points out that this complementariness variable can occur in two ways, type I and type II.

Winch does not seem to view either the concept need or need complementarity as a variable, and he never states his ideas in terms of relationships between variables. The idea of a relationship is implicit in his statements, however, because he seems to be asserting that complementarity produces mate selection and noncomplementarity does not. Thus variables in his theory can be identified and the ideas can be stated in the type of propositions that identify relationships. The phenomenon of need complementarity can be viewed as a variable in that gratification can either occur or not occur, and it can apparently vary in amount. Some relationships can have very little or no complementarity, and others can have a great deal. Moreover, if the needs of individuals change over time, it is possible for the complementarity of a relationship to vary over time. Thus *need complementarity* can apparently be defined as the amount of need gratification in a relationship, and it can be viewed as varying continuously between no complementarity and a high amount. There is some ambiguity in this variable because it could conceivably vary in the number of needs that are gratified or in the strength of these needs, or as a combination of both of these. Eventually it may be necessary to differentiate between these two different components, but at the present time it is proposed that this variable be viewed as a combination of the number of needs involved and the strength of the needs to give an overall variable of need complementarity. The appropriate dependent variable is the same one used in earlier sections of this chapter—the probability of mate selection. The main idea in Winch's formulation can then apparently be stated as the following proposition.

PROPOSITION 4.25:   Need complementarity influences the probability of mate selection and this is a positive, monotonic relationship.

A sizable literature has grown that criticizes various aspects of this theoretical formulation, and these reactions prompted Winch (1967) to reexamine the theory and modify some of the ideas in it. It seems to this author that some of the criticisms of the theory are valid but others are not, and that some aspects of Winch's reexamination of the theory are defensible whereas others are not. Thus a relatively extensive review of this literature seems called for.

One of the first criticisms was by Rosow (1957), who stated that the theory provides no basis for knowing which particular combinations of needs are complementary and which are not. This criticism is important because Rosow is apparently identifying a serious problem with the independent variable in proposition 4.25. He seems to be pointing out that thus far we have no way of even intuitively knowing what it is that is varying when this variable varies, let alone knowing defensible methods of empirically operationalizing it. Levinger (1964) added a refinement to Winch's formulation when he pointed out that the influence that need complementarity has on mate selection should be expected to occur only in regard to those needs that are gratified in the marital relationship.

Tharp (1963) offered an alternative formulation by suggesting that it might be more useful to try to understand the mate selection process by theorizing about the impact that compatibility of role expectations has on relationships rather than focusing on need complementarity. What he proposed was that the compatibility of two individuals' role expectations has an important influence on their selection of a marriage partner. This phenomenon of *compatibility of role expectations* is apparently a continuous variable that denotes variation in the degree to which the role expectations an individual has agree with the expectations of the other individual, or the amount of consensus on role expectations. It can vary from no role compatibility to virtually complete agreement. The proposition suggested by Tharp thus can be stated as follows.

PROPOSITION 4.26:   The compatibility of role expectations influences the probability of mate selection and this is a positive, monotonic relationship.

In 1967 Winch published what he termed "another look" at his theory, and he proposed several changes. One of his suggestions was that the idea suggested earlier by Tharp be incorporated with the complementary need proposals to make a more comprehensive theory. This led him to propose that:

PROPOSITION 4.27:   Need complementarity and compatibility of role expectations interact in an additive manner in influencing the probability of mate selection.

This proposal seems to be different from Tharp's original suggestion, since Tharp seems to argue that the conceptualization of needs and need complementarity are not useful, and they ought to be replaced with the variable of compatibility of role expectations. This apparent difference between Tharp and Winch is an important issue that must be resolved before much progress can be made in subsequent theorizing and research; and it may be that it has to be resolved with conceptual analyses rather than empirical data.

A particular conceptualization such as the concept "need" is useful to science only if it is conceptually clear and precise, and the concept of need may be so unclear and/or imprecise that it will not ever be useful. In Murray's formulation he identifies a certain number of needs, and the fact that he articulated and defined a relatively limited number of them has resulted in other scholars thinking there was utility in using the conceptualization of need. The term need, however, may suffer from exactly the same fatal deficiency that the term instinct did in psychology at the start of the twentieth century. The term instinct was useful as long as scholars had a relatively small list of instincts that were meaningful to them. However, when the list of separate instincts began to be extended virtually infinitely to include minor variations in inclinations it became apparent that the term instinct really was a label for such useless categories of phenomena that it literally fell out of use.

The term need may turn out to be just as useless as the term instinct for exactly the same reasons. It is defined as a force that influences what

Murray labels as "perception, apperception, intellection, conation and action" (1938:123). If this includes virtually all of the mental processes that can be labeled as desires, wants, wishes, perceptions, ideals, values, goals, objectives, and so on, it is so inclusive that it is likely it will turn out to not symbolize any meaningful aspect of reality. If it does not symbolize these things, *it is imperative that the conceptual difference be identified*, and this has not yet been done.

Empirical Tests of the Complementary Needs Theory

There have been a number of empirical studies that have attempted to test the ideas in the complementary needs theory. Winch (1955, 1958) and his co-workers (Winch, Greer, and Blumberg, 1954) investigated 25 married couples, and found what they defined as some support. Several other studies (Huntington, 1958; Kerchoff and Davis, 1962) found some evidence of complementarity. Most of the studies, however, failed to find any supporting evidence, and this includes studies by Bowerman and Day (1956), Schellenberg and Bee (1960), Kernodle (1959), Udry (1963), Lundy (1958), Day (1961), and Murstein (1961, 1967). It is likely that when the conceptual obscurity of the term "need complementarity" is removed the theory can be more conclusively tested.

Summary

This chapter has identified a number of propositions about factors that influence marital choices. These propositions have occasionally been stated very differently from the way they appeared in the earlier writings with the hope that the changes made here will increase the utility of the ideas in the scientific community. The chapter is not an attempt to write any of these ideas in their final form but rather is an attempt to improve this area of theory so others can build on this work by increasing the clarity and sophistication of the theoretical ideas and gathering additional empirical data to test their validity.

CHAPTER 5

THE EFFECTS OF PREMARITAL FACTORS
ON MARRIAGE

Most of the research that has dealt with the relationship between pre-marital variables and later marital variables has been concerned with prediction rather than explanation. This was the case with the initial major monographs by Burgess and Cottrell (1939) and Terman and his associates (1938) and in such longitudinal studies as those by Burgess and Wallin (1953) and Kelley (1939, 1955). The result has been a gradual accumulation of findings that have shown covariation between many premarital variables and later marital success variables, but very little theoretical understanding of which premarital factors influence the marital variables and which of these relationships can be used to make deductions about more specific phenomena.

These prediction studies have, however, provided a base from which theoretical insights might be synthesized. Bowerman, for example, argues as follows:

Not least among the contribution of the prediction studies is the stimulation they have given for other studies, which are providing additional findings and developing basic variables that will contribute to an eventual explanatory theory of pre-marriage behavior and marital interaction (1964:245).

This chapter is an attempt to accomplish two objectives that are related to the theory that Bowerman refers to as a "theory of premarriage behavior and marriage interaction." The first objective is to synthesize some theoretical propositions from the rather atheoretical prediction literature. These propositions should identify relationships between pre-marital variables and marital variables that will be the beginning of explanation and understanding rather than just prediction. This task is being undertaken with an appreciation for its difficulty and an awareness that it is very likely that much of what emerges from any initial foray into an uncharted forest will not stand the test of time. It is hoped, however, that it will lead to more thorough formulations in the future. The second objective of this chapter is to rework some of the few attempts that have been made to develop bona fide theory about how premarital factors influence marital phenomena and to integrate these propositions with the propositions that are synthesized from the prediction literature.

The strategy of theory building that is used in this chapter is somewhat different from the strategy that predominates in the two preceding chapters. Aldous (1970) has identified five different strategies that can be used, and in the last two chapters the one that was used most was what she termed "borrowed" theory. Here concepts and theoretical ideas that were developed in a different substantive area are applied to the family institution. The theories may or may not be revised or extended in this process of borrowing them. In the present chapter the method that is used is close to what Zetterberg refers to as the axiomatic method with definitional reduction (1965:94–96). In this chapter there is almost no concern with extending theories laterally by axiomatic deductions (see Zetterberg, 1965:96–100). Rather, the emphasis here is on inducing more general or abstract propositions from a large body of empirical research.

Bartz and Nye (1970) used this same strategy in their attempt to generate abstract theoretical propositions about the factors that influence age at marriage. First they identified as many relevant empirical relationships as possible. Then, after clarifying such things as the definitions of the concepts and natures of the relationships as much as possible, they logically combined the propositions to not only acquire new relationships at the same level of generality but to induce more abstract formulations. It is possible to go further than Bartz and Nye did by deducing new propositions from the more abstract ones and eventually deducing hypotheses that can test the validity of the ideas. The tests of these hypotheses provide evidence for or against the whole model and provide additional data that can then be used to make revisions or extensions of the model. The basic strategy of the present chapter is to use the method charted by Nye to induce propositions about how premarital variables influence marital phenomena. The next sections hence present an analysis of a large number of empirical relationships followed by an attempt to induce more general propositions and evaluate the resulting formulations.

One comment about the dependent variables that are used is probably necessary before these relationships are analyzed. The predictive studies have operationalized the marital success type of variables in a number of ways, but, as Bowerman (1964:237) has pointed out, most of them have used the method that was initially developed by Burgess (1936, 1939) and his co-workers at the University of Chicago. Of the 60 studies Bowerman reviewed in preparing his chapter for the *Handbook on Marriage and the Family*, 23 used this measure, 10 used a single-item rating, 12 used divorce or separation, and 15 used other types of measures. All of the major studies that investigated a large number of predictive factors used the Burgess type of dependent variable that was labeled "marital adjustment" in the conceptual reformulation that was suggested in Chapter 3.

The conceptualization of "marital adjustment" was severely criticized in Chapter 3 for its lack of rational meaning. It is a general variable that includes many dimensions, and therefore it is difficult to know what is being denoted when it is being used. It does, however, provide an overall measure of the marital success-type of variables and thus is simple to use. It has also been the most extensively used dependent variable in marriage prediction, and because of this it is the most extensively used dependent variable in the present analysis. It is expected, however, that as the theorizing becomes more complex and as the research becomes more sophisticated in this area, this relatively meaningless variable will be used less and less.

Homogamy and Marital Adjustment

One theme that runs through the marriage prediction research is that the similarity of the spouses before the marriage is positively related to their later marital adjustment. This has been found to be the case with a large number of variables, and there are no data indicating an inverse relationship has been found. This persistent finding thus provides a basis for inducing a relatively abstract proposition that the general phenomenon of "homogamy" is positively related to later marital adjustment. Furthermore, since this research deals with independent variables that are clearly operating before the dependent variable can vary, these findings provide a basis for speculating that the homogamy variable may have an influence on the dependent variable.

It is, of course, possible that a different phenomenon influences both homogamy and later marital adjustment and that the relationship between them is hence spurious. This issue, however, is only a possibility until another theoretical formulation is made that suggests different influential relationships, and when or if this is done additional research will be needed to determine which relationships are valid and influential. The empirical relationships that have been found between various types of homogamy and marital adjustments are analyzed in the following sections, and then a more abstract proposition is induced from these relationships.

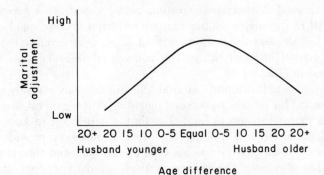

Figure 5.1　The relationship between age differences and marital adjustment.

Age Differences

Differences in age is a continuous variable that is usually operationalized in years. It ranges from the husband being substantially younger to
substantially older than the wife, and a number of studies have found it
to be related to marital adjustment. Bernard (1934), Terman and Oden
(1947), Burgess and Cottrell (1939:406), Locke (1951:343), and Karlsson
(1951:52–53) found that marital adjustment scores are higher when the
couple is the same age or the husband is slightly older. This leads to the
first hypothesis.

HYPOTHESIS 5.1:　The amount of age difference between spouses is related to marital adjustment and this is a curvilinear
relationship.

The curvilinear relationship that seems to best summarize the data from
these studies, as diagramed in Figure 5.1, shows that marital adjustment
tends to decrease more rapidly when the husband is younger than when
he is older than the wife.

Intelligence Differences

Hamilton (1929), Terman (1938), Terman and Oden (1947), Locke
(1951:255, 351) and Karlsson (1951:54) all found that differences in intelligence were related to marital adjustment. This independent variable
can be viewed as a continuous variable that varies between the two extremes of the husband being substantially inferior to the wife and his
being substantially superior. Most of the studies merely found that ex-

treme differences were associated with smaller proportions of the samples being well adjusted. Terman's data, however, also indicate that when there are differences the spouse that is superior will tend to have the largest decrease in adjustment. Hypothesis 5.2 is supported by these findings.

HYPOTHESIS 5.2: The amount of difference between spouses in intelligence is related to marital adjustment and this is a curvilinear relationship in which the more intelligent spouse has the lower adjustment.

Socioeconomic Differences of Couple

There are many different ways to conceptualize socioeconomic status differences, and it is important to note that very few of these methods have been used in the marital prediction research. The research uses only the conceptualization developed by Warner (1941) and Hollingshead (1949). No attention has been paid to more recent innovations such as Lenski's (1954) concept of status crystallization. This conceptualization of social class has lent itself to viewing the variable of class differences as a categorical variable that has categories of being of the same class, one class apart, two classes apart, and so on. Roth and Peck (1951) analyzed the Burgess and Cottrell (1939) data; their findings are presented in hypothesis 5.3.

HYPOTHESIS 5.3: The amount of difference in socioeconomic status between the individuals in a marriage is related to marital adjustment and this is an inverse, monotonic relationship.

Socioeconomic Differences between Parents

Udry (1966) has pointed out that the Roth and Peck (1951) study can be easily misinterpreted if the independent variable is viewed as the social class difference between the parents of the couple at the time of the marriage. He points out that Burgess and Cottrell found no evidence in their data to support this (hypothesis 5.4).

HYPOTHESIS 5.4: The amount of socioeconomic difference between the parents of a couple is related to marital adjustment of the couple.

It is premature to conclude from this one study that there is no relationship between these two variables, but at the present time an analysis of the only data that are available failed to find any.

Racial Differences

Racial difference was defined earlier as a dichotomous variable that denotes variation in what is defined in a culture as a meaningful difference in the physical characteristics of individuals. It varies between the two categories of no racial differences and the existence of racial differences. Unfortunately there are few data on the nature of the relationship between racial differences and marital adjustment. This variable was not included in any of the major prediction studies. There have, however, been several small studies that provide some data. Golden (1954) interviewed 50 Negro-white couples, and Pavela (1964) interviewed nine couples. Both studies report difficulties in the interaction with individuals outside the couple, but neither report anything else about the quality of the marital relationship. Kimura (1957) found marriages of Japanese in Hawaii with non-Japanese had in-law relations that were as good as those who married homogamously. Cheng and Yamamura (1957) found no differences in the divorce rate between interracial marriages and racially homogamous marriages. The findings in a case history analysis (Baber, 1953), however, argue that interracial marriages do have more difficulties. Thus at the present time there is insufficient and conflicting evidence about the following frequently stated relationship.

HYPOTHESIS 5.5:   The existence of racial differences is related to marital adjustment and this is an inverse, monotonic relationship.

Educational Differences

Differences in education have been operationalized by measuring the differences in the number of years of formal schooling. This can be put on the same type of dimensional scale used with age and intelligence differences with one extreme being husbands having much less education than wives and the other being husbands having much more education than wives.

Several studies, including Davis (1929) and Terman and Oden (1947), found that being different as opposed to the same in education tends to be associated with greater frequencies of adjusted couples. Terman (1938) and Burgess and Wallin (1953), however, found no relationship. Blood and Wolfe (1960:256) found a monotonic relationship between the amount of difference and marital satisfaction irrespective of which member of the couple had the greater education. There thus seems to be conflicting evidence about this idea, but most of the data indicates hypothesis 5.6.

HYPOTHESIS 5.6: The amount of educational difference is related to marital adjustment and this is an inverse relationship.

Denominational Heterogamy

Considerable research has focused on whether there is a relationship between religious differences and marital adjustment. This independent variable could be operationalized several different ways, but it has almost always been measured by denominational affiliation. Thus the data deal with a dichotomous variable that has the two categories of having the same or different affiliations. The results from these studies are unfortunately not entirely consistent. Some of the major prediction studies (Burgess and Cottrell, 1939:87; Terman, 1938) found no relationship between the two variables, whereas other studies such as Baber's (1937), Locke's (1951:345), and Heiss' (1961) found a relationship.

Heiss' study is uniquely important because in his analysis of 1600 subjects from the Midtown Mental Health Survey he attempted to control a number of variables that he had previously found (Heiss, 1960) to be related to the occurrence of denominational heterogamy. He controlled economic status, parent's religiosity, and several other variables and still found denominational heterogamy to be significantly related to marital adjustment. He found the relationship strongest for the Catholics and less strong for Jews, and he had conflicting findings for Protestants. His interpretation was that the church and family pressures from Catholic and Jewish religions probably made the religious factor more relevant in these groups. No studies have ever found a positive relationship between denominational heterogamy and adjustment, so the validity of hypothesis 5.7 seems to be uncertain.

HYPOTHESIS 5.7: Denominational heterogamy is related to marital adjustment and this is an inverse relationship.

There is much more conclusive evidence about the relationship between denominational heterogamy and marital stability.

HYPOTHESIS 5.8: Denominational heterogamy is related to marital stability and this is an inverse, monotonic relationship.

Weeks (1943), Bell (1938), Landis (1949), and Zimmerman and Cervantes (1960) all analyzed data from large samples and found that religious heterogamy was related to divorce rates. More recently Christensen and Barber (1967) analyzed marriage and divorce records in Indiana and found interreligious marriages to have slightly more divorce than intrareligious marriages. The most extensive data on this issue were analyzed by Burchinal and Chancelor (1962), who found a significant relationship between these two variables. They also controlled for age at marriage and found the relationship still existed. It is an interesting aside to note that they found age at marriage accounted for more of the variance than did the religious heterogamy variable, and they found the two tended to operate independently of each other. The important finding for the present point, however, is that they found the religious difference to be significant.

A More General Proposition about Premarital Homogamy and Marital Variables

Each of the independent variables in these hypotheses deals with a specific type of homogamy, and this provides a basis for inducing that a more abstract relationship can be identified between an overall condition of homogamy in general and marital adjustment. In doing this, it is probably first necessary to define homogamy, which can be defined as a concept that identifies variation in the similarity of the individuals in a marriage. It varies continuously between a low of not being at all alike to a high of being identical.

Since the homogamy variable varies prior to the adjustment variables, there is temporal priority in it, and it provides some basis for speculating that this relationship is more than just covariational. Thus we have proposition 5.1.

PROPOSITION 5.1:   The amount of premarital homogamy influences later marital adjustment and this is a positive relationship.

This proposition was formulated by inducing it from empirical research, but there are several other bases for this proposition. For example, it is possible to use role theory to arrive at the same theoretical idea. This can be done by identifying a more general proposition and then deducing proposition 5.1 from it. A highly general proposition was stated by Mangus:

The personal and social development and well-being of a person is viewed as a function of factors that facilitate or impede effective role perception and role performance in group situations (1957:206).

Apparently Mangus is identifying a chain sequence in which certain "factors" influence the effectiveness of role performance, and the effectiveness of role performance influences the "personal and social development and well-being" variable. The sequence is diagramed in Figure 5.2. It is a highly abstract formulation in need of some conceptual clarification. However, deductions can be made from it. It is possible to de-

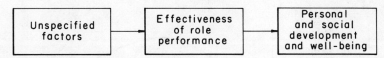

Figure 5.2   Mangus' formulation of role theory.

duce that if marital adjustment can be viewed as a representation of whatever it is that Mangus was identifying by "personal and social development and well-being," and if it is true that heterogamy adversely influences role performance in marital situations, it follows that homogamy would have an indirect, positive influence on marital satisfaction. This conclusion is the theoretical idea in proposition 5.1, arrived at here by deduction within the framework of role theory rather than by induction from empirical data.

Relative Status of Spouse

The eight empirical relationships that were discussed earlier in this chapter also have another regularity that seems to justify attention. The most optimum condition in regard to homogamy is almost always similarity, but when the individuals in a couple deviate from this optimum condition one type of deviation seems to have less detrimental impact than another: Whenever status distinctions are made in regard to a variable, if the female has lower status than the male, this tends to have less undesirable influence than if the male has lower status than the female. This seems to justify the speculation of proposition 5.2.

PROPOSITION 5.2:   The relative status of the husband and wife is related to the marital adjustment and this is a curvilinear relationship.

Figure 5.3 is a speculation about the shape of this relationship. The shape diagramed shows that equal status seems to be associated with the highest probability of marital adjustment, the husband having slightly higher status is next, and the husband having less status is associated with the least adequate adjustment. It is also interesting to speculate that this relationship probably occurs only in a culture that is traditionally male dominated, but further speculation should be postponed until more data are available to test these ideas.

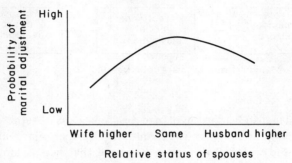

Figure 5.3   The relationship between relative status of spouses and marital adjustment.

Personality Characteristics and
Later Marital Adjustment

A number of personality characteristics have been found to be empirically related to later marital adjustment. These include such diverse characteristics as religiosity, sociability, absence of neuroses, sense of humor—the list could be extended to include over 50 different characteristics. Table 5.1 identifies some of these characteristics and the sources of the data. It is difficult to integrate all of these findings into a theoretical framework, but there are several patterns in the findings that might justify the beginning of the development of theory in this area. One of these patterns that has been identified in reviews of the research (Locke, 1963:320) deals with variation in the *conventionality* of individuals.

Conventionality

From research during the middle of the twentieth century in the United States and Western Europe, characteristics such as those identified in Table 5.1 were found to be related to later marital adjustment. Each of these traits seems to identify the fact that persons who tend to be more conventional in the cultures tend to have a higher probability of success in their marriages. This phenomenon of conventionality can be defined as variation in the degree to which the behavior of individuals conforms to the traditional, dominant culture in the society or subgroup of a society in which they live. It is viewed here as a continuous

Table 5.1 Personality Traits Related to Marital Adjustment

Personality Trait	Studies Finding a Relationship
Adaptability	Terman and Oden (1947); Burgess and Wallin (1953)
Desire for children	Terman and Oden (1947); Burgess and Wallin (1953)
Church attendance	King (1951); Schroeder (1939); Terman and Oden (1947); Burgess and Cottrell (1939)
Church membership	Schroeder (1939); Schnepp and Johnson (1952); Terman and Oden (1947); Locke (1951)
Conventional behavior	Burgess and Wallin (1953); Locke (1951)
Drinking and smoking	Burgess and Wallin (1953)
Emotional stability	Terman and Oden (1947); Burgess and Wallin (1953)
Regularity of employment	Burgess and Cottrell (1939)
Happiness of childhood	Terman (1938); Terman and Oden (1947); Locke (1951); Locke and Karlsson (1951)
Leisure time activities	Burgess and Wallin (1953)
Place of marriage	Burgess and Cottrell (1939); Locke (1951)
Married by religious leader	Schroeder (1939); Burgess and Cottrell (1939); Locke (1951); Terman and Oden (1947)
Membership in organizations	King (1951); Terman and Oden (1947); Burgess and Cottrell (1939); Burgess and Wallin (1953)
Absence of neuroses	Terman (1938)
Savings	King (1951); Burgess and Cottrell (1939); Locke (1951); Terman and Oden (1947)
Attitude toward premarital sex	King (1951); Terman (1938); Terman and Oden (1947)
Not low in sociability	Terman and Oden (1947)

variable that ranges from no conformity to a high degree of conformity. It seems to be conceptually different from conformity to the expectations of a particular role, for it denotes conventionality as a style of life, encompassing many roles. If the dependent variable that is relevant in this idea is later marital adjustment, proposition 5.3 can be deduced.

PROPOSITION 5.3: The amount of conventionality influences marital adjustment and this is a positive, monotonic relationship.

There is an important issue that is raised by stating proposition 5.3 in this manner: each of the specific empirical relationships that are identified in Table 5.1 deals with a specific type of behavior or set of acts, but the independent variable in proposition 5.3 does not identify any particular set of behaviors. It merely denotes variation in conventionality of the behaviors. The proposition asserts that it is the fact that the behavior is conventional in the society or subgroups of a society that determines whether the behavior influences marital success, and this is very different from the idea that certain acts or behaviors influence marital adjustment. There has been voluminous literature that argues that certain behaviors such as emotional maturity and interpersonal competence influence marital adjustment, but it is suggested here that all of the data that show a relationship between behaviors and marital adjustment can be explained by proposition 5.3. Later research may reveal that some behaviors influence marital adjustment independently of cultural definitions, but no currently available data indicate this.

One body of literature that supports the cultural argument rather than the argument that certain behaviors influence marital adjustment is the ethnographic comparisons published by anthropologists. Mead's (1935) analysis of three cultures in New Guinea is one example. She found that the traits that were associated with marital and life adjustment in one of these cultures were radically different from the traits that seemed to promote adjustment in the other cultures. For example, pride, harshness, and violence in the Mundugumor were positively associated with adjustment, whereas gentleness, warmth, and unaggressiveness were associated with adjustment among the Arapesh. The appropriate conclusion seems to be that it is not the traits themselves that influence marital adjustment, but whether the traits conform to the cultural definitions of the social group where they occur.

Another body of research that argues for the cultural point of view is Christensen's (1969) research on premarital sexual attitudes and behavior in three cultures, discussed in more detail in Chapter 8. Christensen demonstrates that it is deviation from the cultural definitions about sexual behavior that is related to divorce, not the specific sexual behaviors themselves.

There is another aspect of proposition 5.3 that should be identified. This is that the heterogeneity of the culture in a society probably influences the relationship in this proposition. Thus far we have no systematic formulations that have identified how this occurs, but future research should provide some. It may be that if a society is highly homogeneous, the relationship in proposition 5.3 is highly influential. But if a society is heterogeneous, behavior would be conventional according to some definitions and unconventional according to others and the relationship in this proposition is less influential because of the resulting conflict in definitions.

Reference Relationship

There are several similar empirical relationships in the marriage prediction literature that can serve as a basis for stating another theoretical proposition. One of these relationships deals with the parent's approval of the prospective partner. This independent variable denotes variation in the degree to which the parents approve or disapprove of the prospective mate. It is a continuous variable that ranges from a low of strongly disapprove through neutrality to strongly approving of the prospective spouse. The data from Burgess and Cottrell (1939:408), Locke (1959:119, 352), Karlsson (1951:61), and Deburger (1961) support this hypothesis.

HYPOTHESIS 5.9:   The amount that parents approve of the mate is related to marital adjustment and this is a positive, monotonic relationship.

In addition, Burgess and Wallin (1953:521) have data on how later adjustment is related to the amount an individual likes his or her future in-laws. This independent variable varies from disliking very much to liking very much.

HYPOTHESIS 5.10:   The amount an individual likes future in-laws is related to subsequent marital adjustment and this is a positive relationship.

If some of the theoretical ideas in symbolic interaction about reference relationships (Rose, 1962:11) are incorporated with these findings it provides a useful theoretical rationale. One of the central ideas in reference group theory is that the meanings that various phenomena have to a person are influenced by the meanings of certain other individuals. If these other individuals are what Mead (1934) referred to as *significant* to a person, then the meanings the person has will tend to conform to the meanings the other individual(s) has. This abstract theoretical idea has not been stated in terms of variables and propositions, but the idea can be translated into variables and propositions that can be used as a theoretical basis for explaining why empirical relationships such as hypotheses 5.9 and 5.10 appear. There seem to be three variables in this idea: (1) variation in meaning to a person; (2) variation in the meaning to another individual or individuals; and (3) variation in the significance of these other individuals with whom the person interacts. It is first necessary to define "meaning" and identify how it varies.

Rose (1962:5) defines meaning as "equivalent to a 'true' dictionary definition, referring to the way in which people actually use a term in their behavior." And, as Mead states, it "does not simply symbolize a situation or object which is already there in advance; it makes possible the existence or the appearance of that situation or object, for it is a part of the mechanism whereby that situation or object is created" (Strauss, 1956:180). A meaning can thus be a belief, an idea, attitude, perspective, and so on. This variable of meaning does not vary in a linear manner but in an infinite variety of ways. In fact, Stone (1962) argues that it varies in such a variety of ways that it is impossible for something to have exactly the same meaning to two individuals. They can have substantially the same definition of what something means, but it will always differ somewhat. Proposition 5.4 states one of the ideas in reference group theory.

PROPOSITION 5.4:   The meaning a phenomenon has to significant others influences the meaning the phenomenon has to a person so the person's meaning tends to be the same as the meaning of these significant others.

If Mead's concept of "significant" is viewed as a variable that identifies variation in the salience or importance of other individuals, it seems reasonable that variation in significance influences the amount of influence the other individual will have on a person. This phenomenon of significant, however, does not seem to be different conceptually from the phenomenon that has been labeled "value" in this book. Both of these variables identify the subjectively experienced salience, worth, or importance of something, and because of this the term *value* is used here. There is a related proposition that seems to be inherent in reference group theory.

PROPOSITION 5.5:   The value of significant others influences the effect that the others' meanings have on an individual's meanings and this is a positive, monotonic relationship.

These relationships are diagrammed in Figure 5.4, which shows that the value variable is a contingent variable influencing the effect that others have on an individual's meanings. It should also be pointed out that these relationships undoubtedly operate only when there is considerable interaction.

It is now possible to integrate this formulation about reference relationships with the empirical relationships identified earlier that dealt with such variables as parental approval of the marriage and marital adjustment. If highly valued others with whom important reference rela-

The Effects of Premarital Factors on Marriage 117

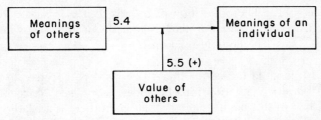

Figure 5.4 Propositions about how reference relationships influence meanings.

tionships are established are opposed to a marriage, the individual's meanings will tend to be similar to the others'. Since the opposition will create incongruity in the individual's mind, it will tend to be more difficult to develop a satisfactory adjustment in the marriage than if the significant others approved of the marriage. This would probably be especially true when the majority or all of the individuals in one's reference relationships either oppose or encourage the marriage. Thus, since reference relationships are important in influencing individual's meanings, the amount they oppose or support the marriage probably influences the subsequent adjustment in the marriage. If the independent variable in this deduction is conceptualized as *opposition* and viewed as varying continuously from high opposition through neutrality to high support, proposition 5.6 can be stated.

PROPOSITION 5.6:   The amount of opposition that significant others have to a marriage influences the adjustment of the marriage and this is an inverse, monotonic relationship.

Furthermore, since the value of the individuals influences the effect these individuals have on a person's life, as indicated in proposition 5.5, proposition 5.7 is likely.

PROPOSITION 5.7:   The value of significant others is related to the amount of influence in proposition 5.6 which asserts their opposition to a marriage influences the marital adjustment, and this is a positive, monotonic relationship.

These last two propositions provide a rationale for deducing that if an individual's friends oppose the marriage, the marriage is likely to have less adequate adjustment. No known data have yet suggested this idea, which is presented in hypothesis 5.11.

HYPOTHESIS 5.11:   The opposition of friends to a marriage is related to subsequent marital adjustment and this is an inverse, monotonic relationship.

It is also possible to use another theoretical perspective to arrive at the same empirical relationship. Balance theory (see Newcomb, 1961; see also Ch. 3 in this book) suggests that when there is a triadic relationship where one individual likes two other persons but one of the other persons does not like the third, this triad is in imbalance and the individual will experience strain. This strain can be resolved, but it is likely that where the disliked individual is one's spouse the strain in these relationships might adversely influence marital adjustment.

Skills to Conform to Prescriptions

Another pattern in the marriage prediction research that suggests theoretical propositions is the pattern of a number of findings that deal with the presence or absence of certain skills. These empirical findings are summarized in the following sections, and then a more general formulation is proposed.

Age at Marriage

Considerable evidence leads to hypothesis 5.12.

HYPOTHESIS 5.12:   Age at the time of first marriage is related to marital adjustment and this is a positive, monotonic, curvilinear relationship.

An attempt is made in Figure 5.5 to summarize the findings from several studies (Burgess and Cottrell, 1939:122, 271; Burgess and Wallin, 1953: 521; Locke, 1956:102, 343; Terman, 1938:181; Karlsson, 1963:56). The age variable is operationalized in terms of years, but it is difficult to draw this line because most of the empirical studies group several years together into categories and different studies use different age categories. At any rate, the evidence is clear that considerable movement is made in the dependent variable while age moves between 15 and the early twenties, and after this time the curve tends to level off.

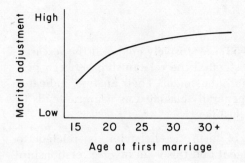

Figure 5.5 The relationship between age at first marriage and marital adjustment.

Education

A number of studies have investigated the relationship between the amount of education and marital adjustment. This independent variable is usually viewed as a categorical variable varying in the number of years of formal schooling. The available date from several studies (Burgess and Cottrell, 1939:271; Burgess and Wallin, 1953:516; Terman, 1938:189) indicate there is a positive relationship between these two variables that is probably almost linear. Some recent evidence by Udry (1968) indicates this relationship may not be monotonic, and that it may be slightly curvilinear in that the proportion adjusted may decrease slightly for those with extensive graduate education. This seems to be a slight decline, however, so the relationship still tends to be essentially positive. The relationship seems to hold for both sexes.

HYPOTHESIS 5.13:   The amount of education is related to marital adjustment and this is a curvilinear relationship.

Considerable research has focused on the relationship between education and marital stability. The findings are consistent in that there seems to be a positive, linear relationship. This has been found by Weeks (1943), Hollingshead (1950), Kephart (1954), Goode (1956), and Udry (1968). Glick (1957) and Hillman (1962) found a curvilinear relationship, but Udry (1967) demonstrated that this appeared because the dependent variable in their analyses was not stability rate but the number of individuals divorced or separated at the time of the 1950 census. Thus there is considerable and consistent evidence for hypothesis 5.14.

HYPOTHESIS 5.14:   The amount of education is related to marital stability and this is a positive, linear relationship.

Neurosis

Burgess and Wallin (1953:523–537) extensively analyzed the research done before their study that investigated the relationship between personality characteristics and marital adjustment. Their analysis indicates that the typical behavior that is generally classified as neurotic tends to be inversely related to marital adjustment.

HYPOTHESIS 5.15:　The amount of neurotic behavior is related to marital adjustment and this is an inverse relationship.

Skills

The role of spouse contains a large number of complex expectations, many of which are formally identified as "laws." Others are clear but are not codified, and others are subtle and highly variable in different subgroups. There are many skills that are necessary if a person is to behave in accordance with these expectations, and if a person does not have the necessary skills he will eventually incur sanctions from his spouse, from his intimate acquaintances, and from the larger society. If it is true that the reason that age at marriage, amount of education, and neurosis are related to marital adjustment is because the younger, less education, and more neurotic individuals do not have the skills to function satisfactorily in the marital role, these empirical findings can be viewed as specific cases of a general idea that the degree to which a person has the skills to behave in the ways prescribed for a role is likely to influence the "adjustment" in the role. This can be stated as a relatively abstract proposition, and then specific deductions can be made from it to the marital role.

The independent variable in this formulation can be labeled amount of skill. It is difficult to define precisely, since it includes many different skills, but it can be defined as the degree to which a person has the skills to behave in the ways prescribed for a social role. It varies continuously from having none to all of them. This suggests the following general proposition.

PROPOSITION 5.8:　The amount of skill a person has to behave in the ways prescribed for a role influences the adjustment the person will have in the role and this is a positive, monotonic relationship.

A less general proposition can be deduced from this highly abstract idea by applying it to marital roles. It can be deduced that since there

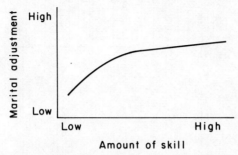

Figure 5.6 The suggested relationship between the amount of skill to behave in accordance with role prescriptions and marital adjustment.

are prescriptions for marital roles and if proposition 5:8 is true, then proposition 5.9 follows.

PROPOSITION 5.9:   The amount of skill a person has to behave in ways prescribed for a marital role influences the marital adjustment and this is a positive, monotonic relationship.

Figure 5.6 diagrams the type of relationship that seems, on an intuitive basis, to occur. It seems likely that this relationship is monotonic but curvilinear. It is drawn this way because it seems reasonable that when an individual is quite deficient in skills this will be highly influential, but that after a moderately high level of skill is attained additional increases in skills probably do not have as much influence.

Motivation for Marriage

There is some evidence accumulating that the reasons for marriage may be related to marital adjustment. One of the findings deals with an empirical relationship between premarital pregnancy and divorce. Christensen's (1969) research on three cultures argues that it is not the premarital pregnancy itself that influences marital instability, but rather the extent to which the pregnancy and the intercourse that preceded it deviated from the culturally provided norms. However, in addition to this finding, Christensen also presents evidence that in some cultural groups there are data that indicate that the pregnancy induces marriage. He found, for example, a large number of marriages occurring shortly after the time when the pregnancy would be discovered in the Utah group, and a very large group of the premaritally pregnant group in this sample were later divorced. It may be that part of the reason for this

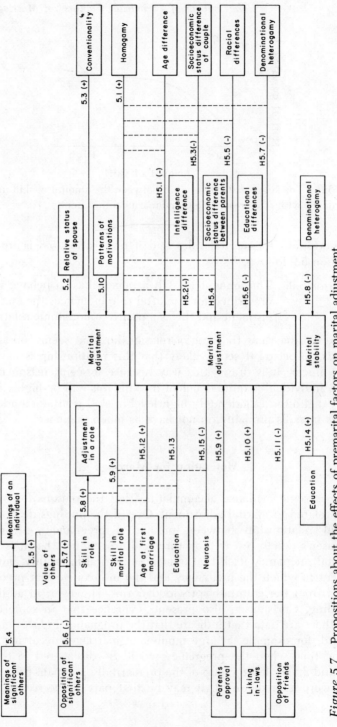

Figure 5.7 Propositions about the effects of premarital factors on marital adjustment.

high divorce rate is that the marriage was precipitated by the pregnancy rather than other factors, and when marriages tend to be caused by pregnancy (especially when other reasons for marriage are absent or are less important) these marriages tend to have more difficulty.

This same reasoning is supported by Popenoe's (1938) analysis of elopements in which he found the reason for the elopment to be related to the proportion of couples that were happy at later times. These findings also suggest that when certain types of motivation predominate in causing marriages the marriages tend to have more difficulty. One relevant proposition can be formulated.

PROPOSITION 5.10:   The unique pattern of motivation for marriage influences the probability of marital adjustment.

Summary

This chapter has attempted to begin the process of generating theory from the marriage prediction literature. The main theoretical ideas that are proposed are that at the time of marriage the amount of homogamy, relative status of spouses, conventionality, supporting reference relationships, and the presence of enough skill that an individual can conform to role prescriptions all influence an individual's adjustment in marriage. These ideas are summarized in Figure 5.7.

THE EASE OF ROLE TRANSITIONS

The process of entering or leaving a social role is known as a role transition (Cottrell, 1942:619). It is a change in the role expectations or norms that are relevant for an individual and hence a change in a set of behaviors. Since so much of what occurs in families is carefully defined role behavior and these roles are continually being entered and exited, this process is certainly one that is important in family theory. Thus Chapter 6 examines a number of theoretical ideas about role transitions.

There are several different aspects of transitions that could be theorized about. For example, propositions could be developed about such things as the causes of role transitions or their effects on other variables. The concern in this chapter, however, is with one relatively narrow aspect of the role transitions—the factors that influence the *ease* of making these transitions. This dependent variable is defined as the degree to which there is freedom from difficulty and the presence of easily available resources to make these changes. It is a continuous variable that varies in degree from its lowest point of a role transition being impossible to the opposite extreme of a transition being highly easy.

There are some dependent variables where the variation can be understood by identifying relationships with a small number of independent variables. This does not, however, seem to be the case with the ease of role transitions. Instead, there seem to be a large number of variables that influence this phenomenon and, to make it more complicated, no ways have yet been found to group these theoretical ideas together to induce any highly general theoretical statements. Instead, there are many factors that seem to operate independently of each other in influencing the ease of making transitions. It will be interesting to see if additional theorizing and research can find ways to induce more general explanations, and if this is not possible this area may be particularly amenable to studying the ways different variables interact with each other in influencing the dependent variable.

Anticipatory Socialization

Leonard Cottrell published a very short paper in 1942 on "Individual Adjustment to Age and Sex Roles," and in it he attempted to identify a number of factors that influence adjustment to social roles. One of his assertions was that experiences such as "emotionally intimate contact which allows identification with persons functioning in the role," "imaginal or incipient rehearsal," and "practice" facilitate role adjustment. These are examples of the more inclusive phenomenon that has come to be known as *anticipatory socialization* (Merton, 1968:316 ff). This variable can be defined as the process of learning the norms of a role before being in a social situation where it is appropriate to actually behave in that role. Anticipatory socialization can be viewed as a continuous variable that varies in amount from being absent to having relatively high amounts of training.

The main idea in Cottrell's formulation is that variation in this variable positively influences the ease of making role transitions. He suggests that all of his propositions probably have linear relationships, but that it is "quite probable that there are limits beyond which a linear relationship does not exist" (1942:620). This particular relationship seems to deviate from a linear pattern. Very likely variation in anticipatory socialization influences the ease of transitions most when it is relatively absent, and additional increases beyond moderate amounts of socialization do not continue to exert the same amount of influence. If this is the case, the relationship in this proposition is positive, monotonic, curvilinear, and the most influence occurs in the low degrees of the independent variable. This relationship is diagramed in Figure 6.1 and stated in the first proposition.

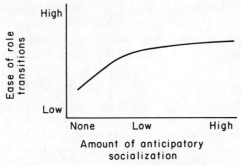

Figure 6.1 The relationship between anticipatory socialization and ease of transitions into roles.

PROPOSITION 6.1:   The amount of anticipatory socialization influences the ease of transitions into roles and this is a positive, monotonic, curvilinear relationship in which the influence decreases as the independent variable increases.

This proposition is probably useful in helping to explain variation in the ease of role transitions in many nonfamilial transitions, but it has been specifically studied in several family transitions. It was one of the major lines of reasoning in Deutscher's (1959) study of the launching process. In fact, he used the reasoning in this proposition as the major explanation of his finding that the postparental stage was in many ways less difficult than its preceding state in the family life cycle:

> *Theoretically* this could be assumed to be a difficult transition to make, largely because of the absence of role models—the absence of socialization to play post-parental roles. However, middle-aged couples whose children have left home indicate that there are opportunities for them to learn these new roles before they are thrust upon them (1962:523).

It is important to note that Deutscher's data have no measures of variation in this independent variable, and hence his study provides no empirical evidence of even the existence of the relationship asserted in this proposition. He merely used it as a rationale for his descriptive finding that the parents were experiencing a certain degree of ease in their role transition.

There is, however, literature that does provide some evidence of the validity of this proposition. In the family field, Dyer's (1963) study of some of the factors that are related to the severity of the crisis when parenthood occurs has supporting data. He found that one factor that is inversely related to the severity of the crisis is whether one of the members of the couple had previously had a preparation for marriage course. If it can be assumed that this type of educational experience would be a type of anticipatory socialization, the finding provides some evidence in support of the particular assertion of this proposition that a relationship exists.

There is considerably more evidence from nonfamilial research in support of this proposition than there is from family research. Davis' (1940, 1947) analyses of several cases of extreme isolation from human interaction is one example. One of the characteristics of extreme isolation is that there is an inadequate opportunity for any type of socialization to occur. The isolated children that were studied were not able to move into roles such as student or friend that most children are able to assume when they have more extensive interaction and the anticipatory socialization that goes with it.

Ellis and Lane's (1967) study of the consequences of social mobility is another related study. They found that male college students who were upwardly mobile by coming to college had more difficulty in making the adjustment to college than did the less mobile students. Upward mobility is a relatively effective empirical indicator of the independent variable in proposition 6.1. Persons who were upwardly mobile would be expected to be less adequately socialized to assume the role of student in a social situation different from the one in which they were reared than boys who were reared in more affluent homes. The fact that the upwardly mobile boys had more difficulty thus adds evidence of the validity of this proposition.

These studies provide some evidence that the relationship that is asserted does exist. They do not, however, permit making any inferences about other aspects of this relationship such as how much variation occurs in the dependent variable when the independent variable varies, or whether the relationship conforms to the pattern diagramed in Figure 6.1. Inferences about these aspects of this proposition will only be possible when additional data are available. These particular studies do not control the variation of other variables and hence do not rule out alternative explanations of the relationships that have been found. This means that the evidence in support of this proposition should be viewed as tentative until additional research provides better data.

Role Clarity

Another of Cottrell's propositions contends that the clarity with which roles are defined positively influences the ability to adjust to transitions from one role to another. By *role clarity* he apparently means the degree to which there is a set of "explicit definitions of the reciprocal behavior expected" (Cottrell, 1942:618) rather than a set of ambiguous or vague definitions. Apparently role clarity is a continuous variable that ranges from a low to high amount of clarity. It seems likely that this is not a linear relationship. There is probably a marginal point beyond which additional increments in clarity do not facilitate the ease of making role transitions (proposition 6.2). If this is true, then this is a second-order or quadratic relationship as diagramed in Figure 6.2.

PROPOSITION 6.2:   The amount of role clarity influences the ease of making transitions into the roles and this is a positive, monotonic, curvilinear relationship in which the amount of influence decreases as the independent variable increases.

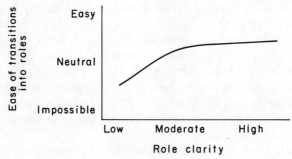

Figure 6.2   The relationship between role clarity and the ease of transitions into roles.

Cottrell did not differentiate between transitions that are made into roles and those made out of roles. These are, however, two different processes, and it is likely that they are influenced differently by different independent variables. Although proposition 6.2 states that role clarity influences transitions into roles in a positive manner, proposition 6.3 is somewhat different.

PROPOSITION 6.3:   The amount of role clarity influences the ease of transitions out of roles and this is an inverse, monotonic relationship.

It is unlikely that this is a linear relationship since variation in clarity when there is very little clarity probably makes more difference than variation in this same independent variable when there is considerable clarity. This speculation, however, is highly tentative.

Proposition 6.3 is probably useful in understanding variation in the ease of role transitions at a societal level and at an individual level. In the case of the societal analysis, the degree of clarity of the definitions of expected behavior in the society is the independent variable. In the case of variation at an individual level, variation in the clarity of the individual's definitions is influential. This proposition seems reasonable, but this far no empirical data have been found that systematically test the asserted relationship.

Role Conflict

After his analysis of the impact of role clarity on the ease of role transitions, Cottrell then speculated on how several other factors influence role clarity. He suggested that such phenomena as inconsistent expectations verbally and behaviorally and contact with members of subcultural groups that have different role expectations influence role clarity. He then suggested that the consistency of expectations influences the adjustment to social roles.

It seems possible to revise these ideas and eliminate some of the conceptual ambiguity and redundance in this part of Cottrell's earlier formulation. The concept of role conflict has emerged in recent years, and it provides a relatively clear conceptualization of the phenomenon that Cottrell seems to be identifying when he discusses inconsistencies, discrepancies, and exposure to multiple cultures. *Role conflict* can be defined as the presence of incompatible expectations for a social role.[1]

If it were possible to isolate and count the conflict this variable could be viewed as a categorical variable varying in number, but at the present time this is not possible. The most practical way to view its variation is probably that it varies continuously from relative absence to a high degree of conflict.

If Cottrell's initial formulation only were to be used to identify the theoretical relationships in regard to role conflict, the relationship that would be proposed would be that role conflict is inversely related to role clarity and to the ease of making role transitions. There is, however, another set of theoretical ideas that probably should be integrated with Cottrell's ideas. These are the formulations in Goode's (1960) theory of role strain.

Goode defines role strain as the stress generated within a person when he either cannot comply or has difficulty complying with the expectations of a role or set of roles. Role strain is apparently a continuous variable that ranges in degree from absence to a high amount. It is important that it be integrated with Cottrell's ideas on role conflict since variation in role conflict probably influences the ease of role transitions only indirectly. It probably influences role strain rather than ease of making role transitions, and then the amount of strain influences the ease of the transitions. These ideas can be expressed in the following three propositions.

PROPOSITION 6.4: The amount of role conflict in a role influences the amount of role strain experienced when occupying this role and this is a positive relationship.

PROPOSITION 6.5: The amount of role strain that results from occupying a role influences the ease of making a transition into this role and this is an inverse relationship.

PROPOSITION 6.6:   The amount of role strain that results from occupying a role influences the ease of making transitions out of this role and this is a positive relationship.

There is, at present, very little basis for speculation about any additional characteristics of the relationships in these propositions. They seem to be relatively influential, and they seem to be monotonic. It also seems plausible that role strain has more influence toward its upper end, but these are mere speculations.

Cottrell speculates that variation in what is here being called role conflict also influences role clarity. It seems doubtful that when empirical data are available to test this relationship it will be found to be valid, but this is only an intuitive observation. Following is Cottrell's proposition.

PROPOSITION 6.7:   The amount of role conflict influences the amount of role clarity and this is an inverse relationship.

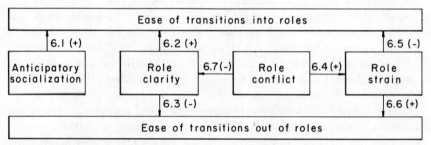

Figure 6.3   The relationships between role conflict, role strain, and the ease of making transitions into roles.

The relationships in these first five propositions can be seen diagramatically in Figure 6.3. The arrows indicate the direction of influence or causality that is asserted and the numbers indicate the propositions that assert the relationships.

No studies have been found that test these ideas with familial variables, but there are a number of studies of phenomena that are quite different from familial processes that have findings that would be expected to occur if the assertions made in these propositions are true. Campbell and Pettigrew (1959), for example, found that the minister's role in the South had an increased strain as a result of the role conflict introduced when the Christian ideals and discriminatory practices of their parishioners met. Gross et al. (1957) demonstrate that strain and complexity are introduced into the school superintendent's role by the conflicting demands of that role. There are thus some published data that indicate a concomitant variation existing between the variables identified in propositions 6.3 and 6.4. Thus far, however, little has been done to isolate the effects of these independent variables from the effects of other variables, so it is difficult to estimate how much influence they have or to say much about the nature of the relationships other than that they apparently exist. It is likely that most scholars would expect these relationships are quite influential in the sense that variation in the independent variable would cause major variation in the dependent variables, but no data have been found to test this.

It is also interesting to note that no studies have been found that have empirically demonstrated temporal priority in the covariation of these variables. Thus, even though there is some basis for inferring that a relationship does exist among the variables, there is the possibility that future research, which demonstrates temporal priority and isolates the effects of role conflict and role strain from the effects of other variables, may find that the influence of the independent variables in these propositions is considerably less than is presently expected.

Role Incompatibility

Both Cottrell (1942) and Goode (1960) identify phenomenon that can be labeled role incompatibility. This identifies the degree to which the demands of one role are incompatible with the demands of other roles a person is occupying. This variable is probably also a continuous variable ranging from two or more roles being completely incompatible to their being highly compatible. Goode suggests that it is a source of role strain and Cottrell proposes that it is related to the adjustment to roles. Both of these assertions are probably correct, and they can be integrated if the role strain variable is viewed as an intervening phenomenon that varies between role incompatibility and the ease of adjusting to new roles. This integrates both Cottrell's and Goode's formulations and identifies an additional factor that influences role strain.

PROPOSITION 6.8: The amount of role incompatibility influences role strain and this is a positive relationship.

On an intuitive basis it is suggested that this is probably a positive, monotonic relationship, but there is no basis for asserting any other characteristics of this relationship. No data have been found that empirically test it.

Other Sources of Role Strain

Goode (1960) identifies a number of other phenomena that influence role strain, but many of the sources of role strain he discusses are specific situations, and theoretical propositions cannot be made about how they systematically influence role transitions. It is, however, possible to state some of his ideas as propositions. One of these formulations is that the degree to which roles are compartmentalized influences the strain that results from incompatible roles.

Goode apparently defines compartmentalization as playing roles in different physical locations or social situations. He does not systematically define just how this varies, but it apparently varies in the degree to which there is overlap in the social circumstances where roles are played. It could thus vary from no compartmentalization in a situation where roles would be played simultaneously to having complete compartmentalization when roles are completely separated. Goode's idea seems to be that when there is role incompatibility, the greater the compartmentalization, the less the role strain. This can be stated as a proposition.

PROPOSITION 6.9:   When there is role incompatibility, the amount of role compartmentalization influences role strain and this is an inverse relationship.

Another of Goode's formulations that can be stated as a theoretical proposition has to do with the total amount of role activity that is prescribed in a person's life. Goode does not state a formal proposition but notes that eliminating roles can decrease strain and adding new roles can increase it. The crucial variable here is probably the total amount of activity that is normatively prescribed. This variable can be viewed as a continuous variable ranging from no activity being prescribed to a high amount of prescribed activity. It is likely that increases in this independent variable up to a moderately high point have little or no influence on role strain, and that the influence increases markedly after a certain marginal point is reached. The relationship that is proposed in this proposition is diagramed in Figure 6.4 and stated in proposition 6.10.

PROPOSITION 6.10:   The amount of activity that is normatively prescribed in a person's life influences the individual's role strain and this is a positive relationship.

It is now possible to expand the number of variables that are identified in Figure 6.3. Propositions 6.8, 6.9, and 6.10 each identify additional factors that are related, and these make the model more complex. Figure 6.5 includes these additional three propositions.

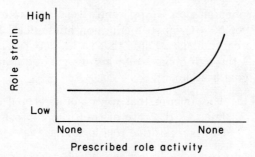

Figure 6.4 The relationship between the amount of normatively prescribed role activity and role strain.

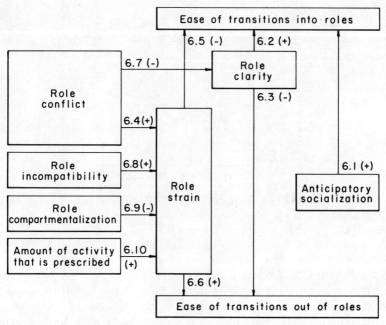

Figure 6.5 The relationships in propositions 6.1 through 6.10.

Goal Attainment

Cottrell (1942) suggests that the degree of adjustment to roles varies directly with the extent to which the role permits individuals to realize dominant goals in their subcultural groups. The crucial independent variable here seems to be the degree to which roles facilitate goal attainment. This phenomenon is apparently very similar to what Biddle and Thomas (1966:60–61) label "facilitation-hindrance." It can be conceptualized as a continuous variable that varies between one extreme of preventing goals through being irrelevant for goal attainment to highly facilitating the goal attainment.

PROPOSITION 6.11:   The amount that roles facilitate goal attainment influences the ease of transitions into these roles and this is a positive relationship.

This relationship could be linear as Cottrell proposed but it may be nonlinear. It may be that when the independent variable is closer to the extremes it has more influence on the ease of transitions. If this is the case, a cubic or third-order relationship exists. Both of these possibilities are diagramed in Figure 6.6.

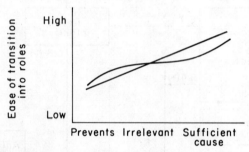

Figure 6.6   The relationship between the facilitation of goal attainment and the ease of role transition.

Cottrell notes that when a role interferes with the attainment of a dominant goal, adjustment varies positively with the extent to which the frustrating role is defined as a path to another role which promises the desired gratifications. This idea does not seem to be a separate theoretical idea but a more specific case of the idea in proposition 6.11, and hence it should be viewed as a deduction from that proposition.

It also seems reasonable that the degree to which a role *transition* facilitates goal attainment is related to the ease of transitions out of roles. If, for example, having a certain status or position is a goal and terminating a role would entail leaving that status or position, this termination would hinder the attainment of a goal. If this reasoning is correct, proposition 6.12 follows.

PROPOSITION 6.12: The degree to which role transitions out of roles facilitate goal attainment influences the ease of transitions out of roles and this is a positive relationship.

There is little basis for speculating about the nature of this relationship. However, a suggestion is made here that the independent variable probably has little influence at the point where there is low facilitation or hindrance, and when either facilitation or hindrance increases it probably has more influence. If this is the case, the relationship is like the curved function in Figure 6.6.

No data have been found that test the validity of these three propositions, but Cavan's (1962) analysis of the difficulty of the transition into the aged role is related. She does not systematically analyze any empirical data but rather analyzes the nature of the aging role in contemporary United States society. Cavan suggests that "old age is more or less of a vacuum culturally" (1962:529), and that this deficiency of gratifying phenomena in the role contributes to the difficulty of the transition into this role. This is more of an analytic argument in favor of the proposition than an analysis of empirical data, but since it is based on a scholarly assessment of conditions in a society, it seems defensible to view her observations as providing some evidence in support of the assertion in this proposition that a relationship exists. It is at best a very low order of proof, but it does seem to be relevant.

The Value of Goals

Variation in a certain type of evaluation seems to have an effect on the influence that occurs in proposition 6.11. The term values was defined earlier as the relative worth or importance of a particular phenomenon, and the variation in it is viewed as continuous between the extremes of being highly negatively valued through neutrality to a very high degree of value. A highly general proposition stated in Chapter 3 about one probable effect of variation in this phenomenon of value is repeated here for convenience.

PROPOSITION 3.5: The value of a phenomenon influences the amount of effect this phenomenon has in social processes and this is a positive, monotonic relationship.

It seems reasonable to use this proposition to extend the idea in proposition 6.11.

Proposition 6.11 asserts that variation in the degree to which a role transition facilitates goal attainment positively influences the ease of this transition. If variation in the "value" of these goals is a more specific instance of the valuing that is identified in proposition 3.5, and if proposition 3.5 is true, this variation in the value of goals can be expected to influence the relationship that the facilitation of goal attainment has with the ease of role transitions. The way this probably occurs is that when a role transition facilitates or hinders the attainment of highly valued or highly devalued goals, this probably has a substantial influence on the ease of the transitions. Conversely, when a transition facilitates or hinders the attainment of goals that are not highly valued or devalued, then assuming no variation in the amount of facilitation, this probably has less influence on the ease of the role transition. Thus proposition 6.13 is deduced from proposition 3.5.

PROPOSITION 6.13:   The value of goals is related to the amount of influence in proposition 6.11 which asserts that the facilitation of goal attainment positively influences the ease of transitions into roles, and this is a positive, monotonic relationship.

This is a positive relationship that is probably monotonic, and it is likely that it has considerable influence. This proposition is an important extension of Cottrell's formulation; he merely states that the relationship in proposition 6.11 operates with "dominant" goals. This refinement introduces precision in that it allows for variation in the value of goals and identifies at least one factor that influences when the facilitation of the goal attainment varies in its influence.

This value variable probably also influences the amount of influence in proposition 6.12, which identifies a relationship between role transitions facilitating goal attainment and the ease of transitions out of roles. If there are value differences in goals, and if proposition 3.5 is true, proposition 6.14 follows.

PROPOSITION 6.14:   The value of goals is related to the amount of influence in proposition 6.12, which states that the degree to which role transitions out of roles influence goal attainment positively influences the ease of transitions out of roles, and this is a positive, monotonic relationship.

Length of Time in a Role

The amount of time to be spent in a role is another variable that probably influences the relationship in proposition 6.11 between goal facilitation and ease of transitions into roles. If the period of time that is to be spent in a role is viewed as relatively short, this probably mitigates somewhat the adverse effects that occur as a result of the role interfering with attaining goals. What probably occurs is that the shorter the time in the role, the more this time factor eliminates the difficulty caused by the frustrated goal attainment. This is diagramed in Figure 6.7 as a curvilinear rather than a linear relationship and is formulated in proposition 6.15.

PROPOSITION 6.15:   When a role prevents the attainment of a goal, the length of time that a person expects to be in a role is related to the amount of influence in proposition 6.11, which asserts that the facilitation of goal attainment influences the ease of transitions into roles, and this is a positive relationship.

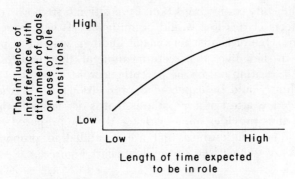

Figure 6.7   The relationship between the length of time in an undesirable role and ease of the role transitions.

Substitute Gratification

Cottrell (1942:619) speculated on how another set of factors makes a difference in the influence that the facilitation of goal attainment has on the ease of adjusting to roles. He suggested that when there is "an excess of deprivation or frustration" in the attainment of goals, the adjustment to a role is influenced by the availability of substitute gratifications. This availability of substitute gratifications can be conceptualized as a variable, and it is probably most meaningful when viewed as a categorical variable that varies in the number of substitute gratifications available. When it is, it varies from none to a large number of them.

What Cottrell seems to be suggesting is that when the independent variable in proposition 6.11 is in its low range (hinders goal attainment) the influence it has is influenced by variation in the availability of substitute gratifications.

PROPOSITION 6.16:   When a role prevents the attainment of goals, the availability of substitute gratifications is related to the amount of influence in proposition 6.11, which asserts the facilitation of goal attainment influences the ease of transition into roles, and this is an inverse relationship.

Deutscher's (1969) study of the adjustment to the postparental role is related to the idea in this proposition. If it is true that this particular role transition is a situation of moving into a role that prevents the attainment of a highly valued goal, parenthood, this hindrance would contribute to difficulty in this transition. Proposition 6.16, however, suggests that the effects of this loss would be mitigated if there were substitute gratifications. One of Deutscher's major findings was that if parents had other roles in their lives that were meaningful, they had less difficulty making the transition out of the parenthood role.

This finding would be expected if proposition 6.16 is true; hence it can be viewed as a test of a hypothesis that is deducible from this proposition and thus provides some evidence that the proposed relationship does exist. The relationships that are identified in propositions 6.11 through 6.6 are summarized in the flow chart Figure 6.8.

Transition Procedures

Cottrell suggested that the adjustment in a role transition "varies directly with the degree of importance attached to and the definiteness of the transitional procedures used by the society in designating the change in the role" (1942:619). He is apparently conceptualizing a continuous variable that ranges from being an unimportant and obscure procedure to a highly important and definite procedure. This concept

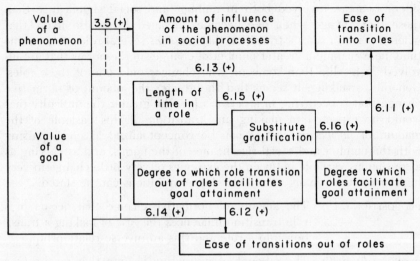

Figure 6.8 The relationships identified in propositions 6.11 to 6.16.

will probably need to be made more precise since it includes two dimensions, but at this stage of these formulations this will not be done. If the relationship in this proposition is linear, positive, and influential, this can be stated as a proposition.

PROPOSITION 6.17: The importance and/or definiteness of the transition procedure in a role transition influences the ease of transitions into roles and this is a positive relationship.

PROPOSITION 6.18: The importance and/or definiteness of the transition procedure in a role transition influences the ease of transitions out of roles and this is a positive relationship.

No empirical data have been found regarding these propositions.

Amount of Normative Change

It is likely that some role transitions consist of only minor changes in the norms and behaviors in a person's life, whereas other transitions require major changes. For example, there is little question that the normative changes that occur when one assumes the parental role are considerably more involved both in number and social significance than those that change when one becomes engaged. It is also likely that when a person makes a transition that involves several roles at the same time, he is making a greater number of changes in the norms that are involved in his life than someone who changes only one of these roles. Generally speaking, it seems that the greater the amount of normative change that is occurring in a person's life, the greater the difficulty that would be expected in making any transition. If this variable of the *amount of normative change* can be conceptualized as encompassing both the number and social significance of the norms, and as varying as a continuous variable between the extremes of very little change to very high amounts of change, the following propositions can be stated.

PROPOSITION 6.19:   The amount of normative change that occurs in a role transition influences the ease of making a transition into a role and this an inverse relationship.

PROPOSITION 6.20:   The amount of normative change that occurs in a role transition influences the ease of making transitions out of a role and this is an inverse relationship.

It is likely that variation in this independent variable while it is still relatively low would not have a great influence on these dependent variables, but additional increases after a relatively large number of changes are involved would have greater influence. If this is the case, the relationships in these propositions are a unique form of a curvilinear relationship. The particular relationship being suggested is diagramed in Figure 6.9, and, as with a number of the propositions in this model, no data have been found that systematically test the idea in this proposition.

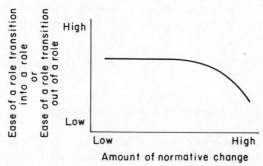

Figure 6.9   The relationship between the amount of normative change and ease of role transitions.

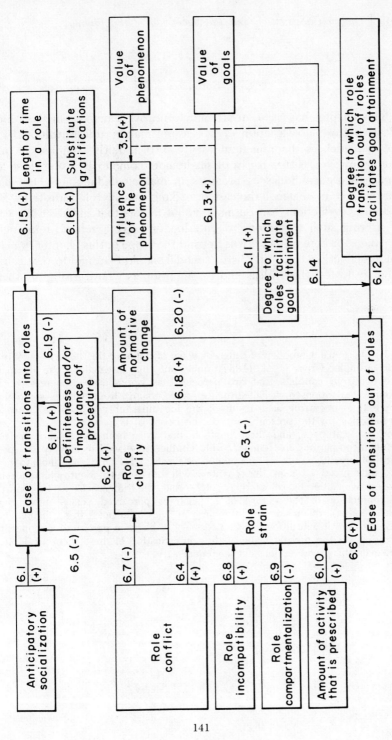

Figure 6.10 Propositions about role transitions.

Summary

This chapter has been an attempt to rework a number of theoretical ideas that explain variation in the ease of making role transitions. The entire model, as diagramed in Figure 6.10, is fairly complex. Its real value, however, is that it can be made more complex by using these abstract theoretical ideas as premises in making deductions about how various factors influence the ease of making specific role transitions. For example, deductions can be made about factors that influence the ease of making such transitions as entering or leaving school, retirement, marriage, or bereavement. It is beyond the scope of this chapter to make these deductions, but this abstract model should be useful to researchers who try to test these ideas and to practitioners who try to apply them.

Note

1. There are a number of different ways of defining this term role conflict. For example, Gross et al. (1957) point out that distinctions can be made between role conflicts that are perceived as opposed to unperceived, legitimate as opposed to illegitimate, and arising from within a role as opposed to occurring as a result of the incompatibility of two or more different roles. In the present context, the issues of the awareness of the conflict, its legitimacy, and those conflicts that arise from more than one role being incompatible are ignored. Role conflict is viewed as merely the presence of conflicting definitions about *one* role. The term role incompatibility, introduced later in this chapter, will be used to identify conflict between two different roles. It is likely that the differences in the sources of conflict or in the nature of it (such as perceived versus unperceived role conflict) do make a difference in the influences this phenomenon has, and that it will ultimately be necessary to be more precise in its conceptualization. At the present stage of the sophistication of these theoretical ideas, however, this precision does not seem necessary.

CHAPTER 7

KINSHIP RELATIONS

Scholars of the family have been highly concerned with the nature of kinship relations and the factors that influence variation in these relations. This concern dates back to the earliest stages of the social sciences when several European sociologists developed the thesis that extensive kinship involvement is incompatible with industrialization and urbanization. Their thesis was later expanded by such scholars as Linton (1959) and Wirth (1938) and was stated in its most elaborate form by Parsons (1943). This proposition was widely accepted until the 1950s when a number of empirical studies found that extensive kinship contact existed in the most industrial and urban centers in England and the United States. These studies ultimately led to the modification of the earlier conclusion, but the controversy between the earlier belief and the research had an important by-product. It generated a great deal of empirical research aimed at finding which variables influence kinship relationships and how they influence them.

The theoretical propositions that were identified in this research were developed by theorists who were working independently of each other and they were usually developed as part of a limited empirical study to test a theorist's ideas. The result of this particular pattern of growth is that there has been little integration of widely different theoretical ideas, and on occasion different theorists have dealt with the same idea while using different conceptual labels. This has created a need for the theoretical ideas in this substantive area to be reworked, and this is the objective of the present chapter. This chapter is, however, more than just an attempt to combine several of the relatively specific propositions in such a way that more general explanatory variables can be identified. The goal of the chapter is to provide greater coherence and generality in the theoretical explanations and, if successful, it will facilitate the deduction of still additional propositions that have not yet been identified.

The Ease of Interaction

There are several propositions in the literature that deal with the general phenomenon of the ease with which various kin groups are able to interact with each other. The first task of this section is to identify several of these and then use them as a basis for inducing a more general proposition about how the ease of interaction influences certain aspects of kinship relationships.

Size of the Food Supply

Nimkoff and Middleton's (1960) comparative analysis of 549 cultures was an attempt to find relationship between economic and familial variables. The dependent variable in their research was what they termed the "type of family," and they operationalized it as a dichotomous variable having the two categories of independent and extended families. The independent type contains those family systems that have only one nuclear family in a residential unit, and the extended type includes those systems where families have more than one nuclear unit. The conceptual phenomenon they were identifying with this dependent variable has been extensively used in both sociology and anthropology, but there are a number of other categories in the variable that have also been identified. Goode (1963), for example, uses the term "conjugal family" to describe a familial system that is intermediate between an extended system and an isolated nuclear system, and Murdock (1949: Ch.2) distinguishes between several other types depending on the relationship between the individuals in the residential unit.

Unfortunately, this variable has never acquired a descriptive label that has found very wide acceptance. Certainly the label "type of family" that Nimkoff and Middleton use is not adequate since there are many different typologies of families in the anthropological and sociological literature. The usual pattern has been to deal with these phenomena as either empirical or ideal types and merely identify different types, as Sussman and Burchinal (1962), Litwak (1960, 1960a), and Murdock (1940) have done. This does not, however, label the variable that is being identified. Several different terms have been used. For example, Rogers and Sebald (1962) suggested the term "kinship orientation," and Winch and his co-workers have used the three different terms, "extended familism" (Winch, Greer, and Blumberg, 1967; Winch and Greer, 1968), "family organization," and "nuclear familism" (Winch and Blumberg, 1968:73). It is suggested here that the term *extendedness* is the best label for this conceptual phenomenon. It can be defined as the degree to which the extended kinship group rather than the nuclear family is the important organizational unit in the family system at one extreme and the isolated nuclear system at the other. It can be collapsed into a dichotomy as studied by Nimkoff and Middleton or viewed as a trichotomy as Goode and Litwak have used it. It is not a very precise concept because there are many aspects of the family structure that vary as systems move from the isolated type to the high extended type, but it is a variable that has been extensively used.

Nimkoff and Middleton's data suggest that there are two propositions that can be identified that explain how economic variables are related to what is being termed the extendedness of kinship systems. One of these proposes that the size of the food supply influences extendedness. They view this independent variable of the *size of the food supply* as the scarcity as opposed to abundance of the food supply. They operationalize it as a dichotomy by considering only variation between the scarcity usually found in hunting and gathering societies and the relatively greater abundance usually found in agricultural societies.

Their logic in making this proposition is that the scarcity of the food supply precludes an extended system because the units securing the food have to be small in order to obtain the scarce food. In societies having a greater supply of food, however, such as most of the agricultural systems, the lack of food does not prevent extendedness from appearing. They thus seem to be suggesting that there is a linear, positive relationship between abundance and extendedness.

It seems possible, however, that the phenomenon denoted by the concept "size of the food supply" actually varies continuously from the extreme of an inadequate supply to a great surplus. This would mean that several points on the variable would be inadequate, scarce, slight surplus, and considerable surplus. If the variable is viewed in this way, the Nimkoff and Middleton analysis is limited to only part of the variation that really ought to be identified in the independent variable. They are concerned only with variation between scarce and adequate levels of the food supply, and they do not consider the relationships involved as the food supply increases into surplus amounts as it does in some societies. When this additional type of variation is taken into account, it seems doubtful that additional increases in the food supply would promote still greater extendedness after a certain degree of extendedness has been attained. Thus the proposition that is stated here is a slight modification of the Nimkoff and Middleton formulation.

PROPOSITION 7.1:   The size of the food supply influences the extendedness of kin systems and this is a positive, curvilinear relationship with the most influence occurring when the variation in size is below a slight surplus.

The relationship that is proposed is thus a curvilinear rather than linear relationship. It is diagrammed in Figure 7.1, and it is a second-order

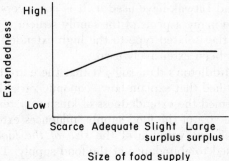

Figure 7.1   The relationship between the size of food supply and extendedness of kinship structure.

or quadratic relationship since the independent variable has an influence on the dependent variable only when it varies in the lower end of its range.

Spatial Mobility

Nimkoff and Middleton (1960:117) suggest that the amount of spatial mobility involved in subsistence activities influences the extendedness of the kinship system. This independent variable is defined as the amount of travel involved in obtaining subsistence. It is apparently a continuous variable, but the only categories that have been developed are relative differences of higher and lower spatial mobility between societies, between groups within a society, or over time. Nimkoff and Middleton deal only with differences between societies. Hence what they are proposing is that when societies differ in the amount of mobility, they also would be expected, all other things being equal, to differ in the extendedness of their kinship systems. Their reasoning, restated in proposition 7.2, is that high mobility prevents the kin groups from being important social structures in the society.

PROPOSITION 7.2:   The amount of spatial mobility involved in obtaining subsistence influences the extendedness of kinship systems and this is an inverse, curvilinear relationship with the greatest influence in the high levels of mobility.

Nimkoff and Middleton initially suggest that this relationship is inverse and linear. They eventually conclude, however, that no influence

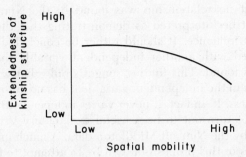

Figure 7.2 The relationship between spatial mobility and extendedness of the Kinship system.

actually occurs as a result of variation in this independent variable. It is proposed here, however, that there is in fact an influence. In addition, it is also speculated here that the influence is greatest in the moderately high levels of mobility and the influence is lowest in the lower levels of mobility. If this is the case, a nonlinear relationship would appear as diagramed in Figure 7.2.

It should be mentioned that Nimkoff and Middleton were only concerned with variation between societies in their spatial mobility. It also seems reasonable that if variation in this independent variable was to occur either between groups within a society or over time within a society, the influence would still be the same. This permits proposition 7.2 to be useful in deducing that if there are differences between occupational groups or social classes in spatial mobility, this would influence their extendedness.

Empirical Data Related to Proposition 7.2

Nimkoff and Middleton argue that their data do not support this proposition. They analyzed data from 549 of the societies in the World Ethnographic Sample (Murdock, 1957) and found a significant relationship between the two variables. However, when they partialed out the general subsistence patterns identified in the independent variable in proposition 7.1, they found no relationship remained. They therefore suggest "that mobility patterns do not constitute an independent variable; rather, they tend to be an integral part of the general pattern of subsistence" (1960:118). There is little reason to question the accuracy of the last phrase of their conclusion in stating that the mobility variable should not be viewed as a meaningful independent variable itself.

The fact that no relationship was found in the Nimkoff-Middleton data should not be interpreted as demonstrating that this independent variable has no influence. It should rather be concluded that it was so highly correlated with another independent variable that no separate covariation was found. This finding suggests only that when no unique variation occurs in the independent variable it has no unique relationship with extendedness. If, in fact, it never varies independently of other variables, it will not turn out to be a useful explanatory variable; but this was not tested by the Nimkoff-Middleton data. A much more crucial test of the usefulness of this proposition will be to attempt to find a situation where it alone varies and then test for existence of a relationship.

It seems that there can be variation in the amount of spatial mobility within certain general types of subsistence. Parsons (1943) argues that the necessity for spatial mobility among some groups in industrial societies tends to reduce the extendedness patterns. He was later shown to have overstated his case, but the later empirical studies (see Sussman and Burchinal, 1962) that demonstrated that Parsons was in error merely showed the industrialization does not eliminate extendedness. They did not test the idea that mobility is related to extendedness. If the influence does occur as Parsons suggested, then less mobility would be expected among those social groups in an industrial society that have high spatial mobility. Data from Winch and Greer's (1968) study supports the validity of this idea. They found that the amount of migration into a large city in their sample was inversely related to extendedness.

Geographical Distance

A study by Reiss (1962) found that *geographical distance* between kin is an important variable in understanding kinship interaction. This independent variable is, of course, continuous, and if it is defined as the amount of space between kinship units it is a variable that is highly clear. The dependent variable in Reiss' study was the amount of interaction occurring between kinship groups. This variable is conceptually different from the more complex phenomenon of the extendedness of kinship systems that was the dependent variable in the last two propositions; yet the two are sufficiently similar that they need to be interdefined.

Winch, Greer, and Blumberg (1967) have suggested a series of concepts that seem to be helpful in interdefining these terms. They make a distinction between what they term extensity of presence, intensity of presence, interaction, and functionality. They define *extensity* of presence as the number of kinship households in a fairly close geographical area. This is thus a continuous variable that can be operationalized with a ratio scale. *Intensity* of presence is the same as what Adams (1968) refers to as degree of relationship. It conceptualized variation in how closely kinship units are related. Winch et al. dichotomized the variable by using only the two categories of whether the kin were in the person's family of orientation or were more distant relatives. They operationalized the *interaction* variable as the number of households interacted with "regularly." Others (Bell and Boat, 1957; Reiss, 1962) have taken into account variation in the amount of interaction with various kin units as well as the number of them, which means that the variable that most have been concerned with identifies variation in the total amount of interaction with kin. *Functionality* was initially defined by Winch (1963) as a continuous variable that denoted the degree to which a social unit carries out basic societal functions. Thus kinship functionality would refer to the extent to which the kinship system performs societal functions.

These four variables can be viewed as four specific factors within the more inclusive, omnibus concept of extendedness. A number of other factors that can be identified (Goode, 1963:10 ff) are also a part of the more general variable of extendedness, but it is not necessary to introduce them to identify the proposition Reiss suggests between geographical distance and the amount of kinship interaction. Reiss suggests that the relationship between these variables exists, and that it is probably a cubic type that is highly influential. A cubic relationship is proposed because it seems reasonable that variation in distance makes little difference when the distance is either very small or very great, but between these extremes it has considerable influence.

PROPOSITION 7.3:   The geographical distance between kin groups influences the interaction of kin and this is an inverse but cubic relationship.

It is impossible to identify the actual distances where the amount of influence in the relationship changes, because it is highly likely that other variables influence when the distance both begins to make a difference and when it ceases to make much difference. For example, the distance involved when traveling on foot is undoubtedly less than in situations such as those in the twentieth-century United States culture where automobiles shrink the impact of previously important distance.

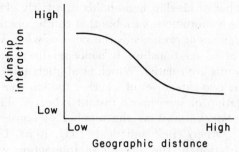

Figure 7.3   The relationship between geographical distance and the amount of kin interaction.

A More General Proposition

These three propositions all deal in one way or another with how easy it is for people in different kin groups to interact with each other. When there is a scarcity of food the kin groups need to break up to maximize the ability of each to secure enough to subsist, but when there is ample food they are able to live close enough to interact. When mobility is high the nuclear unit or members of it move about enough that this either terminates the interaction or at least interferes with it. Further, large distances between kin units interfere with interaction.

The similarities in these propositions suggest that a more general explanatory relationship can be induced between extendedness and what can be conceptualized as the *ease of interaction.* This variable of the ease of interaction is defined as the degree to which there is freedom from difficulty and the presence of easily available resources to interact in what Weber (1947:88 ff) describes as social action. Conceptually this is viewed as a continuous variable ranging from interaction being impossible to a high degree of interaction where the resources needed for interaction are available with no or little cost.

The relationship that is proposed between these two variables is probably highly influential, positive, and cubic, as diagramed in Figure 7.4. The cubic relationship is proposed because it is likely that increases in the ease of interaction while it is very low do not make much difference in the extendedness of the kinship system. Additional increases, however, beyond a marginal level of ease, would have more influence on the extendedness of the kin system. After the ease of interaction has reached a certain point, however, it is likely that other variables influence variation in the extendedness of the kinship system, and additional increases

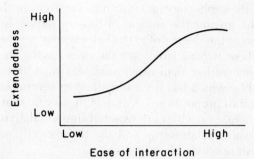

Figure 7.4 The relationship between the ease of interaction and extendedness.

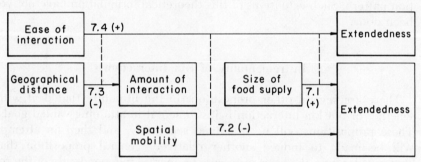

Figure 7.5 The relationships in propositions 7.1 to 7.4.

in the ease of interaction do not have a substantial influence on the dependent variable. Proposition 7.4 results.

PROPOSITION 7.4: The ease of interaction of kin units influences the extendedness of the kinship structure and this is a positive, cubic relationship.

The ideas in these four propositions are summarized in Figure 7.5. This figure shows that the ease of interaction positively influences extendedness, and the other three propositions can be logically deduced from this more abstract proposition.

When this general proposition is used to summarize the knowledge described in the specific propositions, it is possible to deduce new propositions that deal with other specific variables. For example, the author is not aware of anyone systematically dealing with the time dimension in commuting to the residence of kin or the economic costs in this commuting. However, on the basis of proposition 7.4, it can be deduced that

if variation in these phenomena constitute variation in the ease of interacting, then the greater the amount of time or money involved in commuting, the less is the degree of extendedness that is expected. In fact, it
may be that these two variables are the ones having the greatest effect
most of the time rather than other variables such as the geographical
distance variable, which has been identified in several empirical studies
and is identified in proposition 7.3. In fact, it may be that when the temporal and economic variables are inserted into an analysis, both the empirically observable relationship and the theoretically meaningful influence of the distance variable will disappear.

It is also interesting to speculate on the way these independent
variables interact in influencing extendedness. Several of them may be
sufficient to prevent extendedness, or they may have an additive interaction pattern. Such extensions of this theoretical formulation have not yet
been done.

Instrumentality of Kin Interaction

There are several other propositions in the literature that deal with
whether or not kin interaction is instrumental in attaining valued goals.
These propositions will be examined separately, and then an attempt
will be made to induce another relatively general proposition that
seems, at least on the basis of reason, to operate independently of the relationship between the ease of interaction and the extendedness of the
kinship system.

Amount of Family Property

Nimkoff and Middleton (1960) suggest there is a relationship between
the kind and amount of property held by families and extendedness.
Their operationalization and discussion of the independent variable do
not really deal with the "kind" of property, so the apparent independent
variable is the *amount of property* that is owned by families. Apparently
this variable can vary in several ways. It can vary between societies in
the sense that some societies have institutional arrangements where families own properties and some have less familial ownership. This type of
variation is variation between societies in their institutional arrangements. This same conceptual variable can vary between families or social groups such as castes or classes in the amount of property they own.
It can also vary over time. In all of these situations the pattern of variation is viewed as continuous, ranging from none to a relatively high

amount. These distinctions between the ways this independent variable can vary do not, however, seem to make a difference in the nature of the relationship between the variables in the proposition. The relationship that Nimkoff and Middleton suggest, as stated in proposition 7.5, is positive and linear.

PROPOSITION 7.5: The amount of property that is owned by families influences the amount of extendedness and this is a positive, linear relationship.

Nimkoff and Middleton's (1960) analysis of the World Ethnographic Sample served as the basis for initially postulating this relationship. In these data they found that hunting types of societies had the least family ownership and least extended families. Herders had more ownership and extendedness, and stable agriculture economies had the most family ownership and extendedness.

There is another set of data that seems to be relevant for this proposition. This is the research that has investigated the relationship between the amount of kinship involvement and socioeconomic status. If socioeconomic status can be viewed as an indicator of variation in the amount of property owned, this body of literature can be viewed as evidence in support of this proposition since it has been rather extensively documented that there is a positive relationship between extendedness and socioeconomic status.

Several studies that have found a positive relationship between socioeconomic status and kinship extendedness. Bell and Boat (1957) found more interaction among high-status groups than low-status groups in their interview data in San Francisco in 1953. Bradburn (1963) found a positive relationship between socioeconomic status and kinship interaction. There are also data from other cultures that demonstrate the same relationship. In Buck's (1930) analysis of the Chinese society, he found a positive relationship between the size of farms and the size of the extended families. Lewis' (1958) analysis of data from India found the same relationship. He found that the upper castes, which tend to have property, have greater extendedness.

There are some data that at first glance may appear to demonstrate an inverse relationship between socioeconomic status and extendedness. Young and Wilmott (1962), for example, in their analysis of two British communities, found greater interaction between the manual workers than the clerical and professional people. They suggest that the reason for this may be because the higher-status people live farther apart rather than because of class difference. They do not, however, introduce any statistical controls to test this hypothesis. Litwak (1960) found exactly the same relationship Young and Wilmott did, but when he controlled for geographical distance he found that the control of the distance variable actually reversed the relationship with the stable, higher class group having the greatest kin contact. This suggestion of Young and Wilmott's and data from Litwak's study provide evidence in support of the idea that the "ease of interaction" variable probably influences kinship extendedness. It also seems to suggest that the ease of interaction variable may be considerably more influential than the amount of property variable.

It may be defensible to view this finding about a relationship between socioeconomic status and extendedness as supporting the validity of proposition 7.5. It may be that socioeconomic status is related to kinship interaction because of other things besides the fact that variation in the amount of property influences socioeconomic status. If this is the case, a separate relationship will need to be identified between socioeconomic status and kinship extendedness. At the present time, however, none of these other relationships have been systematically formulated. This seems to justify, at least at the present time, the argument that the relationship between socioeconomic status and kinship extendedness is an indication that variation in the amount of property owned by families influences kinship extendedness.

Demand for the Family as a Unit of Labor

In Winch and Blumberg's (1968) analysis of the Nimkoff-Middleton (1960) study, another factor is identified that they contend influences the extendedness of kinship systems. This is the degree to which the family is the *unit of labor* in a society rather than individual members of the family being the active participants as is done in many of the very simple and the highly industrialized systems. Apparently this independent variable can vary in degree and is hence a continuous variable. Winch and Blumberg suggest that the family as the unit of labor is associated with greater extendedness. Neither set of authors discusses the nature of this relationship, so until later evidence indicates a change is in order, the rather intuitive pattern that it is a positive, monotonic relationship that is likely not very influential will be assumed.

PROPOSITION 7.6:   The degree to which the family is the unit of labor influences the extendedness of the kinship system and this is a positive, monotonic relationship.

Openness of Class System

Several theorists have speculated about the relationship between the openness of the class system in a society and the extendedness of kinship systems. Parsons (1943) and Davis (1962) argue that when societies move from feudal to industrial systems, there are usually pressures to move toward a more open class system to facilitate movement into new types of high-status positions. They then argue that this open class system is incompatible with an extended kinship system. The mobility that is necessary in the new industrialization opens the class system, and this inversely influences the extendedness of the kinship structure. This independent variable of the openness of a class system can be defined as the amount of social mobility in a society. The relationship they have proposed is an inverse and apparently linear one.

PROPOSITION 7.7:   The openness of the class system influences the extendedness of the kinship system and this is an inverse relationship.

Facilitation of Social Mobility

Adams (1967, 1968) analyzed the kinship relations of a sample of 800 individuals in Greensboro, North Carolina, in the process of studying relationships between occupational position, social mobility, and kinship relationships. He found that differences in occupational positions and mobility from one occupational status level to another were not systematically related to kinship interaction or to sentiment for kin unless an additional factor was introduced. He summarizes the role of this third factor as follows:

A key conclusion is that those significant others who embody, or who have led us to embody, the dominant societal definitions of success are more likely to be considered worthy of our affectional response (1967:376).

Adams' conceptualization of this third factor, however, is relatively ambiguous. It is unclear just what variable he is talking about when he refers to those who "embody, or who have led us to embody," or in other places in his paper where he attempts to summarize this point by stating: "This paper suggests that adult kin relations cannot be understood apart from the economic achievement values impinging upon them, both during socialization and in adulthood" (1967:365).

He seems to be dealing with a phenomenon that is important in understanding the kinship system, and the relationships involved are fairly clear when this third variable is clarified. Adams demonstrates that when a sib or parent can be viewed as facilitating movement into higher status occupational positions this tends to be associated with positive affect toward kin. If, however, the kin tend to hinder one's own upward affectional distance, there is less positive affect. Thus the important independent variable seems to be the degree to which a relationship facilitates the attainment of upward social mobility. This can apparently vary conceptually between the extremes of hindering to facilitating, and it apparently has an intermediate point at which there is neither facilitation nor hindrance. The dependent variable is the affect felt toward the relative, and this is a continuous variable that varies between a low of high negative affect to high positive affect. Thus proposition 7.8 seems to emerge from Adams' data.

PROPOSITION 7.8:   The amount that kin facilitate the attainment of upward social mobility influences the sentiment toward the kin and this is a positive relationship.

This is apparently a positive, monotonic relationship. Moreover, it seems that this variable of sentiment is one dimension in the multidimensional variable of kinship extendedness.

Instrumentality

It is possible to find similarities in the last four independent variables that seem to justify stating a more abstract proposition. All of these independent variables deal in one way or another with how familial phenomena are instrumental in attaining valued goals. When family units own property, this increases the control the familial unit has over a highly valued aspect of life, and involvement in extended familial relationships is hence engaged in more than in situations where families have less ownership. When the family unit tends to be the essential unit of labor in the economic system, it is again instrumental in attaining desired ends. Furthermore, when an open class system is desired, the degree to which kinship units facilitate upward social mobility seems to influence sentiment toward kin.

Thus each of the independent variables in these four propositions deals with a way that familial phenomena are instrumental or not instrumental in either attaining or not attaining valued ends. The similarity in these propositions suggests that it is useful to conceptualize a more general phenomenon of the instrumentality of the family as an institutional system in attaining either societal or personal goals. *Instrumentality* is defined as the degree to which aspects of the familial institution serve as a means for influencing the attainment of desired goals. It is conceptually a continuous variable that varies from preventing goals through not facilitating their attainment at all to a high degree of instrumentality. Once this phenomenon is conceptually identified, then, on the basis of the ideas in the earlier specific propositions, a proposition can be induced that explains at a more general level the preceding five propositions.

PROPOSITION 7.9: The instrumentality of the family institution in attaining valued goals influences the extendedness of the kinship system and this is a positive, monotonic relationship.

The nature of this relationship is subject to speculation, but it is suggested here that it is apparently a monotonic, positive relationship that is probably not nearly as influential as proposition 7.4.

This formulation about the instrumentality of families is summarized in Figure 7.6, which attempts to show the influence between variables and the logical inductions and deductions that can be made between the propositions. This figure shows that propositions 7.5, 7.6, and 7.7 can be deduced from 7.9 if each of the three independent variables is a more

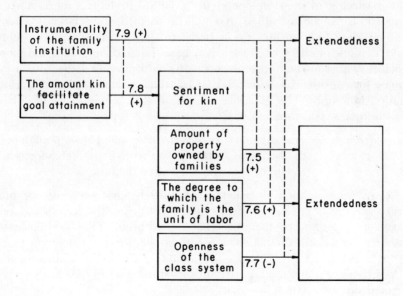

Figure 7.6 The relationships between propositions 7.5 to 7.9.

specific instance of instrumentality in attaining goals. It also shows that proposition 7.8 can be deduced from 7.9 if sentiment is one aspect of extendedness and if facilitating upward social mobility is a more specific instance of instrumentality in attaining valued goals. All of these logical relationships seem defensible, and it seems that it would be a relatively easy task to extend this model to include additional specific aspects of extendedness and other ways familial phenomena can be instrumental in attaining valued goals.

Normative Influence

Several independent variables have been shown to be empirically related to the extendedness of kinship systems, although it is very difficult to find any meaningful influential processes. For example, such independent variables as ethnicity and religion have been repeatedly found to be related to kinship extendedness, and they seem to retain empirically observable relationships even when other variables such as mobility are controlled (Winch and Greer, 1968). Stating propositions, however, about how variation in ethnicity or religion influences extendedness seems to be meaningless since it is so difficult to identify just what it is that is varying in these independent variables. Perhaps a more general proposition can be identified that will be useful in understanding why the empirical relationships occur between these variables. If the more general proposition can be used as a basis for deducing that the more specific, empirical relationships occur, this will provide a theoretical rationale for considerable research that has thus far consisted of empirical relationships only. The general proposition that seems to be useful in this context was introduced in Chapter 4 and is repeated here.

PROPOSITION 4.1:   The existence of norms in a social group influences the bahavior in that group so that the behavior tends to conform to the normative definitions.

Norms were defined as beliefs or definitions that proscribe or prescribe specific behaviors. They proscribe by defining what should not occur and prescribe by defining what should occur. They seldom make absolute definitions about behavior but rather define what ought to be or ought not to be done in specific situations. The two variables in this proposition are dichotomous attributes (Dubin, 1969:34–35) in that they occur or do not occur.

Proposition 4.1 can be applied to kinship extendedness if norms exist about kinship extendedness. On the basis of evidence that these types or norms do exist (Adams, 1968:164), proposition 7.10 can be deduced.

PROPOSITION 7.10:   The existence of norms about extendedness influences the extendedness of kinship systems, so the extendedness tends to conform to the normative definitions.

Two further deductions can be made if ethnic and religious groups differ in their norms about extendedness.

PROPOSITION 7.11:   Ethnicity is related to extendedness.

PROPOSITION 7.12:   Religious differences are related to extendedness.

The empirical finding that in the twentieth-century United States culture, Jewish groups tend to have more extended kinship systems than Catholics and Catholics tend to have more extended kinship systems than Protestants can be viewed as evidence supporting the validity of these propositions if one assumption can be made. This assumption is that they differ in their normative definitions in the same way. Interestingly, the systematic research (Winch, Greer, and Blumberg, 1967; Winch and Greer, 1968) on these differences between kinship groups has extensive data about differences in behavior, but no data have been found that systematically compare the normative dimension. Thus, if this research is to be viewed as supporting the propositions, it must be with the unverified assumption that the normative component varies.

There is another point that can be made about why this research should be viewed as evidence supporting the validity of these propositions. Thus far, no other theoretical formulation has been explicated that would determine why the relationships between extendedness and religion and ethnicity occur. If an alternative theory is suggested from which deductions can be made that these relationships exist, this may decrease the confidence that can be placed in this theory, but until this is done it seems defensible to view these relationships as support of the validity of the theory proposed here.

Closeness

Bott (1957), Reiss (1962), and later Adams (1968) argue that the closeness or degree of relatedness of kinship groups influences the amount of interaction between kin groups. This variable conceptualizes variations in how closely related kin groups are. The parents in a nuclear family are closely related to their parents and sibs. There is greater distance in their closeness to their cousins, and there is still less closeness between them and their parents' cousins. This could be viewed as a categorical variable that has a large number of categories. Adams (1968:168), however, suggests that the most useful way to view the variation in this variable is to collapse the potential categories into a trichotomy that has the three categories of the nuclear family, kin of orientation consisting of parents and siblings, and the wider kin. The proposition that has been suggested is that this variable has a systematic influence on the amount of interaction of kinship groups, and Adams proposes that it is likely that there is a substantial influence between the categories of kin of orientation and wider kin. The particular place in the range of variation of the independent variable where this influence occurs probably also varies according to a number of other variables such as normative definitions and distance.

PROPOSITION 7.13:   The closeness of kinship groups influences the amount of interaction in kinship groups and this is a positive relationship.

Societal Complexity

Goode summarizes the main thesis of his classic monograph on comparative family patterns as follows:

> Wherever the economic system expands through industrialization, family patterns change. Extended ties weaken, lineage patterns dissolve, and a trend toward some form of the conjugal system generally begins to appear—that is, the nuclear family becomes a more independent kinship unit (1963:6).

The variables in this proposition seem to be industrialization and extendedness. Goode never defines industrialization precisely, but the context indicates it apparently conceptualizes variation in the extent to which a society adopts into its structure a highly complex technology and an economic system that is operated through large, complex social organizations. Goode argues that a ranking can be made according to how "advanced" (1963:4) this industrialization is. He does not develop a scale of industrialization, but apparently cultures such as India and Sub-Saharan Africa before the twentieth century are examples of low industrialization. This variable is thus apparently a continuous variable ranging from low to high levels of industrialization. Goode argues that societies change at different rates, some parts of extendedness change in different ways in different cultures, and we know little about how industrialization and/or urbanization affect the family system. He does, however, develop the following general thesis.

PROPOSITION 7.14:   If a society has a relatively extended kinship system, increases in industrialization influence the kinship system so it moves toward the conjugal type.

Goode seems to argue that this is not a linear relationship. He apparently views it as a curvilinear relationship with the influence being confined to the upper part of the dependent variable since high degrees of industrialization do not result in the kinship system moving beyond the conjugal type. An attempt is made to diagram this relationship in Figure 7.7.

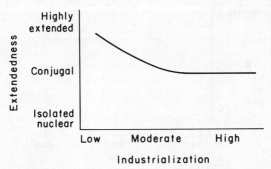

Figure 7.7   Goode's proposition about industrialization and extendedness.

Winch and Blumberg (1968) later took issue with the shape of the relationship that Goode seems to have proposed. They suggest that Goode's independent variable should be replaced with a different conceptualization, which they refer to as "societal complexity." This variable of societal complexity refers to the complexity of the institutional arrangements that provide the subsistence in a society. They contend that societies such as small hunting and gathering tribes have much less complex institutional patterns, and that the modern industrialized-urbanized pattern is the most complex. This variable is a continuous variable on which different cultural patterns can be arrayed in an ordinal manner. They suggest that the societies Goode was analyzing are only societies in the upper half of this new variable, and that because of this the "low" end of the independent variation that Goode conceptualized was really more of a "medium" location on the societal complexity variable.

The theoretical contribution that Winch and Blumberg make is that they then suggest that the relationship Goode proposed occurs only in societies that already have a considerable amount of complexity. They suggest that when the entire range of the societal complexity variable is considered, the relationship between the variables is curvilinear (1968:73). This relationship is diagramed in Figure 7.8 and the idea can be stated in a proposition.

PROPOSITION 7.15: Societal complexity influences the extendedness of the kinship structure and this is a curvilinear relationship.

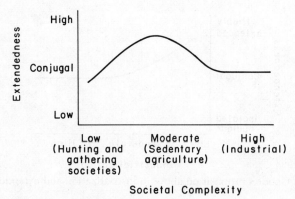

Figure 7.8 The relationship between societal complexity and extendedness of kinship system.

Summary

This chapter has attempted to systematize a number of theoretical ideas about kinship and to integrate them in a way that would permit the induction of several new propositions. These ideas are summarized in Figure 7.9, which reveals that the model is fairly abstract. The ideas in this model will be considerably more useful as additional research and theorizing—perhaps facilitated by this chapter—expand it by adding additional propositions about how various factors influence more specific dependent variables.

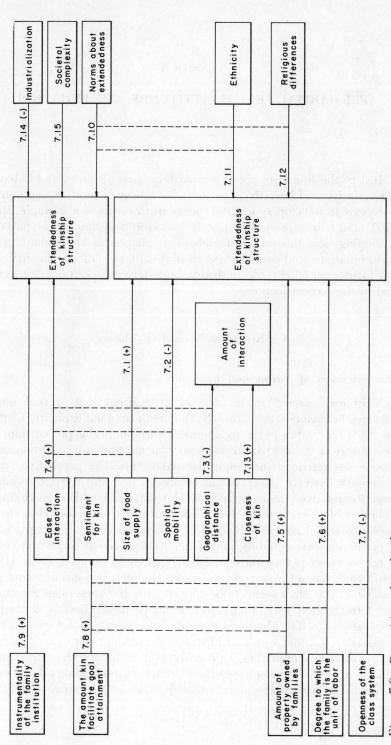

Figure 7.9 Propositions about kinship.

CHAPTER 8

PREMARITAL SEXUAL ATTITUDES AND BEHAVIOR

Most of the literature about premarital sexual attitudes and behavior is descriptive and hortative, but there have been several attempts in recent years to develop systematic theory in this area. For example, Reiss (1967) and Christensen (1969) both used empirical data as the basis for developing new theoretical models. This chapter is an attempt to rework, integrate, and extend these theoretical formulations. The first section focuses on Christensen's theory, and Reiss' propositions are examined in the second section.

Christensen's Normative Theory

Permissiveness of Norms and Behavior

Christensen asserts in his second proposition that "sexual norms influence behavior" (1969:216). His statement does not explicitly identify what it is that varies in the independent variable in this proposition, but the context of the discussion seems to indicate that it is the permissiveness versus restrictiveness of the sexual norms. The permissive norms proscribe relatively fewer sexual behaviors and the restrictive norms proscribe relatively more behaviors. This variable could be labeled with a number of different terms, but it does not seem adequate to merely use the term "sexual norms." The best label is probably the proscriptiveness of premarital sexual norms, and either permissiveness or restrictiveness of norms about permarital sexual behavior could be used. Reiss' (1964, 1967) work has set a precedent of using the term *premarital sexual permissiveness* for what seems to be conceptually the same phenomenon, so this term is used here. Premarital sexual permissiveness is defined by Reiss as indicating "how 'far' people are permitted to go sexually" (1964:189). In other words, it identifies the amount of premarital sexual behavior that is normatively proscribed. It is apparently a continuous variable that can vary between the extremes of proscribing all erotic behavior to not proscribing any. In reality, however, no known society has ever reached either of these extremes.

Another aspect of the way this variable varies is that sexual behaviors do not seem to be randomly proscribed. They seem to be proscribed in a systematic order depending on the amount of intimacy of the behavior involved. When permissiveness is high only those behaviors that are highly intimate are proscribed. As permissiveness decreases, gradually more and more intimate behaviors are proscribed. This has resulted in Reiss (1964) being able to develop a Guttman-type scale of premarital sexual permissiveness.

Christensen merely uses the term "behavior" to identify the dependent variable in his second proposition, but it is somewhat difficult to know from the context of Christensen's summarizing article just what variable he is referring to by this term. He states that "permissive behavior accompanied permissiveness norms, and restrictive behavior, restrictive norms" (1969:216). The terms permissive and restrictive, however, are normative terms rather than descriptions of behavior and hence do not communicate information about the nature of this dependent variable. His operationalization of the variable seems to indicate that what he is really concerned with is variation in what should probably be called the intimacy of the sexual behavior. Christensen measures variation in such things as whether people kiss, neck, or experience coitus. If this is really what is being operationalized, the dependent variable should probably be labeled the *intimacy of sexual behavior*. This variable seems to have such subtle variations that it is probably a continuous variable, but several reference points that have an ordinal nature have been identified and extensively used in this area. Different points have been selected by different researchers such as Ehrmann (1959), Simonsom and Geis (1956), and Reiss (1964), but common reference points are no intimacy, kissing, necking, petting, and coitus.

If this analysis of the nature of the variables in Christensen's formulation is correct, proposition 8.1 follows.

PROPOSITION 8.1: Premarital sexual permissiveness influences the intimacy level of premarital sexual behavior and this is a positive, monotonic relationship.

Christensen's data from Denmark, Indiana, and Utah measure only three points in the variation of the independent variable, and thus his findings provide only fragmentary evidence about the shape of this relationship. His data do, however, suggest that the relationship is monotonic, and it could probably be argued that they provide a basis for arguing the relationship is linear.

A More General Proposition

The proposition identified in the previous section is more meaningful if it is viewed as part of a more inclusive theoretical formulation that has multiple levels of generality. It is possible to do this by pointing out the relationship between this proposition and the following general proposition, which was identified in Chapter 4.

PROPOSITION 4.1:   The existence of norms in a social group influences the behavior in that group so the behavior tends to conform to the normative definitions.

Proposition 8.1 is a specific case of the idea in proposition 4.1, and hence it can be deduced from proposition 4.1. It can be deduced that since variation in premarital sexual permissiveness is variation in the degree to which social norms in a group proscribe premarital sexual behavior, then if proposition 4.1 is true, it follows that premarital permissiveness can be expected to influence premarital sexual behavior. The relationship between these two propositions is summarized in Figure 8.1.

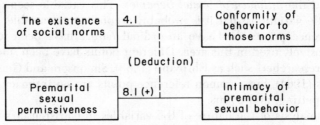

Figure 8.1   The relationship between propositions 4.1 and 8.1.

Premarital Sexual Permissiveness and Deviation

One of Christensen's other propositions provides a basis for making some additional assertions about the nature of the relationships in proposition 8.1. This is his fifth proposition, which states that "deviations from actual sex norms, as these are prescribed by existing societies and internalized within their constituent members, increase with restrictiveness in the culture" (1969:218). Christensen uses the term restrictiveness to refer to the independent variable in this proposition, but it seems to be the same conceptual phenomena as Reiss' premarital sexual permissiveness and what Christensen elsewhere refers to as the "permissiveness-restrictiveness of sexual norms" (1969:216).

The meaning of the dependent variable in this proposition is more difficult to identify. Christensen refers to it as "deviations from actual sex norms," but it is not clear just what it is that varies. It could be variation in the amount of behavior that deviates from proscriptive norms, or it could be variation in the amount of behavior relative to the number of proscriptive norms. If Christensen is referring to the former, then the dependent variable is simply the *amount* of behavior that is deviation. If, however, he is referring to the latter phenomenon, the dependent variable is the *proportion* of norms from which there is deviation. It is difficult to know which of these two variables Christensen intended, but the proposition he asserts can be stated both ways.

PROPOSITION 8.2: Premarital sexual permissiveness is related to the amount of behavior that is deviation from norms and this is an inverse relationship.

PROPOSITION 8.3: Premarital sexual permissiveness is related to the proportion of the proscriptive norms from which there are deviations and this is an inverse relationship.

Proposition 8.2 is very reasonable, since it would be expected a society that had very high permissiveness would find it difficult to deviate greatly from proscriptive norms. It would only be when a society is relatively low in permissiveness that a great amount of deviation could occur. Christensen's cross-cultural data rather conclusively support the fact that this relationship does exist. The proposition is also equally obvious on an individual rather than social level. It would only be possible for much deviation to occur when an individual has a large number of internalized proscriptive norms, and it would be impossible for any to occur if there were no proscriptive norms.

Proposition 8.3 identifies a much less obvious relationship. It asserts that the proportion of norms that are deviated from decreases with increased permissiveness, and there are no logical reasons that this relationship should be expected as there are with proposition 8.2. It is difficult to know if Christensen's data provide supporting evidence for this proposition. His data indicate that among those who say they have restrictive norms the percentage who deviate from these norms decreases with the permissiveness of the culture, but this does not really test the issue of whether there is a greater or smaller proportion of norms deviated from, because the more permissive culture has fewer proscriptive norms. Thus at the present time, these data cannot be viewed as evidence of the validity of this proposition.

One reason these propositions are important is that they have different implications for the nature of the relationship in proposition 8.1. Proposition 8.2 provides a basis for arguing that the independent variable in proposition 8.1 has a limited amount of influence. If it were true that behavior conformed completely to normative definitions, then a linear and highly influential relationship would be expected in proposition 8.1 such as the relationship diagramed with line *A* in Figure 8.2. If, however, proposition 8.2 is true in asserting that the amount of deviation decreases as the permissiveness increases, this means that as permissiveness decreases the level of intimacy of behavior would not decrease as fast as it would if there were complete conformity to the norms. Thus the relationship between proscriptiveness and intimacy (proposition 8.1) would have less influence than line *A* in Figure 8.2 describes, and line *B* would be a more accurate description of the relationship.

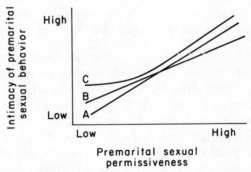

Figure 8.2   Possible relationships between premarital sexual permissiveness and the intimacy of behavior.

On the other hand, if line *B* accurately describes the relationship between the two variables in proposition 8.1, then proposition 8.3 is not accurate in proposing that the proportion of norms that are deviated from is inversely related to permissiveness. If proposition 8.3 is true, the relationship between permissiveness and intimacy (proposition 8.1) is most accurately described with line *C* in Figure 8.2. This is the case because if the proportion of norms that are deviated from increases as permissiveness decreases, the relationship between permissiveness and inti-

Premarital Sexual Attitudes and Behavior 169

macy would not be a linear pattern as shown in line *A* or *B*. It would be a curvilinear relationship with more intimacy occurring in the condition of low permissiveness than would be the case if a linear relationship occurred.

There is considerable evidence in Christensen's data that supports proposition 8.1 and some that supports proposition 8.2. There are, however, no data in Christensen's research that permit making inferences about the validity of proposition 8.3, and it is almost axiomatic to point out that much more research is needed.

Negative Consequences of Premarital Coitus

Christensen identifies a proposition about how the "negative consequences resulting from premarital coitus are positively related to these behavioral deviations from norms" (1969:218). The dependent variable in this proposition is labeled "negative consequences," but the nature of this particular variable is obscure. Christensen operationalizes it by measuring such phenomena as guilt, divorce rate, or hurrying the wedding date upon discovery of premarital pregnancy, so he is including a relatively wide range of specific phenomena as negative consequences.

The phenomenon Christensen is dealing with in this conceptualization may be the same thing that is referred to in exchange theory as profit. Profit was defined earlier following Homans (1961) and Thibaut and Kelley (1959) as variation in the amount of cost or reward received from something. Christensen's concern with negative consequences may be the same as the cost aspect of profit in that it seems to identify phenomena that are negatively valued. Although it is possible that this is distorting Christensen's intent, it seems defensible to suggest that profit is a more appropriate conceptualization of what he is denoting than is the label "negative consequences." The term profit has the advantage of being conceptually more clear, and it is a more useful variable in that its pattern of variation is identifiable.

The concept that is used as the independent variable in this proposition seems to be clear. It is variation in whether coitus deviates from the proscriptive norms or not. Christensen does not, however, identify whether this is a continuous or categorical variable or what the categories are if it is categorical. He merely states that "the negative consequences of premarital coitus adhere, not so much to the act itself, but to how the act lines up or fails to line up with the standards held" (1969:218). Apparently he intends this to be a dichotomous variable, and the two categories are premarital coitus either conforming to norms or deviating from the social norms. It is suggested here that this variable

be viewed as the same conceptual phenomenon that Jackson (1966) refers to as the "behavior dimension" of norms. Jackson suggests that one
"characteristic of a norm is the specification of the amount or degree of
behavior that is expected of a person," and this amount or degree varies
"in degree along a dimension of quantity or quality" (1966:113). Apparently behaviors can vary in the amount they deviate from a "range of
tolerable behavior" on this behavior dimension of norms. Some behaviors could deviate more than others from the range of tolerable acts.
This variable could be called the amount behavior deviates from the tolerable range of behavior of a norm, but this is a fairly unwieldy label.
The *amount of deviance from norms* is a simple and abbreviated label
that conceptualizes what is intended. If this variable is used in stating
Christensen's idea, proposition 8.4 can be stated.

PROPOSITION 8.4:   The amount of premarital coitus that deviates from
norms about premarital coitus influences the profit
from this behavior and this is an inverse relationship.

Christensen does not speculate on the nature of this relationship other
than to assert its existence and direction. He does, however, present
data that argue for the validity of the proposition. He found (1963) that
guilt is higher in the more proscriptive societies in his sample than in
the less proscriptive societies and that the divorce rate of the premaritally pregnant couples is higher in the more proscriptive societies.

The Importance of Proscriptive Norms

One of the propositions that has been applied in several contexts in
this book is that the cultural importance of a phenomenon influences the
impact it has in a social group. It seems reasonable that this proposition is also relevant in understanding the relationship identified in proposition 8.4. The general proposition that is repeated and integrated here
is discussed in detail in Chapter 3.

PROPOSITION 3.5:   The value of a phenomenon influences the amount of
effect this phenomenon has in social processes and this
is a positive, monotonic relationship.

It seems easy to defend the point that social groups differ in the degree to which they value whether behavior conforms to proscriptive
norms about premarital coitus, and that individuals within these social
groups differ in the amount they value it. This particular type of evaluation can be conceptually labeled the *importance* of behavior conforming
to norms about premarital coitus. It is possible to deduce that if this

particular type of importance is a more specific instance of the value variable identified in proposition 3.5, and if proposition 3.5 is true, proposition 8.5 follows.

PROPOSITION 8.5: The importance of behavior conforming to norms about premarital coitus is related to the amount of influence the amount of deviation from these norms has on the profit from premarital coitus and this is a positive, monotonic relationship.

The relationship that occurs in this proposition is probably similar to the relationship expected in similar propositions discussed in Chapters 3 and 4. This is hence probably a positive, monotonic, and relatively influential relationship.

More General Propositions
Induced from Propositions 8.4 and 8.5

Propositions 8.4 and 8.5 are highly specific in that they deal with one rather narrow aspect of sexuality. It seems, however, that the relationships in these two propositions can serve as a basis for stating several more general propositions about what seem to be the same social processes. It is likely that if the amount of deviation from norms about premarital coitus influences the profit from this particular behavior, then the amount of deviation from norms about other premarital sexual behaviors would probably influence the profit from them. Moreover, it is equally likely that the importance that is attached to behavior conforming to these norms would also influence the amount of influence that these discrepancies would have on the profit from the behavior. Two propositions identify these general ideas.

PROPOSITION 8.6: The amount that behavior deviates from norms about sexual behavior influences the profit from the behavior and this is an inverse relationship.

PROPOSITION 8.7: The importance of behavior conforming to norms about sexual behavior is related to the amount of influence that the amount of deviation from these norms has on the profit from the behavior, and this is a positive relationship.

It is also possible that it is useful to induce these same ideas to a still higher level of generality by not limiting them to sexual behaviors. If this is done, two new propositions result.

PROPOSITION 8.8:   The amount behavior deviates from norms influences the profit from the behavior and this is an inverse relationship.

PROPOSITION 8.9:   The importance of behavior conforming to norms is related to the amount of influence that deviation from these norms has on the profit from the behavior, and this is a positive relationship.

These are highly general propositions and it is likely that they can be tested in a wide variety of situations. They were not, however, induced from a wide range of specific propositions. They were acquired from a few assertions in the area of premarital sexual behavior, which argues for caution in applying them before empirical data are related to them. The last six propositions comprise a relatively complex model that has three levels of generality, as diagramed in Figure 8.3.

Permissiveness of Societies

Christensen proposes several other relationships between the permissiveness of societies and other variables. For example, he asserts: "Movement toward greater permissiveness in sexual norms tends to converge both attitudes and behavior as between males and females" (1969:217). The variables in this idea seem to be sociological variables. The independent variable appears to be change in the permissiveness of the premarital sexual norms in a social unit. It is difficult, however, to identify just how this variable varies. It could vary three different ways: (1) it could be a dichotomous variable that varies between changing toward greater permissiveness and not changing at all; (2) it could be a trichotomous variable with the three categories of changing toward less permissiveness, no change at all, and changing toward greater permissiveness; or (3) it could be a continuous variable that varies in the amount of change in permissiveness. If it is type 3 it would have a point at which no change is occurring and then vary continuously in the amount of change toward permissiveness on one side and the amount of change toward restrictiveness on the other.

To keep the present formulation simple enough to work with, it is assumed here that Christensen is identifying the first of these three patterns of variation and that it is hence a dichotomous variable varying between no change and a change toward greater permissiveness. This variable can be labeled *change in permissiveness* of the norms about premarital sexual behavior.

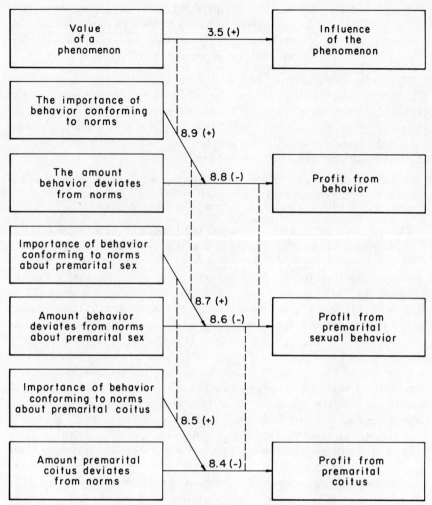

Figure 8.3 The relationships between permissiveness, importance of behavior conforming to norms, and profit from behavior.

The dependent variable can be labeled the amount of *difference* between the sexes in premarital sexual attitudes and behavior. It is apparently a continuous variable ranging between a low point of no difference and a high point of no similarity. When the variables are identified in this manner proposition 8.10 seems to be what Christensen is asserting.

PROPOSITION 8.10:   Change in the permissiveness of norms about premarital sexual behavior influences the difference between the sexes in premarital sexual attitudes and behavior and this is an inverse relationship.

The only characteristics of this relationship that are identified by
Christensen are that it exists and is positive. The proposition is consistent with Christensen's data. He found in his cross-cultural comparisons
the most permissive cultures tended to have the least sex differences and
the most restrictive culture the greatest sex differences. He also notes
the following about the United States:

> During the shift toward greater sexual freedom which has occurred over the
> last half century or so, the great changes have been with females—which have
> made them more like males in attitude and behavior (1969:217).

The proposition is also consistent with some of Christensen's later
data (Christensen and Gregg, 1970) and with Bell and Chaskes' (1970)
data. However, in spite of the congruence of the data with the idea suggested in this proposition, there are reasons to doubt the validity of the
proposition. There seems to be considerable evidence (Terman, 1938;
Kinsey, 1948) that the societies that were investigated in these studies
were investigated at a time when they were moving from relatively low
permissiveness to high permissiveness. However, it is possible that the
norms regarding the male became permissive at an earlier time than for
the female, and if this is the case, the earlier change in permissiveness
would have brought about greater sex differences. If this is true, it
would only be the change at a certain historical period that was inversely related to sex differences.

It thus seems possible that the phenomenon identified in proposition
8.10 is a spurious relationship that appeared because the data were
gathered at a certain historic period, and differences between the sexes
in attitudes and behavior tend to be caused by other variables than the
change in permissiveness. This proposition should thus be held tentative
until additional theoretical work is done, and the ideas are tested with
additional data. Some of Reiss' formulations in the next section are relevant for this proposition, and after they are explicated they can be integrated with this analysis.

There are several other conclusions in Christensen's formulation, but
before these conclusions can be stated in propositional form and inserted into a deductive theoretical model the variables, relationships,
and logical connections between the relationships need to be made more
clear. Many of these conclusions are statements like the fact that "there
is always some individual deviation" (1969:216), and movement toward

greater permissiveness in sexual norms tends to encourage the persistence of certain "subcultures" (1969:217). Such statements do not seem to identify relationships between variables.

Reiss' Formulations

Responsibility for Other Family Members

In the book *The social Context of Premarital Sexual Permissiveness* (1967), Reiss identifies a number of propositions about premarital sexual attitudes and behavior. One of these deals with a variable that he refers to as the "responsibility for other family members" (1967:156), defined as the degree to which a person or a social position is accountable or answerable for the actions of other family members. It is apparently a continuous variable varying from no responsibility to a relatively high degree as is usually found in the socializing roles of parenthood. The dependent variable in this proposition is the *permissiveness* of the norms about premarital sexual behavior.

PROPOSITION 8.11:   The amount of responsibility for other family members influences the permissiveness of premarital sexual norms and this is an inverse relationship.

This proposition was induced from several more specific empirical findings in Reiss' data that seemed to have the dimension of responsibility in them. He found that older siblings were lower in permissiveness than younger siblings, that only children were highest in permissiveness, and that as the number of children increases and as their ages increase the permissiveness of parents tends to decrease. Reiss proposes that the factor that seems to explain these variations is the responsibility dimension. He implies that this relationship is linear, but this is not made explicit. It also seems likely that this is a fairly influential relationship, but there are no data to test this speculation.

Courtship Participation

Another of Reiss' theoretical ideas identified in this same proposition deals with the relationship between courtship participation and permissiveness (1967:156). He suggests that involvement in the courtship process tends to increase permissiveness. Apparently the independent variable in the proposition is not just a dichotomous variable identifying participation and no participation, because individuals can gradually become increasingly involved and uninvolved over a period of time. It seems to be viewed as a continuous variable varying in the amount of time and energy spent in heterosexual dating. When the independent variable is defined in this way proposition 8.12 follows.

PROPOSITION 8.12:   The amount of participation in courtship influences the permissiveness of the individual's norms and this is a positive relationship.

Reiss asserts the existence and direction of this relationship but does not speculate about other characteristics of it. He induced its existence from a more specific, empirical finding that divorced parents are more permissive than nondivorced parents (1967:147–150).

There is research in addition to Reiss' data that is relevant for assessing the validity of this proposition. Several studies have investigated changes in permissiveness as individuals move through the courtship process from casual dating to engagement. If it is true that individuals are "participating" more or are more "involved" in the courtship institution as they move toward marriage, then the findings in this research that there are changes in permissiveness would add support either for or against the validity of the assertion in this proposition that a relationship exists between the two variables of participation and permissiveness. Ehrmann (1959:161), for example, found that women became more permissive as their relationships approached marriage, but that men had a curvilinear pattern, being most permissive with friends and less permissive with acquaintances and lovers. This finding argues for the validity of the proposition for women but not for men. It may be, however, that Reiss' proposition is valid for the changes in participation occurring by entering and exiting the courtship process and not for increasing personal involvement while in the courting stage of life.

Autonomy of the Courtship Institution

The last proposition on the relationship between involvement in the courtship process and permissiveness is intricately related with another of Reiss' propositions. This is his proposition that the autonomy of the courtship institution influences the permissiveness of the norms in this institution. Reiss (1967:165–168; 1965) views the courtship process as a separate institution and suggests that this institution can vary in the degree to which it is autonomous from the control of the family institution. This variable is labeled the *autonomy of the courtship institution,* and it apparently varies continuously between the familial institution having complete control over the courtship institution to having no control. An ideal type at the low-autonomy end of this scale would be where marriages are arranged by parents, and the relatively free courtship system in the contemporary United States probably typifies as autonomous a courtship system as currently exists. The dependent variable is permissiveness of the norms in the courtship institution. Proposition 8.13 presents Reiss' suggested relationship between these variables.

PROPOSITION 8.13:   The autonomy of the courtship institution influences the permissiveness of the premarital sexual norms in the courtship institution and this is a positive relationship.

Reiss specifies only that this relationship is positive, but it seems likely that it is also monotonic. It may even be linear and highly influential, but there is no empirical basis for these added speculations. Reiss views this proposition as a highly general formulation from which it is possible to deduce a number of specific propositions. In fact, he seems to argue that it is a more general proposition that can be related to each of his other seven propositions through deductive logic. The logical connection between this proposition and the other seven propositions is not, however, made explicit in Reiss' formulation. It does seem possible, however, to identify one way that proposition 8.13 is related to proposition 8.12.

It can be reasoned that if proposition 8.13 is true in asserting that the autonomy of the courtship institution positively influences the permissiveness of the norms in the courtship institution, ·then, when the courtship institution is relatively autonomous of the familial institution, the relationship that is asserted in proposition 8.12 would occur in that courtship participation would positively influence the permissiveness of the norms of individuals involved in that institution. However, if proposition 8.13 is true in asserting that autonomy positively influences the permissiveness of the norms in the courtship institution, then, when the courtship institution is low in autonomy, it follows that the relationship asserted in proposition 8.12 would probably not exist, or that it would at least be less influential.

The relationship between proposition 8.12 and 8.13 that is being proposed here is relatively complex, but it is not a case of one of the propositions being deduced from the other. It is instead a case of one of them influencing the relationship in the other. An attempt is made in Figure 8.4 to diagram this relationship, and, as can be seen in the figure, what is proposed here is that the autonomy of the courtship institution probably influences the permissiveness of the norms in the courtship institution, and the permissiveness of the norms in the courtship institution

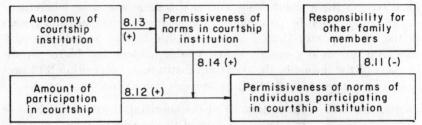

Figure 8.4   The proposed relationships between propositions 8.11 to 8.14.

probably influences the amount of influence that the amount of participation in courtship has on the permissiveness of the norms of the individuals participating in courtship. Thus the following proposition is suggested.

PROPOSITION 8.14:   The permissiveness of the norms about premarital
sexual behavior in the courtship institution is related
to the amount of influence in proposition 8.12, which
asserts that the amount of participation in courtship
influences the permissiveness of the norms of individuals participating in the courtship institution, and
this is a positive relationship.

Social Forces

A substantial part of Reiss' concern is with how various "social forces"
alter individual levels of sexual permissiveness. He includes such variables as religiosity, race, sex, number of love affairs, romantic love orientation, and age when began dating as social factors, and one of his initial formulations is the proposition that the "lower the traditional level
of sexual permissiveness in a group, the greater the likelihood that social
forces will alter individual levels of sexual permissiveness" (1967:51).
This conclusion can be stated as a proposition, but first attention needs
to be directed to the nature of the variables. The independent variable
is the "traditional level of sexual permissiveness." Apparently it conceptualizes variation in the permissiveness of the sexual norms traditionally
existing in a group. This is apparently a continuous variable ranging
from low to high traditional permissiveness.

The dependent variable is the likelihood that social forces will influence individual levels of permissiveness. This being a statement of probability, it apparently varies continuously from 0 to 1.0. This can be
stated in the format used in this book as follows.

PROPOSITION 8.15: The traditional level of sexual permissiveness in a group influences the probability that social forces will influence individual levels of permissiveness and this is an inverse relationship.

Table 8.1 Race and Permissiveness by Sex in the Student and Adult Samples (Reiss, 1967:42)

	Male	*Female*
Student sample		
White	61%; $N=287$	27%; $N=324$
Negro	85%; $N=115$	45%; $N=118$
Adult sample		
White	30%; $N=607$	6%; $N=649$
Negro	65%; $N=62$	30%; $N=81$

There are data in Reiss' study that can be interpreted as arguing against the validity of this proposition. One table in the study shows that men tend to be influenced more by certain "social forces" than women. Part of this table is reproduced here as Table 8.1, and it shows that in these samples there is more difference in permissiveness between the student and adult males than the student and adult females among both Negroes and whites. Proposition 8.11 asserts that responsibility for family members decreases permissiveness and proposition 8.12 argues that participating in courtship increases permissiveness. If these are also "social forces" that influence permissiveness, then if proposition 8.15 is true in asserting that the less permissive groups tend to be the most influenced by "social forces," it would be expected that since women tend to be traditionally less permissive than men, the women would be more influenced by these social forces than the men. In actual fact, however, there is more difference between the student and adult sample for the men than the women, and this argues against the validity of proposition 8.15.[1]

This proposition also has the additional problem that the unique historical events occurring in the past century might influence the way that Reiss' data should be interpreted. There is some evidence that during the twentieth century the United States society has been in the process of increasing in permissiveness about premarital sexual norms (Terman, 1939:321; Kinsey, 1948), and that the males have either always been more permissive than females or they increased in permissiveness first.

Moreover, Negroes have tended to be more permissive than whites (Reiss, 1967:38–39). At a time when the increasing permissiveness is spreading to whites and to women, it seems reasonable that social forces would *at that time* exert more influence on these less permissive groups. However, it seems reasonable to ponder about which social groups would be the most influenced during those periods of time when the permissiveness increased for the males and during periods like the pre-Victorian era when the society experienced decreases in permissiveness. If, in fact, there was a period some decades ago when United States society experienced an increase in permissiveness, for me, it seems reasonable that at that particular time the social forces would have been the most likely to influence not the groups that were lowest in permissiveness, which would have been women, but the more permissive males. The question of which groups would be the most susceptible to the social forces during periods of generally decreasing permissiveness is an open question, but one that complicates the issues with which the proposition deals.

One other aspect of this very involved proposition is that if the relationship exists as Reiss proposes it, there is some basis for expecting a curvilinear relationship. There seems to be little question that recent changes in permissiveness in the United States have been more pronounced for women than men, but there is some reason to believe that it is not the women that have traditionally been the very lowest in permissiveness that are changing the most. Rather it seems that those that have been in an intermediate level of permissiveness tend to move toward less proscriptiveness. The sociological literature contends that changes such as these changes in permissiveness occur only as people change their *reference relationships,* and those who are the least permissive very probably have the most homogeneous reference relationships in the mid-twentieth-century United States. Permissiveness probably responds to the social forces that tend to increase it when there is a social situation where there is enough heterogeneity that there are multiple reference relationships, and this probably occurs most among those who are intermediate in their permissiveness. If this is the case, the relationship in proposition 8.15 would be curvilinear, with social forces having the greatest probability of having an influence on those who have an intermediate level of permissiveness.

The reasoning that gives rise to this suggestion of curvilinearity in proposition 8.15 is literature on the processes that occur in social revolutions and social movements and the relative deprivation literature (Merton, 1968: Ch. 10, 11). There is evidence that those who are the most absolutely deprived or socially isolated are relatively unresponsive to the social movements around them. It is the group that is in an intermediate position between the extremes that is the most sensitized to the differences in the total situation and that responds to it. This, of course, is a considerable leap in generalizing from findings in the literature on social revolutions to changing attitudes about sexual permissiveness, but the situations do seem to have some similarity.

Broderick and Heltsley (1969) published a study that attempted to at least partially test this proposition. They found no differences in the permissiveness of groups they had previously identified as being traditionally low and high in permissiveness, and they suggested this argues against the validity of the proposition. Their sample of college students who were all white and who were high on religiosity was probably not the best group to use to test this idea, but it does provide some related data. After arguing against Reiss' proposition, Broderick and Heltsley then use their finding that religiosity is related to permissiveness among their white sample but not their black sample to assert a slightly different idea. They suggested that religiosity is related to sexual permissiveness only when the religion makes normative proscriptions about permissiveness. This finding does not seem to be related to proposition 8.14, but it does argue for the validity of proposition 8.1, which states that normative definitions influence behavior.

Ties to the Marital and Family Institution

Reiss' third proposition is closely related to propositions 8.12 and 8.13 and it states that "to the extent that individual ties to the marital and family institutions differ, individuals will tend to display a different type of sensitivity of permissiveness to social forces" (1967:89). The independent variable in this proposition is labeled as ties to the marital and family institutions, but it is difficult to know just what it is that is being conceptualized with this variable. It could be something such as different amounts of integration into the familial institution or something such as the amount of activity in the family.

The context of the statement of the proposition, however, indicates that Reiss is concerned with how males differ from females in their "ties" to the familial institution, and he argues that female's courtship "is more marriage-oriented and less free from family influences" (1967:89). It may be that the term "influence" in this statement provides the best clue about what it is that is varying as "ties" to families vary. It may be that it is variation in the amount individuals are influenced by family members. If this is the case, this is very close to identifying variation in the extent to which the individual uses family members for reference relationships. It is suggested here that probably the best conceptualization of the independent variable in this proposition is *the extent to which significant reference relationships exist with family members,* and it probably varies continuously from no influence to a high degree of influence.

The dependent variable in this proposition is also obscure. Reiss states that the way it varies is that individuals display a "different type of sensitivity of permissiveness to social forces" (1967:89). The context of the discussion of the proposition, however, indicates that this conceptualization might be a typology of sensitivities, but the different "types" of sensitivity are not made explicit. It is also possible that he is conceptualizing the *amount* that an individual's normative definitions about premarital sexual behavior are sensitive to social forces. If this is the case, this variable could be labeled *sensitivity of premarital sexual norms to social forces,* and it could be viewed as a continuous variable denoting variation in the amount that permissiveness of an individual's definitions about premarital sexual behaviors is influenced by other social forces. This interpretation seems to be the one in Reiss' formulation. Reiss does not specify anything about the nature of the relationship in this proposition other than to speculate that it exists, but if the variables are defined as suggested here, there is probably an inverse relationship between them.

PROPOSITION 8.16:   The extent to which significant reference relationships exist with family members is related to the sensitivity of premarital sexual norms to social forces and this is an inverse relationship.

It is interesting to speculate about how this proposition is related to propositions 8.12, 8.13, and 8.14. The amount of courtship participation may influence the extent to which reference relationships exist with family members. Or the autonomy of the courtship institution may influence the extent to which reference relationships exist in the family, and this relationship may be influenced by the amount of participation in courtship. It may also be that the sensitivity of premarital sexual norms to social forces influences the amount of influence in proposition 8.13, which speculates that the amount of participation in courtship influences the permissiveness of the norms of an individual. These suggested relationships are highly speculative, but they are suggested here because clear explication at this point will probably facilitate a careful examination of the conceptualization involved and subsequent empirical research to test these ideas. There are three relevant propositions.

PROPOSITION 8.17: The amount of courtship participation influences the extent to which signiflcant references exist with family members and this is an inverse relationship.

PROPOSITION 8.18: When individuals are involved in courtship, the autonomy of the courtship institution influences the extent to which reference relationships exist with family members and this is an inverse relationship.

PROPOSITION 8.19: The amount of courtship participation is related to the amount of influence in proposition 8.18, which asserts that the autonomy of the courtship institution influences the extent to which reference relationships exist with family members, and this is a positive relationship.

Since these propositions are highly speculative, no attempt is made to identify aspects of the relationships in them other than their existence and direction. Figure 8.5, however, illustrates the relationships between the seven propositions in this formulation.[2]

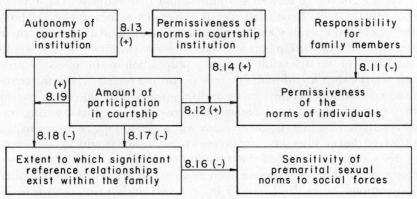

Figure 8.5   A flow chart of propositions 8.10 to 8.17.

Liberality

Reiss' second proposition states that "the stronger the amount of general liberality in a group, the greater the likelihood that social forces will maintain high levels of sexual permissiveness" (1967:613). He arrived at this proposition by finding that variation in what he conceptualizes as the "liberality" of the style of life helped explain the relationship between socioeconomic status and permissiveness. "Liberality" is not defined precisely but Reiss notes the following:

> A liberal would favor change other than tradition, particularly change that involved use of his intellect. He would emphasize individual expression and a universal ethic that stressed concern for all men, including those unlike himself. A conservative would be more likely to support the traditional social order and would place less value on individual expression and a universal ethic than the liberal would. This conception is, of course, debatable, and others are possible; but it has the virtue of attempting to get at some key underlying factors rather than just at attitudes toward specific issues (1967:61–62).

The independent variable in this proposition is thus apparently a continuous variable ranging in degree from low to high liberality. The dependent variable in this proposition, however, is considerably more obscure. Reiss refers to social forces "maintaining" permissiveness, which implies that a permissive attitude that already exists is being continued, but he does not specify what it is that can vary. The only way that maintenance could be a variable would be to conceptualize variation in whether the permissiveness is maintained or not maintained, and there is nothing in the context of the proposition that addresses this type of conceptualization. Reiss' data do, however, have meaningful relationships between liberality and permissiveness, and the data indicate there is a positive relationship between liberality and permissiveness. It would not, however, be defensible to state a proposition to this effect because this relationship would probably only occur in a society where the traditions favored low permissiveness and the groups favoring change rather than tradition would favor higher permissiveness. In a social setting traditionally having high permissiveness where the groups favoring change preferred lower liberality, an inverse relationship would be expected.

Reiss' data indicate that the direction of the relationship between socioeconomic status and permissiveness changes as the level of liberality in the group varies. He found an inverse relationship between socioeconomic status and permissiveness in the conservative setting, and a positive relationship in the liberal setting (1967:71). This finding is summarized by the following proposition.

PROPOSITION 8.20:   The amount of liberality changes the relationship between socioeconomic status and permissiveness such that high liberality is associated with a positive relationship and low liberality is associated with a negative relationship.

It may be that this is the idea Reiss was attempting to summarize in his proposition about liberality maintaining high levels of permissiveness, but his statement does not seem to identify this relationship. For example, the conservative and high-status phenomena converge to decrease permissiveness, and Reiss' statement does not state that. His proposition also does not point out that conversely the conservatism and low status would be expected to increase permissiveness. This proposition is unique and thought provoking, but it should be held tentative until additional data are available to test its existence.

Other Propositions

Reiss has three other propositions that deal with such issues as permissiveness and equalitarianism and how individuals perceive their parents' and peer's permissiveness. These propositions present several problems that make it necessary to do more conceptual and theoretical refining before they can be integrated into the present formulation. For example, his sixth proposition states that "there is a general tendency for the individual to perceive of his parents' permissiveness as a low point on a permissive continuum and his peers' permissiveness as a high point, and to place himself somewhat closer to his peers, particularly to those he regards as his close friends" (1967:139). This seems to be a descriptive statement identifying that sexual standards are closer to peers than parents. It does not identify a relationship between variables, and it seems reasonable that these standards gradually move from being relatively close to the parents to being relatively close to the peers as the individuals increase in age and in independence from the parents. It is likely that additional empirical data and theorizing about these issues will identify relationships that will explain when and why these attitudes vary, but these do not yet seem to be developed.

Summary

This chapter has attempted to identify a number of propositions about factors that influence premarital sexual attitudes and behavior. The theoretical work of Ira Reiss and Harold Christensen has served as the basis for most of the theoretical ideas, and it is hoped that the current formulation moves this earlier work one step further in the slow process of developing comprehensive, integrated, and testable theories in this area. The ideas reviewed in this chapter are summarized in Figure 8.6, which attempts to diagram the relationships between each of the vari-

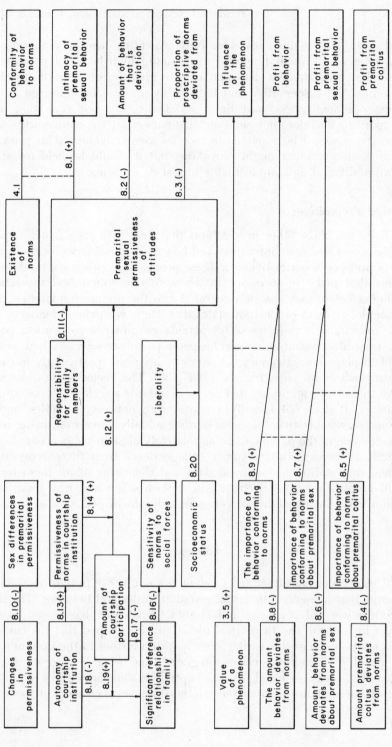

Figure 8.6 Propositions about premarital sexual attitudes and behavior.

ables in the resulting theory of premarital sexual attitudes and behavior. This theory is still in its elementary stages; future conceptual, theoretical, and empirical work should bring substantial additions.

Notes

1. Reiss has pointed out in a personal communication that this interpretation focuses on the absolute percentage change, and that if the proportionate change is taken into account, the data for the white sample are consistent with his proposition. The change from 6 to 27% is an increase of 4½ times while the increase from 30 to 61% is only double. This emphasizes the complexities of the issue and the need for additional data to test these propositions.

2. Reiss, in responding to an earlier draft of this chapter, pointed out that the interpretation made here of his third proposition is not the interpretation he intended. The phrase in Reiss' book that was used as the starting point in the present formulation was the statement that "female courtship is more marriage-oriented and less free from family influences" (1967:89), and the formulation here picked up on the freedom from family influences part of this statement. Reiss indicated that his intention was to emphasize the "marriage-orientedness" part by dealing with the fact that the female is more oriented to the mother-wife role than the male is oriented to the father-husband role. In other words, he was interested in variation in the priority of roles, and he suggested his third proposition could be reworded as follows: "The extent to which one's primary future role orientation is to family roles is directly related to the extent to which one will require affection as a prerequisite for sexual permissiveness." It seems defensible to argue that this proposition suggested by Reiss and the propositions 8.16, 8.17, 8.18, and 8.19 generated in the present formulation both deserve additional empirical testing.

CHAPTER 9

POWER AS A DEPENDENT VARIABLE

The analysis of antecedents and consequences of power has gradually become one of the major areas of inquiry in the study of the family. In fact, research in this area has become sufficiently large that the area was considered one of the major areas of research in the 1960s in the decade-review articles published in the *Journal of Marriage and the Family* (Safilios-Rothschild, 1970). This chapter is an attempt to analyze some of the theoretical ideas in this literature that deal with power as a dependent variable.

The Conceptualization of Power

Safilios-Rothschild (1970:539–541) points out that there are numerous conceptual and operationalization problems in studying the concept of power. Different conceptual labels have been used for the same phenomenon, and in some literature the same term has been used for very different phenomena. In addition, she points out there is reason to question the validity of some of the empirical indicators that have been used to measure what has been conceptualized as power.

It is suggested here that several of the conceptual problems can be resolved if a distinction is made between two things that have both been labeled as power. One of these is the phenomenon that was defined by Max Weber as power, which refers to the "ability" an individual or social group has to get its own way. Weber states, "Power is the probability that one actor within a social relationship will be in a position to carry out his own will despite resistance, regardless of the basis on which this probability rests" (1947:152). This concept can apparently vary between the extremes of an individual having no power or ability to control and having all the ability to control. In most social situations, these extremes would never occur since most of the variation would be between an individual or social group having a small amount of power versus large amounts relative to others.

The other phenomenon that has been referred to as power in many contexts is the actual exertion of control. This was defined by Straus as "actions which control, initiate, change, or modify the behavior of another member of the family" (1964:318). It is suggested here that it would eliminate conceptual confusion if this phenomenon were referred to as *control* rather than power. The difference between these two concepts is that power would be viewed as the ability to control and control would be viewed as the actual occurrence of the control. In family research the control variable usually has been viewed as varying between extremes of permissiveness and restrictiveness, and hence it seems to be a continuous variable varying in amount.

It also seems important to conceptually distinguish between these concepts and the different methods that are used in controlling. For example, attempts to control can be made verbally or nonverbally, overtly or covertly, with physical threats or without them. Moreover, other phenomena such as the legitimacy of power (Weber, 1947:324–329) are conceptually different from the amount of power or the amount of control.

Rodman's Synthesis

A relatively short paper by Rodman (1967) synthesized a number of theoretical ideas about factors that influence power. He referred to his synthesis as a "theory of resources in cultural context." It is an attempt to integrate the earlier ideas of a number of writers such as French and Raven (1960), Blood and Wolfe (1960), Blood (1963), and Heer (1963, 1963a) with some cross-cultural data that had been published since the earlier theoretical speculations were made.

Resources

One of the major theoretical ideas in this literature was initially suggested by Blood and Wolfe (1960:12).

PROPOSITION 9.1: The amount of resources an individual has positively influences the power the individual has in a relationship and this is a positive, monotonic relationship.

The main concept in the independent variable in this proposition is resources, and Blood and Wolfe define them as "anything that one partner may make available to the other, helping the latter satisfy his needs or attain his goals" (1960:12). They apparently vary continuously from a low to a high number of resources, and this relationship is suggested to be a positive, monotonic function.

Heer (1963) proposed that the "exchange value" of the resources is also involved. This idea was initially suggested as an alternative to the idea in proposition 9.1, but later data prompted Rodman to suggest that the value dimension comes into play by influencing the effect that resources have on power. The more the resources are valued, the more they influence power. This idea seems to identify a contingent variable that influences the relationship in proposition 9.1. If this is the case, a further proposition can be identified.

PROPOSITION 9.2:   The value of resources is related to the amount of influence in proposition 9.1, which states that resources influence power, and this is a positive, monotonic relationship.

This idea can be integrated with the following theoretical idea from Chapter 3.

PROPOSITION 3.5:   The value of a phenomenon influences the amount of effect this phenomenon has in social processes and this is a positive, monotonic relationship.

Proposition 9.2 is a specific case of the inclusive idea in proposition 3.5. The logical relationship between these two propositions is that since evaluative distinctions about resources are one specific type of value, and since proposition 9.2 deals with a social process, then if proposition 3.5 is true, it follows that variation in the value of resources would influence the effect of resources on power.

Social Norms

One of the other major ideas in this theory has to do with the effect that social norms have on power. Blood and Wolfe initially suggested that cultural definitions about who ought to have power probably influence power, but their empirical tests of the idea did not support it. They reasoned that several variables would identify variation in normative beliefs. They then examined their data to see if farm families, immigrants, older couples, low education couples, and Catholic families would have relatively patriarchal power structures. They found no statistically significant differences, and they interpreted these findings as evidence that normative definitions did not have an effect on power. Heer (1963) later argued, however, that these data probably do not justify rejecting the proposition. Still later Rodman (1967) used what seemed to be conflicting findings from different cultures as a basis for suggesting that not only do normative definitions about who should have power probably influence who has power, but they also operate as a contingent variable influencing the effect that resources have on power.

The independent variable in this idea has been loosely referred to as cultural factors, norms about power, prescribed authority patterns, and so on. Unfortunately, none of the previous theoretical formulations have been specific in defining this variable and specifying how it varies. It is suggested here that the phenomenon that has been referred to is variation in the amount of power that is normatively prescribed for a social role. It is apparently a continuous variable ranging from no power to total power, and in a dyadic relationship such as marriage it has a mid-point of an equal distribution of power. If this is a correct definition of the independent variable, proposition 9.3 seems to be implicit in Rodman's model.

PROPOSITION 9.3:   The amount of power that is normatively prescribed for a role influences the power of an occupant of the role and this is a positive, monotonic relationship.

It is possible to integrate this proposition with the earlier normative theory in Chapter 4 given in proposition 4.1.

PROPOSITION 4.1:   The existence of norms in a social group influences the behavior in that group so the behavior tends to conform to the normative definitions.

Since the idea in proposition 9.3 asserts that the amount of power will be influenced by normative definitions about power, it seems to be a specific case of the general idea identified in proposition 4.1.

Rodman also suggests that the amount of power normatively prescribed for a role influences the effect that resources have on power. He argues that one of the reasons resources seem to be highly influential in the United States is because the normative definitions are fairly equalitarian. The converse of this is that in situations where the normative definitions are closer to the extremes on this variable (partriarchal or matriarchal) the resources would have less influence. If this interpretation of Rodman's argument is correct, this idea can be summarized as a proposition.

PROPOSITION 9.4:   The amount of power that is normatively prescribed for a role is related to the amount of influence in proposition 9.1, which asserts that resources influence power, and this is a curvilinear relationship in which resources have the most influence in the intermediate part of the normative variable and less influence at both extremes of the normative variable.

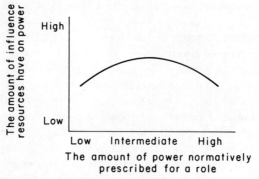

Figure 9.1   The relationship between normative prescriptions about power and the amount of influence resources have on power.

Since this is a relatively unusual relationship, an attempt is made to diagram it in Figure 9.1. This figure shows that resources have the greatest influence when there are intermediate norms, and that when the norms are at either extreme (either patriarchial or matriarchal) there is less influence.

Rodman suggests that the "flexibility" and the "importance" of the normative definitions about power are also involved. He does not, however, define these two variables, and it is not clear just how these two dimensions differ from each other. The context of his discussion, however, seems to indicate that he is referring to the two dimensions of norms that Jackson (1966) identifies as the "evaluative" dimension and the "range of tolerable behavior." The evaluative dimension in Jackson's taxonomy identifies variation in how important or serious the behaviors are that are being normatively defined; earlier in this book this was called the importance of role discrepancies. It is a continuous variable that is the relative value of behavior conforming to norms, and it varies in degree from a high negative value to a high positive value.

The variable Jackson terms the range of tolerable behavior assumes there can be variation in the quantity or quality of a behavior that is normatively approved. In the case of the relative distribution of control in marriage, it would be possible to have a normative definition that defines very narrowly or precisely who should have the control; or, on the other hand, the norms could permit considerable flexibility in who has the control. In the former example there would be a narrow range of tolerable behavior, and in the latter the range would be larger. This variable seems to be a continuous variable ranging between a small and large "range" of tolerable behavior. If these two variables are actually those of Rodman's model, and if the present interpretation of Rodman's ideas is correct, the following two propositions use these variables.

PROPOSITION 9.5: The range of tolerable behavior in norms about power is related to the amount of influence in proposition 9.1, which states that resources influence power, and this is a positive, monotonic relationship.

PROPOSITION 9.6: The importance of role discrepancies about power is related to the amount of influence in proposition 9.1, which states that resources influence power, and this is an inverse, monotonic relationship.

There are two other propositions that should probably be stated with these two independent variables. The basis for asserting them here is partly because they seem implicit in Rodman's model, and partly because of their reasonableness.

PROPOSITION 9.7: The range of tolerable behavior in norms about power is related to the amount of influence in proposition 9.2, which states that norms influence power, and this is an inverse, monotonic relationship.

PROPOSITION 9.8: The importance of role discrepancies about power is related to the amount of influence in proposition 9.2, which states that norms influence power, and this is a positive, monotonic relationship.

Rodman's theory is fairly complex, but an attempt is made to diagram it in Figure 9.2. As can be seen in this figure, the theory suggests that resources and norms about power both influence power and that the norms influence the effect the resources have. The value of resources also influences the effect of resources. The importance of conformity to these norms and the range of tolerable behavior influence the effect that both norms and resources have on power. The dotted lines identify the logical relationships between several of the propositions. Proposition 9.2 can be deduced from 3.5, and proposition 9.3 can be deduced from 4.1.

One of the ingenious contributions of Rodman's synthesis is that he used conflicting findings in previous research as the basis for stating some of his ideas. The earlier data found that certain resources were positively associated with power in the United States and negatively associated with power in several other countries such as Greece. This seemed to question the validity of the idea in proposition 9.1 that states that resources influence power.[1] Rodman, however, suggests that movement from a patriarchal normative system toward equalitarian norms in-

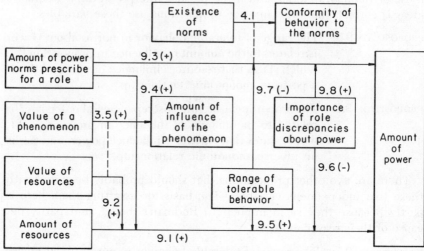

Figure 9.2   The theory of resources in cultural context.

creases wives' power relative to their husbands and decreases husbands' relative power, even though the same change tends to increase the influence of resources. Since the highly educated and high-income groups would be the first to adopt the new normative definitions, they would be the ones in the society who would first experience the relative rise in wives' power. Furthermore, since the social norms seem to have priority over resources (when they are fairly important, inflexible norms), the husbands in the society who have high resources also tend to have relatively low power.

It is also possible to use Rodman's theory as a basis for several other speculations. The inverse relationship between resources and power that were found in Greece and Yugoslavia would only be expected when a society is in the process of changing from a patriarchal normative system. The more educated and higher income families that experienced relatively more wife power than the less educated and lower income families probably experienced this because they changed their norms first. After the entire society makes the change to the equalitarian ethic, then the variation in resources would be expected to account for more of the difference between the high and low education and income groups, and a positive relationship would appear between resources and power. If this is true, and if the Westernization processes continue in the directions speculated by Goode (1963) and others, it can be predicted that in the future the negative relationships between resources and power found in Greece and Yugoslavia will become positive relationships.

Deductions from the Marital Relationship

Socioeconomic Status

It is possible to make a number of deductions from the relatively abstract theory presented in the preceding pages. One has to do with the relationship that seems to occur between socioeconomic status and the power structure in marital relationships. Socioeconomic status in the contemporary United States culture is determined primarily by the success of the husband in his occupational status and the economic rewards that this provides (Simpson, 1965). If the husband is successful, the family tends to be in a proportionately higher status level, and if he is unsuccessful, the family has a lessened status. Socioeconomic status can be placed along a continuum varying from low to high, and since socioeconomic status is determined primarily by the husband's occupational success, and since it is highly valued in the contemporary society, and if proposition 9.1 is true, proposition 9.9 can be deduced.

PROPOSITION 9.9: Socioeconomic status is related to the amount of husband's power in the marital dyad and this is a positive relationship.

Empirical data in the United States (Blood and Wolfe, 1960:31–43) and France (Michel, 1967) are generally consistent with this proposition, but there are exceptions. Blood and Wolfe (1960) and Komarovsky (1962:Ch. 10) both found that at the lower end of the socioeconomic status continuum the relationship between status indicators and power is inverse. Komarovsky (1962:225), however, also found that the lowest status men had a more patriarchal ideology. If they do, and if proposition 9.3 is true in asserting that norms influence power, and if it is true that norms have more influence than resources, the finding of any inverse relationship in the low socioeconomic status levels is consistent with Rodman's theory and argues for its validity.

Occupational Prestige

It is possible to deduce from proposition 9.1 or 9.9 that the husband's occupational prestige is related to his power. The logical connection with proposition 9.9 is that occupational prestige is an important component in all the major conceptualizations of socioeconomic status. Since it is a major component, it follows that if proposition 9.9 is true, occupational prestige is positively related to husband's power.

If this idea is deduced from proposition 9.1, however, an influential relationship between prestige and power can also be deduced. Socioeconomic status cannot be considered an influential variable, because it is so clearly a nominal rather than real variable and therefore can hardly influence something else. Occupational prestige, however, is a definition that occurs in the minds of individuals, and as such it can be viewed as a resource. When it is defined as a resource, if proposition 9.1 is true in asserting that variation in resources positively influences power, proposition 9.10 follows.

PROPOSITION 9.10:   The amount of occupational prestige influences the amount of power and this is a positive, monotonic relationship.

Education

The same logic that is used in deducing proposition 9.10 is applicable in deducing that education undoubtedly influences power. In addition, it can be reasoned that education is probably indirectly related to power because it influences skills, such as amount of information or verbal skills, that are also frequently resources. This leads to another relevant, direct proposition.

PROPOSITION 9.11:   The amount of education influences power and this is a positive relationship.

Employment of Wives

One major concern in the family research is whether wives' employment influences their power. Proposition 9.12 can be deduced from proposition 9.1 if it is true that time spent in economic activity helps the family attain goals (in other words, if it is a resource), especially when this type of activity is highly valued.

PROPOSITION 9.12:   The amount of time spent in economic activity influences the power of a person in the marital dyad and this is a positive relationship.

The data that are related to this proposition are conflicting. Some studies such as Blood and Hamblin's (1958) and Hoffman's (1960) found no relationship between employment and what they termed power; other studies such as those by Heer (1958) and Middleton and Putney (1960) found the predicted relationship.

Blood suggests in his review of this research that the net results of the research indicate the following:

The wife's employment: (*a*) decreases the decisions she makes in household task areas, (*b*) but increases her share in major economic decision-making, while (*c*) leaving unchanged the amount of influence of husband and wife *over* each other (1963:294; italics his).

A slightly different interpretation is suggested here. Blood is clearly dealing with empirical indicators that measure control rather than power, and this may be a situation where the use of control as a measure of power distorts conclusions about power rather than justifying them. It seems defensible to argue that since the wife increases her control in "major" decisions when she is employed she actually has more power when she is employed. Moreover, the research is fairly clear (Blood, 1963:285–290) that when the wife is employed the husband will be relatively more involved in household task performance. It follows that his involvement positively influences the number of decisions he has to make in these minor areas of life. This helps explain the observation that there is a decrease in the "minor" decisions the wife makes when she is employed. Even though the wife loses control in this area, this does not seem to justify the argument that she loses power, or if she does, it would be very little power. Thus the conclusion that is suggested here is that the data indicate that the wife loses *control* in "routine" aspects of the maintenance of the home but that she has greater *power* when she is employed. This interpretation of the data is consistent with Hoffman's (1960) argument that the wife may again power through her employment but be very careful to not exert more control because it would be against her normative definitions about who should do the controlling.

One additional point that seems relevant in this context is that Blood and Wolfe also have data on husbands who are employed overtime, and they attempt to determine who has the greater control in their sample when the husband is unemployed. They find that the more time either spouse spends in economic activity, the greater is his or her power relative to other conditions. This certainly argues for the validity of proposition 9.12, even though there is the possibility that an exorbitant amount of time in economic activity might not continue to increase power—especially for the wife.

Summary

This chapter has analyzed a number of propositions about power as a dependent variable. Rodman's resource theory in cultural context was revised, extended, and integrated with several other propositions introduced in other contexts. Figure 9.3 summarizes the entire model.

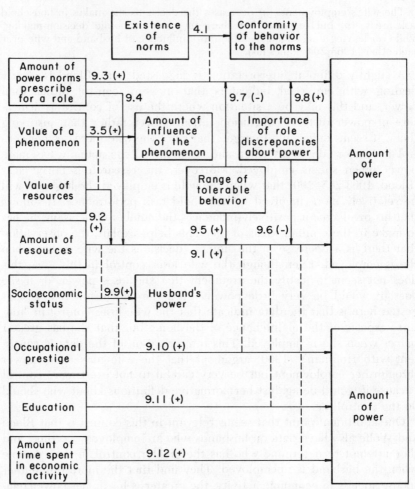

Figure 9.3   Propositions about power as the dependent variable.

Note

1. It should be parenthetically noted that the empirical indicators of the dependent variable in these studies measured what has been conceptualized here as control. However, their operationalizations probably could be viewed as a fairly indirect measure of what is conceptualized here as power, and this seems to be the intent of the researchers.

CHAPTER 10

FAMILIES UNDER STRESS

A number of research projects were undertaken in the 1930s to study the effect of an economic depression on families. The hypotheses that emerged from this research were later retested in a number of other situations where families experience stress such as bereavement, alcoholism, war separation and reunion, unemployment. This research on how families react to and are influenced by stress has generated numerous theoretical ideas, which form an important part of the family sociology literature. This chapter is an attempt to summarize and analyze many of the ideas in this literature that can be stated as parts of deductive theory.

The A, B, C, X Formulation

One of the major formulations in the family crisis literature was developed by Hill (1949) in his study of war separation and reunion. This model was later slightly modified (Hill, 1958; Hansen and Hill, 1964), but it has remained virtually unchanged for over 20 years. Briefly, it is:

A (the event)—interacting with B (the family's crisis-meeting resources)—interacting with C (the definition the family makes of the event)—produces X (the crisis). The second and third determinants—the family resources and definition of the event—lie within the family itself and must be seen in terms of the family's structures and values. The hardships of the event, which go to make up the first determinant, lies outside the family and are an attribute of the event itself (Hill, 1958:141).

The main idea in this model is that the X factor is influenced by several other phenomena. The first step in reworking this model so it can be a bona fide part of deductive theory is to determine what the X factor is and how it varies. Hill defined crisis and "any sharp or decisive change from which old patterns are inadequate" (1949:51), but he did not explain how this phenomenon of "crises" varies. The context of his discussion seems to indicate that he views some crises as more severe than others, but this is not made explicit. Later investigators seem to have viewed this factor as a continuous variable, but none of them ever explain just what it is that is varying or how it varies. LeMasters (1957) suggested that crises vary in their severity, but he did not define this.

Hobbs (1965, 1968) came closer to viewing this factor as a continuous variable when he developed an index of the difficulty of a crises.

Since there has been no previous attempt to systematically explicate just what it is that is varying in Hill's X factor or to identify the way this variable varies, an attempt is made here to identify the phenomen denoted in this earlier research. It seems to be implicit in the early research such as Angell (1936) and Hill (1949) and explicit in later writings such as LeMasters (1957) and Hobbs (1965, 1968) that the students of family crisis view the family as a social system in the same way Rodgers defines system in the developmental conceptual framework. Rodgers states the family is a "semiclosed system . . . which is composed of interrelated positions and roles defined by the society of which it is a part as unique to that system" (1964:264). The students of family crisis also seem to view crises as disruptions in the routine operation of the family social system. The less disrupted the system is, the less severe is the crisis; the more disrupted the system is, the greater is the crisis. Thus the phenomenon that seems to be denoted is the amount of disruption in the family social system.

There are several complications in using a "social system" type of definition of Hill's X factor because there are a number of different schools of thought that make different assumptions about the nature of social systems. Hansen and Hill (1964), for example, seem to assume that systems have a number of characteristics that Allport (1960) asserted systems have, and Buckley (1967: Ch.2) argues that there are important differences between what he terms equilibrium-seeking systems, organismic systems, and process systems. In the present context it does not seem necessary to make the assumption Hansen and Hill make, nor should it be assumed that the family social system fits only one of Buckley's three types. It is only assumed here that the family social system is an organization consisting of intricately related social positions that have complex sets of roles and norms, and that the system exists to accomplish a wide variety of objectives such as reproduction, socialization, and emotionally intimate interaction.

The X factor in Hill's A, B, C, X formulation could be labeled with a number of different terms. The one that seems most useful is the *amount of crisis*, because the term crisis has been used so extensively in the previous literature. It denotes variation in the amount of disruptiveness, incapacitatedness, or disorganization of the family social system, and it varies continuously from no crisis to a high amount of crisis. It is probably also important to point out that when no crisis exists this does not mean there are no stresses or problems in the system. It merely connotes that the problems are of a routine rather than unusual nature.

Hill's *A* factor is the stressor event, but before his idea that stressor events produce crises can be stated in a proposition it is necessary to define this variable. It has been repeatedly pointed out in the literature that the same type of event produces varying amounts of crisis in different situations, yet there has been no attempt to define this "eventness" as a variable. It has been pointed out that there are many different types of stressor events, and a very elaborate paradigm has been developed that differentiates between types of stressor events (Hansen and Hill, 1964:793–794), but thus far no attempt has been found to define this variable and identify how it varies.

It is suggested here that the phenomenon that has been conceptualized in the family crisis literature as the *stressor event* is an event that produces a change in the family social system. Anything that changes some aspect of the system such as the boundaries, structure, goals, processes, role, or values can produce what has been conceptualized in this chapter as some amount of crisis in the system. Some of these stressor events or "changes" produce large amounts of crisis or disruption in the routine operation of the system, and some produce very little crisis. This variable denotes something different from the routine changes within a system that are expected as a part of its regular, routine operation. It conceptualizes events that are sufficiently unusual that the system itself changes. For example, the husband being laid off his job is a routine event in many blue-collar families, and hence, even though it is a "change," it is not the type of event that is referred to as a stress or event. However, if this husband were to become unemployed for a sufficiently long period of time that the routine activities of the family could not continue, this would be a change in the system and thus a stressor event. This variable is a dichotomy that varies between an event not changing the system and one changing the system. It is being labeled in the present context as a stressor event, and the idea in Hill's model that relates stressor events and the amount of crisis is stated in the first proposition.

PROPOSITION 10.1:   A stressor event in a family social system influences the amount of crisis in the system, and this is a positive relationship.

The major contribution of Hill's *A, B, C, X* formulation is that it identifies two variables that influence the relationship in proposition 10.1. The *B* factor is what Hill refers to as the crisis-meeting resources of the family. Hansen (1965) later developed a theoretical model in which he used the term vulnerability to label what seems to be the same conceptual phenomenon. Neither of these theorists define this variable, but it apparently denotes variation in a family's ability to prevent a stressor event of change in a family social system from creating some crisis or disruptiveness in the system. It is apparently a continuous variable.

PROPOSITION 10.2:   When a stressor event occurs, the vulnerability to stress influences the amount of influence the stressor event has on the amount of crisis and this is a positive relationship.

The third major independent variable in the A, B, C, X formulation is the definition the family makes of the event. Unfortunately, this concept is also not defined, and there is no explanation of how it varies. It is therefore necessary to infer from the context of the literature just what it is that is varying. Hill (1949) differentiates between three types of definitions and then explains that his model deals with only one of these. He points out that definitions formulated by an impartial observer, those formulated by a community, and those made by the family are very different types of definitions; and he suggests that the subjective definitions are the ones he is dealing with in his theoretical model. This does not identify just what it is about these definitions that is varying, but the context of his monograph report seems to indicate that the main difference is probably whether the family defines the change in the system as easy or difficult. If this is a correct analysis of what is varying in this variable, the best label for this phenomenon is probably the subjective definition of the severity of the change. It may be that Hill was referring to other aspects than the seriousness of the event, but it seems fairly clear that this is at least one type of definition he was identifying.

The theoretical idea that deals with the definition of the severity of changes is that the definition makes a difference in the amount of crisis. It is impossible, however, to tell whether the definition of the severity of the change (*a*) influences the amount of crisis directly, (*b*) influences the amount of crisis indirectly by influencing the family's vulnerability to stress, or (*c*) is just one of many specific types of resources that make up the more inclusive phenomenon of the family's vulnerability to stress. It is suggested here that the second of these three alternatives is probably the most defensible, and hence the balance of this reformulation will use this idea.

PROPOSITION 10.3:   The definition a family makes of the severity of changes in the family social system influences the family's vulnerability to stress and this is a positive, monotonic relationship.

This idea has a long tradition in social psychology. The statement that "if something is perceived as real it is real in its consequences," and the "self-fulfilling prophecy" both seem to be more abstract statements of the idea summarized in proposition 10.3.

There is one additional idea in Hill's original formulation that was not included in later statements of the model. What he termed the "hardships of the event" (1949:41) are also involved in determining whether or not a crisis occurs. Hill (1949) operationalized this variable by counting the number of changes that were required, so one way to label this variable is the *amount of change* in the system. The way this variable probably fits into the present model is by influencing the amount of crisis that is caused by stressor events in the system, and if this is the case, a further proposition can be stated.

PROPOSITION 10.4:   The amount of change that occurs when a stressor event occurs in the family social system influences the amount of crisis that results from the event and this is a positive relationship.

The theoretical ideas in the *A, B, C, X* formulation are summarized in Figure 10.1. This figure attempts to show that a stressor event influences the amount of crisis. The amount of change in the system and the family's vulnerability to stress influence this relationship, and the definition the family makes of the seriousness of the change influences the vulnerability to stress.

Hansen (1965) published a formulation about how several other factors influence the vulnerability families have to stress. In addition, he in-

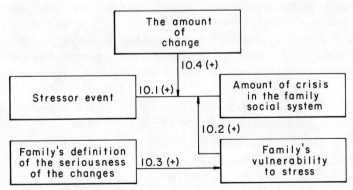

Figure 10.1   The A-B-C-X model.

troduced a variable that he referred to as the *regenerative power* of families, and he developed some propositions about how this variable is influenced. Hansen suggested that difference in "influence" has an effect on both vulnerability to stress and regenerative power. He makes a distinction in the way that individuals influence the action of others by differentiating between "personal" and "positional" influence:

> The distinction arises from the insight that an individual tends to develop both a personal relationship, or the relation of ego to alter as individuals, and a positional relationship or the relation of ego to alter as status or position holders in a group. That is, there are two kinds of cohesiveness in a group: the first involves the influence members have on one another because of their personal relationship; the second involves the influence they have on one another because of their position in the group structure (1965:203).

Hansen argues that these two types of influence are separate variables and that each varies in amount. He does not explicitly state that they are continuous variables, but the context seems to indicate that even though he dichotomizes them in stating his hypothesis, he views them as continuous variables. His major dependent variables are family vulnerability to stress and regenerate power. Neither of these variables were defined by Hansen, but vulnerability to stress was defined in this chapter as variation in a family's ability to prevent a stressor event or change in a family social system from creating some crisis or disruptiveness in the system. Regenerative power apparently denotes variation in the ability of the family to recover from a crisis. It seems to be a continuous variable varying between low and high power.

Hansen uses the term "proposition" in his paper, but his propositions are definitional statements that are used to identify several characteristics of the two variables of positional influence and personal influence. He does not summarize his theoretical ideas with the type of propositions that identify relationship between variables. It seems possible, however, to translate his ideas into propositional statements, and the following four propositions are an attempt to do this.

PROPOSITION 10.5: The amount of positional influence in a social system influences the vulnerability of families to stress and this is an inverse relationship.

PROPOSITION 10.6: The amount of positional influence in a social system influences the regenerative power and this is an inverse relationship.

PROPOSITION 10.7: The amount of personal influence in a social system influences the vulnerability of families to stress and this is a positive relationship.

PROPOSITION 10.8: The amount of personal influence in a social system influences the regenerative power and this is a positive relationship.

Hansen does not speculate on the nature of the individual relationships in these propositions other than to specify their direction. There does, however, seem to be an indication that he believes that more influence is exerted in propositions 10.5 and 10.8 than in the other two. In other words, positional influence probably makes slightly more difference in vulnerability and personal influence makes slightly more difference in regenerative power. This is diagrammed in Figure 10.2.

		Personal influence	
		Low	High
Positional influence	High	Lowest disruption Lowest regenerative power	Low disruption High regenerative power
	Low	High disruption Low regenerative	Highest disruption Highest regenerative power

Figure 10.2   The interaction of personal and positional influence in their relationship with vulnerability and regenerative power.

Hansen also attempts to integrate his formulation with some of the theoretical ideas that were developed in earlier research. He suggests that the type of stress, the type of reaction of the larger community, the externalization of blame, and the severity of the stress are also important variables. He seems to view the severity of stress as the amount of change that occurs in the family social system and seems to argue for the same relationship that was asserted in proposition 10.4. It is also possible to identify a proposition about the externalization of blame and family vulnerability. Externalization of blame is apparently a dichotomous variable denoting variation in whether the blame or responsibility for a stressor event is placed on a family member or on an external source.

PROPOSITION 10.9:   The externalization of blame for changes in the family social system influences the vulnerability of the family to stress and this is an inverse relationship.

Hansen does not speculate on the nature of other aspects of this relationship, and the rest of this part of his model is not as clear as the earlier parts of his theory. This results in it being difficult to know just what relationships he proposes between the type of stress and the type of reaction of the community and other variables. It is possible to integrate these last propositions with the ideas in the A, B, C, X model and diagram the entire formulation (Figure 10.3).

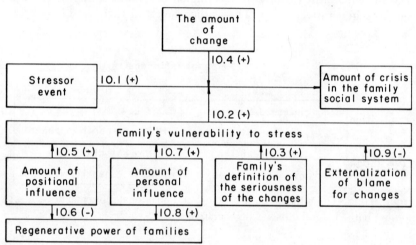

Figure 10.3   Nine propositions on families under stress.

Level of Reorganization

One of the major goals in the research on families in stress has been to identify factors that are related to whether or not the families recover from the disruptive effects of stress. Unfortunately, however, the dependent variable in this research is unclear. It has had a number of different labels such as type of adjustment (Cavan and Ranck, 1938), level of adjustment (Hill, 1949:74 ff), recovery from the crisis (Dyer, 1963:210), and level of reorganization (Hansen and Hill, 1964), but it has never been carefully defined. The context of its use in the literature, however, seems to indicate that it denotes variation whether or not the family social system is able to recover from the disruptiveness that results from a stressor event. If the system is able to recover, this apparently means that it returns to a routine pattern of operation. This does not seem to imply that the recovery eliminates such things as disorganization, change in the system, or inefficiency. It merely means that the system resumes its typical, routine level of operation after having to cope with an unusual change. If the system does not recover, this means that the system is not able to eliminate the disruptiveness introduced by the stressor event.

The most extensively used label for this dependent variable, introduced by Koos (1946), is the *level of reorganization*. This term seems acceptable if it does not eliminate the connotation that when a family social system is highly organized it is in many ways flexible, changing, inefficient, and so on. It would probably be more defensible to use a term such as level of recovery, but since the other term has been so extensively used in the literature, it is used here.

There is another complication in the literature that should be resolved before the propositions relating variables to the level of reorganization are identified. This is that most of the literature tests for a relationship between the level of reorganization and various specific factors such as amount of adaptability, integration, or affection. However, the variable Hansen (1965) refers to as regenerative power complicates these relationships. There are two different and incompatible ways that a theoretical model can be built by using both the specific factors that have been studied empirically and Hansen's regenerative power. One of the ways is to view the specific factors as variables that influence the regenerative power of families and then postulate that the regenerative power influences the level of reorganization. The other method is to view the specific factors as components of regenerative power. If the second method is used, this means that the idea that regenerative power influences the level of recovery is a more abstract proposition, and the propositions that relate the specific factors to level of recovery are more specific deductions from the general propositions.

There are unfortunately no clear-cut rules in theory building that provide a basis for making a choice between these two alternatives. In the present project, it was decided that the best alternative would be to view the specific factors as influential variables rather than as components of regenerative power. The theoretical model that is thus proposed is that the phenomenon Hansen (1965) has termed the regenerative power of families influences the level of reorganization and the various intrafamilial factors that have been found to be related to level of reorganization influence the regenerative power of families. If this is the case, the following proposition should be identified.

PROPOSITION 10.10:   The regenerative power of families influences the level of reorganization after a period of crisis and this is a positive relationship.

Factors Influencing Regenerative Power

Integration and Adaptability

Angell (1936) made the first systematic analysis of factors that were related to the ability of families to recover from crisis. His study dealt with the ability of families to recover from the disruption introduced by the economic depression of the 1930s and he found family integration and adaptability to be two important variables. He defined family integration as the "bonds of coherence and unity running through family life, of which common interests, affection, and a sense of economic interdependence are perhaps the most prominent." Hill later pointed out that this factor "is, in effect, adequacy-inadequacy of family organization" (1965:144). It is apparently variation in the degree to which a family is harmoniously well organized, and it seems to be viewed as a continuous variable. Family adaptability is also a continuous variable that apparently denotes variation in the ability of a family to change its structure or way of operating with little psychic or organizational discomfort. The ideas in Angell's research seem to identify the two following propositions.

PROPOSITION 10.11:   Family intergration influences regenerative power and this is a positive relationship.

PROPOSITION 10.12:   Family adaptability influences regenerative power and this is a positive relationship.

There is some basis for making inferences about the amount of influence in these two proposotions. Waller and Hill report that in an "unpublished restudy of the cases in Angell's study in 1942–1945 by the Social Science Research Council Committee on Appraisal of Research, the factor of adaptability was shown to be much the more important of the two" (1951:461). It is premature to speculate about how much more influential adaptability is, but this does give an indication about relative differences in influence.

It should also be pointed out that Angell (1936) was not just interested in factors that were related to the family's ability to recover from the disruptive effects of stress. He was also interested in identifying factors that would assist families in avoiding the panic of a severe crisis in the stressful situation. He did not differentiate between the avoidance and the recovery variables as clearly as Hansen (1965) did later, but Angell's analysis of his data was very clearly an attempt to deal with both phenomena. His findings suggest that in addition to adaptability and integration being useful in recovering from a crisis, they also seem to be important in preventing stress from creating crisis. This leads to two additional propositions.

PROPOSITION 10.13: The amount of family integration influences the vulnerability to stress and this is an inverse relationship.

PROPOSITION 10.14: The amount of family adaptability influences the vulnerability to stress and this is an inverse relationship.

Hansen and Hill also suggest that the adaptability variable differs in its impact on vulnerability according to the severity of the stressor. They suggest that low adaptability may "isolate the family from small stresses" (1964:814). If this is true, a contingent proposition could be stated identifying this type of interaction. This speculation has not, however, been worked through sufficiently well that a proposition is identified here.

There are empirical data that argue for the validity of proposition 10.13. Koos (1946) and Hill (1949:317) both found that when the amount of "hardships" in the crisis event were held constant, those families who were less well "organized" tended to have more severe crises. Hill then tended to classify these families as more crisis-prone than other families. In a sense, Hill's crisis-proneness is another label for what has been conceptualized as family vulnerability to stress. Those families that have low vulnerability tend to be less prone to have crises when stressful changes occur, and those families with more vulnerability tend to be more crisis-prone.

Hill's Reviews of Factors
Influencing Crisis Recovery

Hill has periodically reviewed the research in this area and attempted to revise and update a list of factors that have been found to be related to the ability of families to recover from crisis. He initially reviewed the literature in his study of war separation and reunion (Hill, 1949) and then again in his revision of Waller's monograph (Waller and Hill, 1951). His last review was with Hansen in the *Handbook of Marriage and the Family* (Hansen and Hill, 1964). His analysis includes several variables that have already been dealt with in the present chapter—severity of the event, family's definition of the situation, externalization of blame for the stressful event, adaptability and integration. His analysis also includes a number of other variables such as the suddenness of the event, individuated versus kinship type of community, affectional relations among family members, marital adjustment, family council type of control in decision making, participation of the wife in roles outside the home, and previous successful experience with similar types of stress. The role of each of these variables seems to deserve individual analysis.

Suddenness of the Event: Hansen and Hill (1964:794–795) argue that the more sudden or unanticipated a stressor event is, the greater the disruptiveness that will result. The conceptual phenomenon they seem to be most concerned with is not whether the change itself occurs in a short period of time, but rather whether it is anticipated for some time before it occurs. If it is anticipated for a sufficiently long period of time, then apparently preparations are usually made and there is less disruption. The variable involved seems to be the *amount of time changes are anticipated*. It can vary between no period of anticipation to long periods of anticipation.

PROPOSITION 10.15:   The amount of time stressful events are anticipated influences the vulnerability to stress and this is an inverse relationship.

Individuated Versus Kinship Type of Community: Hill and Hansen (1962) developed a typology of types of communities. They created two ideal types, labeled kinship-oriented and individual-oriented communities:

> The distinction rests on the networks of relationships that connect kin to one another. In the kinship community there is a predominance of tightly meshed families with little activity between neighbors. In the individual community, loosely knit, nuclear families predominate, and there is a great deal of activity between neighbors and friends. Many rural and countain villages are of the first type, and most urban, industrial communities of the second (1962:200–201).

Later research and conceptual developments have refined this type of conceptualization, and it is now probably defensible to use conceptual revisions such as Winch's (1968) to replace this typology. Winch's (1968) conceptualization of what he terms *extended familism,* for example, seems to conceptualize the main ideas in Hill and Hansen's typology. He views extended familism as a composite variable denoting variation in the interaction, intensity, extensity, and functionality of the kinship system. *Extensity* deals with the number of kin in close proximity. *Intensity* has to do with how closely the kin are related. *Interaction* denotes variation in the amount of activity engaged in with the kin, and *functionality* refers to the instrumental value of the interaction such as receiving goods and services. Winch's continuous variable has a number of advantages over Hill and Hansen's typology. It does not have the connotation that urban areas have low extended familism. It has been defensibly operationalized, and when continuous variables are used rather than typologies that have only two types much more can be learned about the nature of relationships.

Hill and Hansen's thesis is that low extended familism tends to better prepare families "for disaster and short-term recovery than does the kinship community (high extended familism)." But in meeting the long-term effects of disaster, it is probable that the individuated (low extended familism) community loses its advantage (1962:202). What Hill and Hansen thus seem to be proposing is that the length of time of the disruption influences the effect the extended familism has on the regenerative power of families. When the stress is for a short period there is a negative relationship between extended familism and regenerative power, and when there is a long period of disruption there is positive relationship.

PROPOSITION 10.16:   The amount of extended familism influences the regenerative power of families.

PROPOSITION 10.17:   The length of time a family system experiences disruption influences the relationship in proposition 10.16, which asserts that extended familism influences the regenerative power of families, and this is a quadratic relationship in which variation in short periods of time are inversely related and variation in long periods are positively related to the regenerative power.

Affectional Patterns: Hill argues that "affectional relations among family members" are related to what is conceptualized in the present chapter as the level of recovery from crisis (1958:148). This variable was operationalized in his study of war crisis (Hill, 1949) as the presence or absence of affectional cliques. Hill found in his study that the absence of cliques was related to the quality of adjustment to the war separation and reunion. The independent variable in this idea is thus apparently the amount of *similarity of sentiment* in a family. This then is a fairly similar sentiment felt toward all members of the family. This is a condition of high similarity, and the more differences there are between family members in their sentiment toward others, the greater is the clique formation and the less the similarity.

PROPOSITION 10.18:   The amount of similarity of sentiment in a family influences the regenerative power of families and this is a positive relationship.

Marital Adjustment: One of the other variables Hill identifies in his reviews as being important is marital adjustment. This variable was defined earlier in this book in apparently the same way Hill uses it. It is a multidimensional variable designed to denote variation in overall adjustment in marriage. It includes specific dimensions such as consensus, satisfaction, happiness, and stability, and it is a continuous variable. The data Hill uses in his reviews seems to come primarily from Angell (1936), Cavan and Ranck (1938), Koos (1946), and Hill (1949); these data indicate there is a positive relationship between marital adjustment and satisfactory crisis recovery.

In the context of the present formulation, this relationship seems to be an indirect relationship, and any influence that marital adjustment has on the level of recovery from crises probably is exerted through influencing the regenerative power of families. Thus a new proposition can be stated.

PROPOSITION 10.19:   The amount of marital adjustment influences the regenerative power of families and this is a positive relationship.

Power: The empirical research has investigated whether or not different types of power structure are related to recovery from crises. Unfortunately, however, there is considerable ambiguity in the conceptualization of power in this research and in the findings. In Hill's case study analysis of the subjects in his crisis study he found that what he refers to as "family council type of family control" was related to adequacy of adjustment of crises (1949:325). This relationship did not appear in his statistical analysis. It is possible, however, that if some conceptual refinements are made in his analyses, the inconsistencies in these empirical findings can be resolved.

Hill's independent variable in his statistical analyses is labeled the "type of family control," but he is obviously interested in only one narrow aspect of control. His operationalization of this variable is built around the differences between husband-dominant, equalitarian, and wife-dominant distributions of power. This indicates that he is conceptually dealing with the relative *amount of power*. Conceptually this seems to be the same phenomenon that Straus (1964) argues is such a pervading factor in understanding human interaction.

Hill's independent variable in his case study analysis (1949:215–216, 223–226) seems to be conceptually somewhat different from the amount of power. It seems to have amount of power as one of its dimensions, but it also takes into account variation in the way the power is implemented. Hill differentiates, for example, between whether authority is imposed (1949:216) or not, and whether or not there is consultation in the process of making decisions. His discussion of just what it is that seems to be significantly different in the adjustment to crises suggests that it may be that *"the consultive process* in the family is more important than the seat of ultimate authority" (1949:224; italics his). This indicates that conceptually differentiating between the amount of power and the amount of consultation in decision making might reconcile the conflicting findings in his study. The data seem to indicate that the relative amount of power of individuals is not related to regenerative power, but that the amount of consultation is. If it is defensible to speculate that the amount of consultation actually has an influence on other variables rather than just covarying with them, the two following propositions in this analysis seem to be justified.

PROPOSITION 10.20:   The amount of relative power of spouses is not related to the regenerative power of families.

PROPOSITION 10.21:   The amount of consultation in decision making influences the regenerative power of families and this is a positive relationship.

Hill differentiates only between the presence and absence of a consultative process and hence does not view the independent variable in proposition 10.21 as a continuous variable. This means that there is no empirical basis for making assertions about the shape of this relationship. Intuitively, however, it seems that it would be a curvilinear relationship, as diagramed in Figure 10.4. It probably has much less if any influence when there is a large amount of consultation. In fact, it may be that excessive consultation might actually decrease the regenerative power.

Social Participation of Wives Outside the Home: Duvall (1945) found that the amount of social participation of wives outside the home was

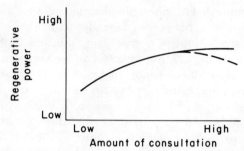

Figure 10.4   The relationship between amount of consultation and regenerative power.

related to satisfactory adjustment to war separation. Hill (1949:205) found this same factor to be positively related to both war separation and reunion crises. Rose (1955) and Deutscher (1962) also found participation in external roles to be positively related to mothers' ability to cope with the stress of launching their children. If this independent variable is defined as the amount of activity spent by wives in nonwife-mother roles, these findings seem to justify one proposition.

PROPOSITION 10.22:   The amount of social activity of wives outside the home is related to the regenerative power of families and this is a positive relationship.

There is no empirical basis for making assertions about the shape of this relationship. There is some empirical evidence in the studies referred to that this is a valid proposition, but there is also one negative finding. Hill (1949:146) found a nonsignificant negative relationship between maternal employment and crisis-adjustment in his study of war separation and reunion.

Previous Successful Experience with Stress: Hill (1949) found that previous successful experience with a similar crisis was related to what has been conceptualized in this chapter as the level of recovery. This independent variable is probably valuable for predictive purposes, but it seems that its only value for theory is that it probably is an effective operationalization of the amount of anticipatory socialization for coping with changes in the family social system. The previous experience would provide an opportunity to develop skills and insights that would help cope with later changes. The conceptual phenomenon of anticipatory socialization was defined earlier as the process of learning norms of a role before being in a social situation where it is appropriate to actually behave in the role. If this variable is viewed as the important theoretical variable in Hill's idea that previous experience is related to adjustment to crises, it seems defensible to suggest the two following propositions.

PROPOSITION 10.23: The amount of anticipatory socialization for changes in the family social system influences the vulnerability of families and this is an inverse relationship.

PROPOSITION 10.24: The amount of anticipatory socialization for changes in the family social system influences the regenerative power of families and this is a positive relationship.

If Hill's variable of previous experience with crises can be viewed as operationalization of the amount of anticipatory socialization for changes, his finding that it is related to the level of recovery can be viewed as empirical support for proposition 10.24.

An attempt is made in Figure 10.5 to diagram the various relationships identified in this chapter. As can be seen in the diagram, this chapter is essentially an analysis of the factors that influence family vulnerability to stress and regenerative power, and these two variables are important because they play such an important role (*a*) in determining whether a family will experience a crisis when they encounter changes in the system and (*b*) in determining how adequately the family will be able to recover from the crisis situation.

Legitimacy of Power

One other variable may be relevant in understanding several aspects of family crises. This is the legitimacy of the power structure. Komarovsky (1940) found that the legitimacy of the power structure influenced the amount of change that a stressful event produced in the power structure. This can be stated in a proposition as follows.

PROPOSITION 10.25: The legitimacy of the power structure in a family influences the amount of change in the power structure that occurs in family crises and this is an inverse relationship.

Komarovsky operationalized the legitimacy of the power by differentiating between primary authority, instrumental authority, and a mixture

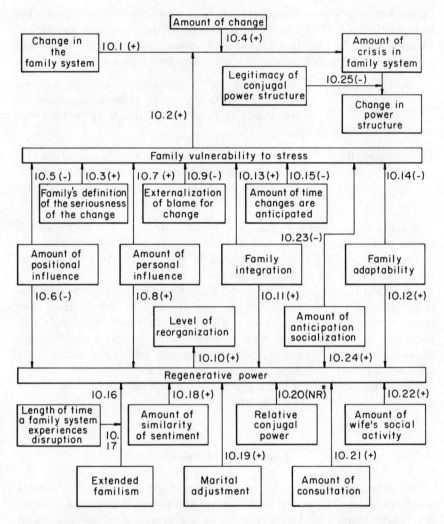

*No relationship thought to exist.

Figure 10.5 Propositions about families under stress. (NR indicates no relationship is thought to exist.)

216

of the two. Primary authority is legitimate in terms of either personal or positional factors, and instrumental power, as she defined the term, is power based on fear or coercion. She found that the most change in power occurred in the power structure with the instrumental type of power and an intermediate amount of change occurred in those families with a mixture of primary and instrumental power. This finding is consistent with the assertion in proposition 10.25 that a relationship exists between these two variables and it thus provides some empirical support. In addition, these findings provide evidence of some monotonicity in this relationship. Since these data were the data that led to the initial formulation of the idea, however, these findings should not be viewed as conclusive empirical proof of the validity of the proposition.

Summary

This chapter has analyzed a number of propositions about family crises. The entire model is summarized in Figure 10.5, and it is a fairly abstract theory. The model can be extended in a number of different ways. One method would be to test the propositions in different crises to see if additional contingent variables that influence the impact of variables can be identified, and to see if some of the propositions are not valid for some crises. This type of additional theoretical and empirical work should be facilitated by the modifications made in this chapter.

CHAPTER 11

THE FAMILY LIFE CYCLE

One of the recent developments in family research has been the effort by Hill and several others to study the family from a developmental point of view (Hill and Hansen, 1960; Hill and Rodgers, 1964). Their efforts have been unique in that their strategy of theory building differs from the strategies used by most theorists. The usual strategy has been to create an elaborate conceptual apparatus only as a by-product of theoretical ideas, but the developmental theorists reversed this procedure. They developed the conceptual framework first with the hope that these concepts would facilitate the generation of theory.

At the present time the theoretical ideas that have been generated in the developmental approach have been minimal, and only a small number of the concepts in this framework have been used in these theoretical ideas. There have, however, been several propositions explicated, and they deserve analysis. This chapter is an attempt to identify and rework these theoretical ideas. The first section of the chapter is an analysis of the family life cycle as a variable, and the second section is an analysis of some of the ways that theorists have suggested that variation in the life cycle is related to or influences other variables.

The Family Life Cycle as a Variable

The family life cycle is a variable that identifies the changes that occur as a result of routinely expected variation in the size of families and in the roles of family members. Its variation is usually viewed as progression through a series of stages or life cycle categories, but there are a number of different ways of dividing the cycle into these sets of stages or categories. For example, some have divided the cycle into two categories such as the expanding and contracting stages (Duvall, 1967:6). Others, including Sorokin et al. (1931), have used a four-stage system, and Rodgers (1962) has divided the life cycle into 24 stages. Probably the most extensively used system of life-cycle stages was formulated by Duvall (1967) in her eight-stage paradigm. Her categories are (1) beginning families, which are married couples before children are born, (2) child-bearing families with the oldest child between birth and 30 months, (3) families with preschool children when the oldest child is 2½ to 6 years of age, (4) families where the oldest child is between 6 and 12 years, (5) families in which the oldest child is in the teens, (6) families as launching centers while the children are leaving their family of orientations, (7) families in the middle years between the launching period and retirement, and (8) aging families from retirement to death.

It is likely that there are more differences in family size and processes between some of these stages than others. For example, there is no change in size and little change in roles as families move from Duvall's stage 3 to stage 4. On the other hand, there is a major change in size and roles as families enter stage 2. This suggests that some of Duvall's distinctions between stages are probably more crucial than others. The Duvall system seems to be a useful compromise between brevity and unnecessary detail, and it was found by Rodgers (1962) to be as efficient as his more intricate 24-stage system in identifying a number of changes in families. Thus Duvall's stages will be used to conceptualize most of the propositions in this chapter.

It has not yet been proved that the family life cycle will turn out to be a very useful concept in deductive theories. It is at best a conglomeration of several specific variables. It varies partly due to changes in the size of families, partly due to the age composition of them, and partly due to changes in social roles such as the occupational status of the members of the family. Yet it does not include all of the variation in any of these variables. For example, variation in size from two to three in the family is an important determinant of movement from one stage to another at the birth of the first child, but variation above three or four members is unimportant in terms of variation in the family life cycle. Some changes in occupational status such as retirement make a difference, but many other changes in occupational status such as promotions or whether the wife is employed make no difference. It is also difficult to define this variable. No definitions have been found in the literature and the best developed in the present project is that the family life cycle is variation that is routinely expected over time in the size, age, composition, and social roles in a family of procreation. This is a complex definition, and it lacks clarity and precision.

One conceptual innovation may replace the life cycle variable. Future research may demonstrate that theorizing about the individual components of the life cycle variable will be more useful. Identification of variables such as the size of families, length of time married, and occupational status, separately may explain all of the phenomena that we are now attempting to explain with the omnibus concept of family life cycle. This possibility, however, is one that remains to be seen because at the present neophyte stage of theory building the family life cycle variable seems to be useful. In fact, both Lansing and Kish (1957) and Rodgers (1962) found the life cycle variable to be more useful in predicting some economic aspects of family processes than single variables such as the age of the head of the household. The life cycle variable is an obscure conceptualization that is difficult to define, but it is probably appropriate for the very rudimentary theories being developed with it.

Role Segregation

Bott's interviews with English couples provided a basis for concluding that systematic variation occurs over the life cycle in role segregation:

> The research couples make it clear that there had been important changes in their degree of conjugal segregation during their married life. In the first phase, before they had children, all couples had had far more joint activities, especially in the form of shared recreation outside the home. After their children were born the activities of all couples had become more sharply differentiated and they had to cut down on joint external recreation. Data from the group discussions with wives in the third phase, when the children were adolescent and leaving home, suggest that most husbands and wives do not return to the extensive joint organization of the first phase even when the necessity for differentiation produced by the presence of young children is no longer so great (1957:54).

This independent variable of role segregation can be defined as variation in the degree to which spouses perform household tasks jointly or separately. It should probably be viewed as a continuous variable varying in amount. Data from studies by Blood and Wolfe (1960) and later Hill (1965) also found that role segregation increased over the life cycle, and they provide a basis for speculating that the relationship in the relevant proposition is monotonic and perhaps even linear.

PROPOSITION 11.1:   The family life cycle influences the amount of marital role segregation and this is a positive, linear relationship.

The three studies that have data on this subject used different sampling procedures and data gathering methods. Bott's study consisted of extensive participant observation and interviewing with a small group of families. Blood and Wolfe's data came from interviews with about 800 wives who had been randomly selected from an urban population, and Hill's data came from interviewing a sample consisting of families where three generations could be contacted. Since there are no data that have failed to find this relationship or have found conflicting findings, this provides substantial evidence that the relationship asserted in this proposition tends to occur.

Intergenerational Aid

Hill's (1965) three-generation study provides a basis for theorizing about how the family life cycle influences the direction of aid giving in intergenerational groups. This dependent variable can be conceptualized as varying in degrees from being high receivers of aid, to a balance of giving and receiving, and to a condition of being high givers of aid. His data indicate that there are some differences according to the specific type of aid that is given, but that generally in the early years there is a relatively balanced reciprocity in the relationship. In the middle years there is a patronlike giving more than receiving, and then in the aging years there is more receiving than giving. If these differences are genuinely influenced by variation in the family life cycle, this relationship can be stated in the following proposition. It is also diagramed in Figure 11.1.

PROPOSITION 11.2: The family life cycle influences the aid given to kinship groups and this is a curvilinear relationship.

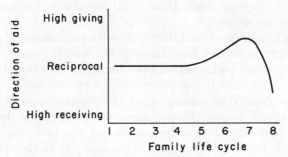

Figure 11.1 The relationship between family life cycle and direction of aid to kinship groups.

Task Participation

There is some evidence that variation in the family life cycle may be related to the involvement of the spouses in household tasks. This phenomenon of task participation is closely related to role segregation but is different in an important way. Role segregation refers to whether spouses engage in tasks separately or together. It denotes specialization. Task performance identifies variation in what Blood and Wolfe refer to as "the amount of work done at home by each partner" (1960:49), and this amount can be either high or low with high segregation or low segregation.

The phenomenon of task performance can vary in two different ways. There can be variation in the *relative task participation* of the two spouses or in the absolute *amount of task participation*. Relative task participation identifies variation in the equality of the task participation of spouses. It varies continuously from the one extreme of having the wife do all the household tasks to the other extreme of the husband doing all of the tasks. The amount of participation can be viewed as the amount of activity in household tasks. It has been operationalized in terms of the number of tasks performed (Blood and Wolfe, 1960; Zelditch, 1955) and in the number of hours an individual devotes to these tasks.

These two variables are identical if there are no changes in the total amount of work that has to be done, but if the amount of work needed to maintain families varies, it is important to distinguish between these two different types of variation. For example, it is possible that when the first child is born in a family the total number of tasks increases, and since the wife usually does most of them, the husband's relative task performance may decrease while there is an increase in the amount of his task performance.

No research has been found that deals with the amount of task performance, but several studies have investigated whether there are changes in the relative task participation over the life cycle. Blood and Wolfe (1960:71) found a curvilinear relationship with the wife's relative task participation slightly increasing up to the preadolescent stage and remaining steady thereafter. They suggest, however, that if the phenomenon of task performance is to be understood, the most important variable is not the family life cycle but the availability of the spouses.

Blood and Wolfe never define this phenomenon of spouse availability, but from the context of their discussion they seem to be denoting the degree to which a spouse is readily accessible or at hand to perform household tasks. It is apparently a continuous variable ranging from being highly unavailable to being highly available. Note, however, that the number of hours an individual is available may not vary directly as a result of variation in life cycle stages. Rather, it seems that there are several intervening variables that should be identified. Thus a more comprehensive theoretical model is proposed here.

The major variables that are included in this more comprehensive model are the family life cycle, the amount of task participation that is normatively prescribed, role strain, relative task performance, the amount of activity that is normatively prescribed in roles other than household tasks, and the freedom to leave these other roles. What is proposed is that variation in the family life cycle influences the amount of task participation that is normatively prescribed in each person's life. These normative prescriptions positively influence role strain, and role strain inversely influences the relative task participation of spouses. The amount of activity that is normatively prescribed in other roles also positively influences role strain. In addition, the freedom to leave the other roles inversely influences the amount of activity prescribed in these other roles.

Since this theoretical model is relatively complex, before the various propositions are identified and examined, it is useful to diagram these relationships as Figure 11.2. The numbers that are used to identify the relationships are the proposition numbers that are identified in the next few pages.

Before these ideas are stated in formal propositions it is necessary to define the concepts and identify how the variables vary. The family life

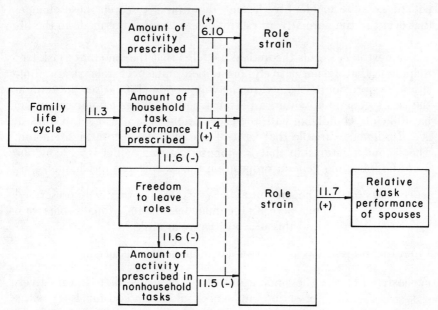

Figure 11.2 The indirect relationship between family life cycle and relative task participation.

cycle was defined earlier. The amount of task participation that is normatively prescribed identifies variation in the extent to which there are normative definitions that state that a person occupying a certain social position should or ought to do certain household tasks. It is a continuous variable that denotes variation in that amount of task participation that is prescribed. Proposition 11.3 indicates the relationship between the life cycle and these prescriptions.

PROPOSITION 11.3:   Changes in the family life cycle influence the amount of task participation that is normatively prescribed for social positions in the family.

The idea in this proposition does not mean that changes in the life cycle invent or destroy norms in a social group. Rather, what is asserted is that the norms that previously exist in a social group are relevant for members of the family social system at some stages of their life cycle and are not relevant at other times. They become operative or inoperative when certain stages are entered and exited.

The relationship in this proposition is sufficiently amorphous that it cannot be easily described. The various changes in life cycle probably have different effects on different norms, and it is only when specific tasks such as changing diapers or mowing the lawn are identified that it will be possible to identify through descriptive research those changes that occur in the normative prescriptions as changes are made in the life cycle.

The next idea in this theoretical model is that the amount of task participation that is normatively prescribed influences role strain. Role strain was previously defined in the way Goode (1960) uses the term as the stress generated within a person when he either cannot comply or has difficulty complying with the expectations of a role or set of roles. It is a continuous variable that varies from an absence to a high amount. The second relationship that is proposed in this model is a deduction from the following general proposition that was stated in Chapter 6.

PROPOSITION 6.10:   The amount of activity that is normatively prescribed in a person's life influences the individual's role strain and this is a positive relationship.

From this proposition another proposition can be deduced.

PROPOSITION 11.4:   The amount of task performance that is normatively prescribed influences role strain and this is a positive relationship.

This is undoubtedly a positive relationship, but there is little basis for speculating about other aspects of this relationship. It may be that it has the greatest influence in the high range of the independent variable, but this is only an intuitive guess.

The other variable that is theorized to influence role strain is the amount of activity that is normatively prescribed in other roles. This variable identifies variation in the extent to which normative definitions prescribe that an individual should or ought to engage in activities in roles other than household task participation. It is a continuous variable varying from none to a large amount of activity. This proposition is also a deduction from proposition 6.10.

PROPOSITION 11.5: The amount of activity that is normatively prescribed in nonhousehold task roles influences role strain and this is a positive relationship.

Another idea in this theory is that the freedom an individual has to terminate roles influences the amount of activity that is normatively prescribed for him. It seems reasonable that individuals in some situations would have considerable freedom to terminate roles, and that this freedom would not result in them decreasing their roles when they are not experiencing a large amount of role strain. However, when role strain is high it is expected that there would be a negative relationship between this particular type of freedom and the amount of prescribed activity. The independent variable in this formulation can be defined as variation in the ability a person has to terminate a role without experiencing high costs. It conceptually can vary between no freedom and complete freedom.

PROPOSITION 11.6: When role strain exists, the amount of freedom to terminate a role influences the amount of activity that is normatively prescribed and this is an inverse relationship.

The last proposition in this model identifies the relationship between role strain and relative task participation.

PROPOSITION 11.7: The amount of role strain a spouse experiences influences relative task participation and this is an inverse relationship.

This relationship is probably generally positive, but it also seems to be a cubic relationship. It seems likely that when role strain is either very high or very low it would have more influence on relative task performance than it would in its middle stages. The person who has very high

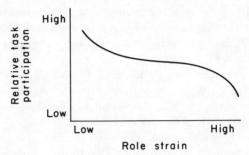

Figure 11.3   The relationship between role strain and relative task participation.

role strain would have more leverage in bargaining his way out of household tasks, and the person with very low strain would have the least. Goode (1960) argues that most people routinely experience considerable role strain in their lives, and if this is the case, then individuals in the middle stages of role strain would have fairly equal bargaining power. An attempt is made in Figure 11.3 to diagram this relationship.

This particular theoretical formulation turned out to be considerably more complex than was anticipated when the relationship between the family life cycle and task participation was initially analyzed. It may be, however, that this type of complexity is only the beginning if adequate theoretical models are to be developed with the family life cycle as the independent variable.

Conventionality in Task Performance

Hill's (1965) three-generation study provided some interesting data on how conventionality in task performance varies in different stages of the life cycle. Conventionality in task performance conceptualizes the degree to which there is deviation from the traditional pattern of division of labor in a culture. The data in this sample indicated that a positive, linear relationship exists between conventionality and progression through the life cycle, and also that radical departure from conventionality tends to occur more in the later stages of the life cycle. These findings can be stated as covariational propositions.

PROPOSITION 11.8:   The family life cycle is related to conventionality of task performance and this is a positive, linear relationship.

PROPOSITION 11.9:   The family life cycle is related to the amount of radical departure from conventional sex roles and this is a positive relationship.

It will be interesting to see if these relationships are also found in replicative research and in other cultural situations. The data from Hill's study identified certain behavior as conventional and certain other behavior as unconventional. If it is conventionality that is the crucial variable, then the validity of this proposition can only be known when it is tested in other cultures where different behaviors are the conventional and unconventional ways of defining roles.

Marital Stability

There is considerable evidence that the length of time married is related to the divorce rate. Kephart (1961:614–617) and The National Office of Vital Statistics (1957) have published data on the length of time between marriage and divorces, and a curvilinear relationship tends to occur. The peak in this curve seems to be in the second and third years of marriage. If the length of time married is viewed as an indicator of variation in the life cycle, this seems to justify the following assertion.

PROPOSITION 11.10:   The family life cycle is related to marital stability and this is a curvilinear relationship.

It is tempting to ponder the question of what it is about variation in the life cycle that is related to this phenomenon of marital stability, and there are a number of ideas in the literature that speculate about this. One idea that is almost a maxim in family sociology is that the presence of children in a family is a deterrent to divorce. Writers have suggested that a number of factors such as the investment the parents feel in the children, the sense of responsibility, religiosity, emotional ties that are strengthened with parenthood, social pressures, and beliefs that divorce would have adverse consequences for the children all operate to make this variable influence the likelihood of getting a divorce. These other variables are temporarily ignored in the present formulation, but the *presence of dependent children* is separately identified. This varies dichotomously between the categories of no children and children being present. This is a very prevalent idea in the literature.

PROPOSITION 11.11:   The presence of dependent children influences marital stability and this is a positive relationship.

It is difficult to know just how the last two propositions are related. It could be that proposition 11.11 is more abstract than proposition 11.10, and 11.10 can be deduced from 11.11. For example, it could be deduced that if proposition 11.11 is true, then since progress through the life cycle is partly a process of variation in the presence of children, a relationship can be expected between the presence of children and stability. However, if proposition 11.11 is used to deduce proposition 11.10, the relationship that would be expected is that the divorce rate would be high during the first few years, low during the next 15 or 20 years, and then higher again after children leave. In actual fact, the relationship is slightly different from this in that the rate stays high for a number of years after the first two years of marriage and it never increases after 15 or 20 years of marriage. On the other hand, the fact that a relatively sharp decrease does occur after the third year of marriage may be partly because of the validity of proposition 11.11, and it may be that other things such as interhabituation prevent an increase in instability after the children leave.

There are two other possible ways that propositions 11.10 and 11.11 might be related. It may be that they should be viewed as a chain sequence in which the family life cycle influences the presence of children and the presence of children influences divorce. Or it may be that the presence of children is merely one aspect of variation in the life cycle and proposition 11.11 is just a specification of one particular part of the phenomenon involved in proposition 11.10. If this is the case, then only one of these propositions should be used and a proposition such as 11.11 may replace the more imprecise idea in proposition 11.10. These theoretical formulations are still sufficiently immature that this problem will need to be resolved by future research and theorizing.

Considerable data (Kephart, 1961) have been gathered on how the divorce rate varies according to the number of years married. Kephart's analysis indicated that the greatest instability occurs in the first 18 months of the marriage, and that there is a sharp decrease after this period. It would be valuable to have data on the nature of this decrease according to movement from stage 1 to stage 2 of the family life cycle, but no data are presently known that provide this. The data during stages 6 and 7, however, are not as supporting of proposition 11.11. There have been no data that indicate an increase in instability during this period. It is likely, however, that there need not be an increase for the proposition to be valid. It may be that the factors that influence marital stability change systematically over the life cycle, and that even though the rate does not change upward during stages 6 and 7, the actual reasons for divorce are consistent with proposition 11.11. This will need to wait for subsequent data that will ferret out the influential patterns suggested.

*Possible Normative Components in
the Effects of the Family Life Cycle on Stability*

Some recent changes in the United States seem to justify the statement of a proposition that has not been fully appreciated in the developmental literature. This has to do with a possible way that norms may influence the extent to which the presence of dependent children is a deterrent to divorce. Proposition 4.1 asserted that normative definitions influence the behavior of individuals so the behavior tends to conform to the normative definitions. If this proposition is true, it can be expected that if cultural norms define the presence of children as a reason to try to avoid divorce, these norms will influence the behavior of people considering getting a divorce. This can be stated as a proposition.

PROPOSITION 11.12: The amount that normative definitions prescribe that the presence of children should be a deterrent to divorce influences the amount of influence in proposition 11.11, which states that the presence of children influences marital stability, and this is a positive relationship.

This proposition was formulated as a separate proposition resulting from a combination of events in the United States. On the basis of a relatively informal analysis of changes in norms, it seems that during the 1950s and 1960s a shift occurred in the norms about divorcing when children were in the home. Before this period there was a rather pervasive belief that divorce had important detrimental effects on children. A great deal of literature suggested that divorce contributed to delinquency, personality problems of children, and so on, and this was widely read during the first half of the twentieth century. The major change that occurred during these two decades was that it became a common belief that it was not divorce itself but rather the psychological and emotional trauma that had the important detrimental effects on children. Several empirical studies published findings to this effect (Nye, 1957; Landis, 1963), and these have been widely quoted. The normative definition changed to prescribing that families should do their best to provide adequate homes, but if this is not possible, then keeping the couple intact can result in more harm to everyone concerned than divorcing. This is especially the case if children are in the home; they will be the victims of the unhappy, unbroken home.

If this analysis of normative change is correct and if it is combined with the changes during this same period in the proportion of divorces that have children involved, this seems to make a case for concomitant variation between the variables in proposition 11.12. The census data for 1959 indicate that the proportion of divorces where there were children involved rose from 48.2% in 1953 to 59.6% in 1960. Moreover, the Vital Statistics Bulletin (1969) reports the number of children involved in divorce rose during the 1950s and 1960s. If proposition 11.12 is true and if the normative change did occur as is argued in this analysis, these changes are exactly what would be expected to occur.

It should be pointed out that this analysis of the normative change and the data indicating there was a change in the proportion of divorces that have children involved served as the basis for formulating proposition 11.12. This means that these data cannot be viewed as anything but a low level of evidence in support of the proposition. Additional evidence either for or against the proposition is needed.

Decision Making

Volume of Economic Plans and Activity

Hill's (1965) study of decision-making processes in three generations provided a basis for theorizing about how the family life cycle influences several aspects of family decision making. He found, for example, that the volume of economic planning and activity differed in the three generations. He gathered data on both the number of plans each family was making about economic activity and the number of actual acquisitions. He found an inverse linear relationship between both of these variables and progression through the life cycle. If these relationships constitute genuinely influential processes, then it is justifiable to state them as propositions.

PROPOSITION 11.13:   The family life cycle influences the volume of economic planning and this is an inverse, linear relationship.

PROPOSITION 11.14:   Variation in the family life cycle influences the volume of economic acquistitions and this is an inverse, linear relationship.

Hill's data deal with only three stages of the life cycle. His sample consisted of families in what could be termed early, middle, and late stages of the family life cycle, which means that the linearity suggested in this relationship is only germane to this abbreviated set of life cycle categories. The data from this one study are the only data that have been found that are relevant in assessing the validity of this proposition.

Length of Time Involved in Economic Plans

Hill (1965) found that the length of time involved in economic plans systematically varied over his three-generation sample. There was a linear relationship with the younger couples planning for the longest time period and the grandparent generation making plans that were projected over the shortest period. This relationship is stated in the following proposition.

PROPOSITION 11.15:   The family life cycle influences the length of time involved in economic plans and this is an inverse relationship.

Rationality in Planning

Hill (1965) developed a measure of rationality and gathered data on how the three generation groups differed in their degree of rationality. Apparently rationality is defined as the amount of careful, intellectual analysis of alternatives in making plans. It is a continuous variable ranging from low to high rationality. Again, the same type of linear relationship was found.

PROPOSITION 11.16:   The family life cycle influences the rationality used in economic planning and this is an inverse relationship.

Other Relationships

Hill (1965:118) suggests relationships between family life cycle and demands on income, value orientation, the content of plans, and in the degree of satisfaction with them. However, before propositions can be stated about these there needs to be more specification of the nature of these variables. It may also be possible to identify relationships between the family life cycle and such variables as where families live in cities, home ownership, or mobility. There are some data about these phenomena, but thus far no attempts have been made to analyze the data sufficiently thoroughly to identify propositions.

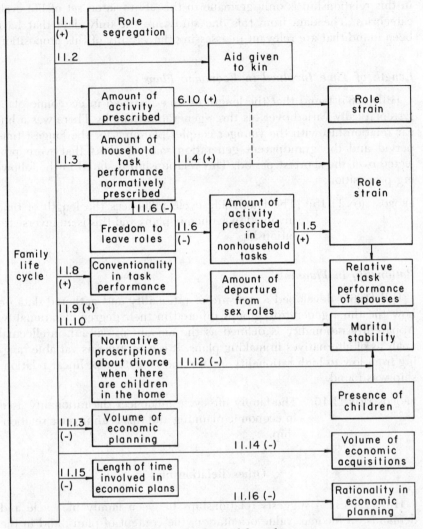

Figure 11.4 Propositions about the family life cycle.

Summary

There is some question about how useful the family life cycle variable is. It is a composite of several variables and hence is not precise. It may be better to separate it into component parts such as age, size, and occupational status, and to identify the relationships for each of these factors separately. It may, on the other hand, be a useful conceptualization at the present stage of theorizing, and we should not now try to be more conceptually precise in this area.

There is another problem with using the family life cycle as an explanatory independent variable. Many of the propositions that are identified are probably so indirect that they really provide little understanding. We might gain an advantage by attempting to specify the various influential processes between the influence that the family life cycle has and the dependent variables that are of greatest interest. Again, however, this could be a function of the beginning stage of these theoretical ideas, and this type of progress is slow. In sum, this conceptualization has severe limitations, but at the present stage of knowledge we have found no better alternatives.

CHAPTER 12

WIFE-MOTHER EMPLOYMENT

There are many different roles that an individual can occupy or not occupy while being a family member. For example, such roles as student, club member, sports fan, church member, and political activist are all optional activities. It seems almost axiomatic to point out that the particular combination of roles that an individual occupies and the unique way he elects to behave in these roles have an influence on many aspects of the family situation. Although few theories have attempted to identify how these role arrangements are systematically related to other familial variables, there has been considerable research on how one particular role is related to a number of other variables. This is whether the wife and/or mother is employed outside the home. There was a great deal of research in the late 1950s and early 1960s that focused on this issue, and the present chapter is an attempt to summarize and rework the theoretical ideas in this literature.

It is important that this variable of the employment of wives and mothers is viewed in the proper context. As Blood (1963) has pointed out, it is merely one of a number of roles that women can occupy in social systems that are external to the family. It is therefore likely that relationships between this role and other familial variables are highly similar to relationships between the number of other roles and family variables. The research, however, has seemed to give disproportionate emphasis to this particular extrafamilial role, neglecting relationships with a number of very similar roles such as community service worker, member of voluntary organizations, or student. One consequence of this emphasis is that the theoretical ideas in this literature are highly specific formulations that are limited to the relationships between this particular role and other familial phenomena. If these specific formulations can be integrated with existing theoretical propositions of a more general nature, they probably can be used as a basis for inducing some new propositions of a more general nature. This will provide a basis for speculating about how some of the other extrafamily roles are related to family variables.

One of the two main objectives in this chapter is to review empirical research and theoretical essays to try to identify how other variables operate either as contingent variables or as intervening variables in the relationships between employment variables and familial variables. The second objective is to attempt to identify theoretical formulations that suggest that employment variables have an influence on other family variables when in fact this variation is caused by different variables. In some of these cases it is suggested in this chapter that a third variable causes the employment variables to vary and the other dependent variable(s) to vary, which results in a covariation but not influential relationship between the employment variables and dependent variables. In other cases it suggested that a proposed relationship between the employment variables and a dependent variable just does not exist.

Employment Variables as Independent Variables

Virtually every reviewer (Stolz, 1960; Nye and Hoffman, 1963, Ch. 14, 20, 27) of the research on the employed wife-mother argues that one of the reasons that scientific knowledge has not advanced more in this area is because there are problems in conceptualizing the employment variables. Thus it seems imperative that this conceptualization be reviewed before the substantive ideas are examined.

A number of different employment variables have been studied. The one that has been used the most denotes variation in whether the wife-mother is employed outside the home or not, and this is usually viewed as a dichotomy labeled something like "maternal employment." Blood (1963) argues that it is important to conceptually differentiate between this variable and similar factors such as the amount of income of the wife and the amount of time and/or energy spent each week away from home in the worker role. Glueck and Glueck (1957) differentiated between mothers working regularly and those working sporadically, and others have argued that phenomena such as the length of time a mother is employed are also important independent variables. No attempt thus far has been made to define each of these variables and explicate the manner in which they vary, so an attempt is made here.

There seems to be little empirical or theoretical value in conceptually separating the following three phenomena that have occasionally been studied separately: (a) the dichotomous variable of employment, which apparently denotes variation in whether an individual is employed or not, (b) the full-timeness of employment, which differentiates between unemployed, part-time, full-time, and overtime employment, and (c) the amount of time spent in employment. Blood (1963:282–283) seems to refer to all of these as the "degree" or "amount" of participation in the economic system. This could be viewed as a categorical variable having the categories of unemployed, part-time, full-time, overtime. This, however, would mask variations in the categories of part-time and overtime, and there is some variation in what is considered full-time. Variation in *the amount of time* spent in the economic system is a meaningful variable that would be easy to operationalize in most situations by identifying the number of hours per week spent at work. It is a continuous variable, and the low extreme identifies the category of being unemployed.

The amount of time working is a different conceptual phenomenon from the *regularity of employment*. This is the variable identified by Glueck and Glueck (1957) to differentiate between those who are regularly employed and those who are sporadically employed. This could be viewed as a dichotomous variable having the categories of regular and sporadic, but it seems more desirable to view it as a continuous variable ranging in degree from very irregularly employed to highly regularly employed. One way it could be operationalized would be to identify the number of times an individual became unemployed during a certain period of time.

The *amount of income* is a conceptually distinct variable that denotes the variation in the amount of money received. It is a continuous variable that in most research situations could be easily measured with monthly or yearly income.

Important Contingent and Intervening Variables

Probably the most conclusive finding to emerge from the research on employed females is that variation in the amount of time women spend working outside the home provides very little if any understanding of why other familial variables vary when it is the only variable that is taken into account. Attempts have been made to see if it is related to such other factors as marital satisfaction, personality problems in children, problems that children have outside the home (e.g., difficulty in school, juvenile delinquence), but it does not seem to be systematically associated with any of them when tested by itself. Reviewers such as Stolz (1960), Hoffman (1961, 1963), Blood (1963), and Nye (1963) thus suggest that if the phenomenon of employed females is to help understand variation in other variables, it will be necessary to not only increase the conceptual precision of the employment variables, but to investigate how these variables interact with other factors such as socioeconomic status and education.

In her review of the research that has dealt with the effects of employment variables on children, Hoffman (1963) identifies several variables that seem to influence the relationships that employment variables have with other familial phenomena. She suggests that the following eleven variables are important: social class, age of child, sex of child, mother's attitude toward employment, adequacy of substitute supervision, duration of the mother's employment, urbanity, hours the mother is away, attitudes of the community, response of the father, and the nature of the mother's work. Douvan (1963:159) and later Orden and Bradburn (1969) suggested that another variable is probably also important in understanding the relationship female employment has with family variables. This is the freedom the wife has to choose the amount of time she is employed outside the home. These variables are defined in the following sections of the chapter as they are needed for substantive propositions.

Employment and Child Variables

Personality Maladjustment

There have been a number of tests of the general idea that maternal employment is associated with problems in the personalities of children. For example, data have been gathered about how employment is related to anxiety (Nye, 1959; Burchinal and Rossman, 1961); antisocial behavior, withdrawing tendencies, and nervous symptoms (Nye, Perry and Ogles, 1963); negative self-image; psychosomatic symptoms; bedwetting and thumbsucking (Douglas and Bloomfield, 1938). It seems most meaningful to first identify the relatively general proposition that summarizes this idea. Unfortunately, the dependent variable in this proposition has had a number of conceptual labels such as personality maladjustment (Power, 1960; Hand, 1957), personality damage (Nye, Perry, and Ogles, 1963), and personality adjustment (Nolan and Tuttle, 1959). The variable seems to have considerable ambiguity, but for the present the term personality maladjustment will be used.

PROPOSITION 12.1:   The amount of time a wife-mother works is related to the amount of personality maladjustment of her children.

The existing data indicate that the relationship in this proposition probably does not exist. The data in all of the studies referred to earlier found no relationship between the specific type of maladjustment studied and whether or not the mother spent time working. Some of the other specific personality maladjustment variables that have been studied are psychosomatic problems and oversensitivity (Burchinal, 1961) and achievement, affiliation, and power motives (Powell, 1960), and none of these have been found to be related to maternal employment.

Several studies have introduced additional variables into the analysis of the data to determine whether there are other variables that influence the finding that no relationship exists between employment and personality maladjustment. Seigel, Stolz, Hitchcock, and Adamson (1959) and Nye, Perry, and Ogles (1963) attempted to control a number of variables by matching their control and working groups. They controlled age, sex, social status, size of family, and ordinal position, and both studies still found no relationship between employment and maladjustment. This provides additional evidence of the invalidity of proposition 12.1, but it does not eliminate the possibility that employment may interact with some other variables in such a way that the interaction may influence personality maladjustment. At the present time, however, no systematic theoretical formulation has been found that identifies this types of interaction, and no empirical data seem to provide a basis for asserting one.

Independence

There is some basis for the idea that employment is systematically related to the amount of independence of children, at least during adolescence. Mering (1955) and Yarrow (1961) both found some evidence of this. Independence can be viewed as a continuous variable varying in amount from low independent (high dependence) to high independence (low dependence), and it can be defined as variation in the autonomy of children in the family. The independent variable is apparently the time the mother works, and the following proposition can be stated.

PROPOSITION 12.2:   The amount of time mothers work influences the independence of their children and this is a positive relationship.

Siegel, Stolz, Hitchcock, and Adamson (1959) attempted to control several other variables that are associated with maternal employment and at the same time determine whether the relationship in this proposition exists. They matched 26 pairs of kindergarten children on family size, ages of children, intactness, and prestige of husband's occupation, and they found no differences in independence between those with employed mothers and those with unemployed mothers. Thus the empirical evidence regarding this proposition is, at present, contradictory and inconclusive.

Role Definitions of Children

There is some evidence that the role expectations of children of employed mothers are systematically different from the expectations of children of unemployed mothers. Consistent with what would be expected if children identified with their parents as they are, the children of employed mothers express less of what has been termed "traditional" attitudes toward the mother role. The dependent variable in this formulation could be viewed as a continuum between "traditional" and "modern," but this is too limited to a particular historical period in a unique culture to be useful to science. It seems more defensible to limit concern to the attitudes of the children toward maternal employment. This can be viewed as variation in the *approval of maternal employment* and as varying between the extremes of strong negative attitudes upward to strong positive attitudes. This dependent variable is undoubtedly also influenced by other factors that influence the modeling process, but these have not been considered in postulating the relationship between these variables.

PROPOSITION 12.3:   The amount of time mothers work influences the amount children in the home approve of maternal employment and this is a positive relationship.

Hartley (1959–1960) found that more of the daughters of working mothers in her sample wanted to work and to have children when they were older, and Peterson (1958, 1961) reported the same finding with adolescent girls. Douvan (1963) and Roy (1961) both found that more of the adolescent girls who had employed mothers in their samples were currently employed and Douvan (1963) also found that daughters of employed mothers scored lower on the index of "traditional femininity."

There is thus some evidence this relationshp does exist, and there are no contradictory findings. It should be pointed out that no controls were introduced in these analyses, and a number of other variables such as socioeconomic status and female educational level are known to be associated with employment. This means that the supporting evidence should be viewed only as partial and tentative support of this proposition.

Hoffman's Model: Hoffman (1961) developed a theoretical model that speculates that the amount a mother likes her work influences the consequences of the work. Hoffman does not state her ideas in propositions. In fact, many of her ideas only state that an independent variable is related to a category of another variable rather than to a variable, so that much of her theoretical formulation is vague. It appears useful to attempt to translate her ideas into propositional language, and specify the role of a contingent variable, and if they can be translated into propositions, it will be possible to integrate her findings with several other studies.

Hoffman argues that maternal employment is positively related to guilt and to withdrawing from the maternal role, but that the degree to which the mother likes her work influences both of these relationships (1961:188). There are four variables and several theoretical ideas in this proposal, but before these ideas can be stated as propositions, it is necessary to define each of the variables. Maternal employment in Hoffman's formulation is apparently the same as the *time spent working* variable that was defined earlier. It is a continuous variable that varies between no time spent working to very large amounts of time (60–70 hours per week).

Guilt is not defined by Hoffman, but she apparently does not intend to denote anything more specific or inclusive than the denotations that are understood in common use of the term in the English language. It is apparently a negative effect experienced with the perception that one's behavior is different from his ethics. This could be viewed as a dichotomous variable that varies between having no guilt and experiencing guilt. It is, however, more likely to be a continuous variable ranging from the absence of guilt to high amounts of it.

Hoffman uses the term "withdrawal" to conceptualize one of her variables. She does not define this term, but the context indicates it may be very similar to what Peterson (1961) seems to be referring to with his term involvement, and what Cumming et al. (1960) refer to as disengagement. The thing that seems to be conceptualized is variation in the degree to which a person fully or partially occupies a social role. It is apparently a continuous variable in that a person can occupy a social role and decide to engage in a few or a large number of the behaviors that are normatively defined as appropriate for that role. Since the term *disengagement* has been widely used to conceptualize this phenomenon, this term is used in the present book. It is a continuous variable that can vary between no disengagements when a person attempts to perform all the behaviors defined for a role to a high amount of disengagement when a person disengages himself from virtually all of the behaviors appropriate for a role.

Hoffman uses several terms to refer to the contingent variable in her formulation. She refers to it as the degree to which a person likes the work, enjoys the work, gains pleasure from the work, and has a positive or negative attitude toward the work. It is thus difficult to identify one term to label the variable that is denoted. It is difficult to know if it is the same as what is termed "profit" in exchange theory or if it denotes variation in the affect the individual feels toward the work (see Ch. 3). After some deliberation it was decided to label this variable as the degree to which a person *likes* her work and to view it as a continuous variable varying from one extreme of having strongly negative effect to the other extreme of having strongly positive effect. When these variables are defined in this way, the ideas in Hoffman's model can be stated in four propositions.

PROPOSITION 12.4:   The time the wife-mother spends working influences her guilt and this is a positive relationship.

PROPOSITION 12.5:   The time the wife-mother spends working influences her disengagement from the maternal role and this is a positive relationship.

PROPOSITION 12.6:   The amount the wife-mother likes her work is related to the amount of influence in proposition 12.4, which asserts that economic activity influences guilt, and this is a positive relationship.

PROPOSITION 12.7:   The amount the wife-mother likes her work is related to the amount of influence in proposition 12.4, which asserts that time spent in economic activity influences disengagement from the maternal role, and this is an inverse relationship.

Hoffman's formulation does not speculate about any of the other characteristics of these relationships. Thus the influence could occur at any point on the independent variable, and it is not known if the relationships are monotonic. This means that much is left unspecific in this part of her model. Hoffman interprets her data as supporting proposition 12.5, but her operationalization of the dependent variable in this proposition (1961:190–191) is so different from the conceptualization that it is highly questionable that the data provide evidence of the validity of this proposition.

Hoffman then seems to speculate that guilt and withdrawal on the part of the mother are related to three other variables, (1) the severity of the mother's discipline, (2) the amount of affection shown by the mother, and (3) the amount the mother demands the child to perform household tasks (1961:188–189). These three variables are not defined, but they are apparently viewed as continuous variables ranging from low to high amounts. Six propositions relate to these ideas.

PROPOSITION 12.8:   The amount of guilt a mother experiences about working influences the severity of her discipline and this is an inverse relationship.

PROPOSITION 12.9:   The amount of guilt a mother experiences about her work influences the demands she makes on the children to perform household tasks and this is an inverse relationship.

PROPOSITION 12.10:   The amount of guilt a mother experiences about her work influences the amount of affection shown to the children in the home and this is a positive relationship.

PROPOSITION 12.11:   The amount the mother disengages from the maternal role inversely influences the severity of her discipline.

PROPOSITION 12.12:   The amount the mother disengages from the maternal role influences the demands the mother makes on the children to perform household tasks and this is a positive relationship.

PROPOSITION 12.13:   The amount the mother disengages from the maternal role influences the amount of affection she shows to the children in the home and this is an inverse relationship.

An attempt is made in Figure 12.1 to summarize these relationships in Hoffman's theoretical model.

Unfortunately Hoffman's data are less useful than her theoretical model. Her theory suggests that guilt and withdrawal are intervening variables between the amount of time the mother is employed and such maternal behaviors as amount of discipline and amount of affection. Her empirical tests, however, ignore these intervening variables and test only the indirect relationships between the amount of time employed and the amount of affection, discipline, and task demands. This means that even though some of the relationships in her data are statistically significant, they shed little light on the question of the validity of the ideas she has identified. Hoffman found significant differences between working and nonworking mothers who like their work in their affec-

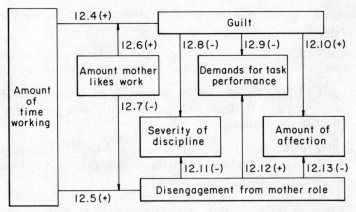

Figure 12.1   Hoffman's theory about the effects of maternal employment.

tion toward their children and in the severity of their discipline. This
provides some supporting evidence that the chain sequence identified in
propositions 12.4 and 12.8 and the sequence identified in 12.4 and 12.9
may have validity. No relationship was found between employment and
the amount the mother who likes her work demands task performance of
the child, and thus at the present time the chain sequence identified in
propositions 12.4 and 12.9 has no supporting data. She found significant
relationships between working and nonworking mothers who did not
like their work in the child's participation in household tasks, and she
found no relationships for these mothers regarding affection and severity
of discipline. This argues that the chain sequence idea expressed in
propositions 12.5 and 12.12 may have validity, but it provides no support for the sequence of 12.5 and 12.11 or the sequence of 12.5 and
12.12.

There is an additional question that should be raised about the value
of Hoffman's data as tests of the validity of her theoretical ideas. Although she found that the amount mothers like their work is related to
the occupational prestige of the mother's work (1861:195), she does not
introduce this variable as a control variable in the analysis of the data.
This means that whenever the amount mothers like their work is used as
an explanatory variable, there is a question as to whether it is the liking
or the socioeconomic status variable that is really involved. It may be
that it is socioeconomic differences rather than liking one's work that influences whether mothers feel guilty about their work or disengage from
the mother's role.

Hoffman also tests hypotheses about how maternal employment might be related to several other variables. Three relationships emerge from these tests.

PROPOSITION 12.14:   The time mothers work is related to the social problems a child has and this is a positive relationship.

PROPOSITION 12.15:   The time mothers work is related to the child's intellectual performance and this is an inverse relationship.

PROPOSITION 12.16:   The time mothers work is related to the child using nonadaptive responses to frustration, and this is a positive relationship.

Hoffman used teacher ratings of responses to frustration and intellectual preformance and a sociometric test in school classes to determine the amount children are liked by others as a measure of social problems. The data were consistent with proposition 12.14, but they provided no support for 12.16 and were conflicting for 12.15.

Employment and Disengagement from Maternal Role

Peterson's (1961) study of the relationship between maternal employment and the mother-daughter relationship seems to suggest some different relationships from Hoffman's formulation. Peterson argues there are conflicting demands in the employee and mother roles, and that because of this the more an individual is involved in one of these roles, the less she will tend to be involved in the other. It also seems to be implicit in Peterson's formulation that the more an individual likes one of these roles, the more she will "devalue" the other role and hence disengage from it. What he seems to be proposing is the same general idea that is suggested in proposition 12.5 that the amount of time the wife-mother spends in economic activity is positively associated with her disengagement from her maternal role, but he seems to be suggesting that the degree the individual likes the economic activity has just the opposite effect from what Hoffman proposes. Hoffman proposes that employment creates disengagement when the mother dislikes her work, whereas Peterson argues that liking work creates the disengagement. Thus two different propositions are suggested by Peterson.

PROPOSITION 12.17:   The amount of time the wife-mother spends in economic activity influences disengagement from noneconomic roles and this is a positive relationship.

PROPOSITION 12.18: The amount the individual likes the economic activity role is related to the amount of influence in proposition 12.17, which asserts that time spent in the economic activity role influences disengagement from other roles, and this is a positive relationship.

Proposition 12.17, which states that the amount of time in the economic role influences disengagement from *all* other roles, is more general than proposition 12.5, which states only that economic activity influences disengagement from the maternal role. The main difference between the Hoffman and Peterson proposals can be deduced from proposition 12.18.

PROPOSITION 12.19: The amount the wife-mother likes her economic activity is related to the influence that her economic activity has on disengagement from the mother role, and this is a positive relationship.

This assertion is just the opposite of the idea in proposition 12.7, and, unfortunately, the data that are relevant for assessing the validity of these propositions are very meager. Peterson, however, has some data that are relevant for proposition 12.5. He deduced from this proposition the testable hypotheses that employed mothers would be expected to have less control over adolescent daughters and have less interest in them, but there were no differences between the employed and unemployed mothers on either of these variables. He also deduced that if the idea identified in proposition 12.19 is true, it can be expected that mothers who like their work have less control and interest in their daughters; and Peterson indicates that the data partially confirm this hypotheses. Hoffman's data do not provide a basis for making inferences about the validity of proposition 12.7 or of the opposing idea suggested in proposition 12.19. Thus at the present time, they are conflicting theoretical proposals. The slight bit of evidence available suggest that the amount mothers like their work increases the amount employment positively influences disengagement from the mother role, but this is highly tentative.

Wife-Mother Employment and Family Relationship Variables

Several studies have gathered data on how time working is related to various familial variables. Locke and Mackeprang (1959), Blood and Wolfe (1960), and others, have studied relationships between wife-mother employment and such marital variables as marital satisfaction, marital conflict, and the division of labor in performing household tasks. Nye (1952, 1959) studied whether employment is related to affection in the parent-child relationship. Essig and Morgan (1945) studied whether employment is related to communication deficiency, feelings of rejection by father, parental approval, and a happy home life. Peterson (1961) investigated the relationship between employment and the interest and control that mothers have over teenage daughters. These dependent variables do not seem to have any overall dimensionality, so each relationship has to be analyzed separately.

Marital Conflict

There is some evidence that the employment of wives may be related to marital conflict, and Nye (1958, 1959, and 1963) argues that the evidence is fairly conclusive. The dependent variable in this formulation is the amount the individuals differ in opinions, attitudes, beliefs, and so forth. Conflict is apparently a continuous variable ranging between none and a high amount, and the main independent variable is the amount of time the wife works.

PROPOSITION 12.20:   The amount of time the wife works influences the amount of marital conflict and this is a positive relationship.

This is asserted as a positive relationship, and it is also probably monotonic. It may not, however, be linear in that increasing the amount of time working from none to a slight amount may make more difference than increasing from part-time to full-time participation.

Nye's data provide some support for the validity of the relationship asserted in this proposition. He operationalized the independent variables in a dichotomous way by dealing with employment versus nonemployment, and he operationalized the dependent variable by measuring the frequency of arguing about six familial subjects. His data were gathered from 1993 mothers in three Washington towns in 1957. Nye found that the employed mothers did argue more with their husbands at a statistically significant but not highly different amount.

It seems doubtful that this is a direct, influential relationship; rather, it is probably either indirect in that the employment causes greater variety in reference relationships and this increases conflict in the marriage, or it is a spurious relationship in which the two variables covary but have no influential relationship. No theoretical formulations have yet been found that assert either of these two conditions, so these ideas are at present mere speculations.

Marital Satisfaction

Several studies have investigated the relationship between the wife's employment and marital satisfaction (Locke and Mackeprang, 1949; Orden and Bradburn, 1969; etc.). The general consensus is that when the employment variable is studied apart from other variables it is probably not related to assessments of marital satisfaction. There is, however, some evidence that when other variables are taken into account there may be an identifiable relationship, so this proposition should probably be identified. The independent variable that apparently receives the most attention is the amount of time the wife works. The dependent variable is a continuous variable defined in Chapter 3 as marital satisfaction.

PROPOSITION 12.21: The Amount of time the wife works is related to marital satisfaction.

Three variables have been suggested as being related to this proposition. Gianopulos and Mitchell (1957) suggested that the husband's attitude (approval toward the employment) influences whether the employment will influence the marital satisfaction. They hypothesized that disapproving husbands with employed wives would have lower satisfaction. Their data supported this, but the data also indicated that approving husbands with unemployed wives also tended to have lower satisfaction. The appropriate conclusion is thus that the amount the husband approves of his wife's employment influences the direction of the relationship in proposition 12.21. If he approves, then the time his wife spends working is positively related to his marital satisfaction, but if he disapproves, it is inversely related to his marital satisfaction. This independent variable can be viewed as a dichotomous variable having the two categories of disapprove and approve. The dependent variable in this idea is the direction of the relationship in proposition 12.21, which can vary between the two categories of negative and positive.

PROPOSITION 12.22: The husband's approval of the wife working influences the direction of the relationship in proposition 12.21, which asserts that the time wives spend working influences marital satisfaction, and this is a positive relationship.

Blood and Wolfe (1960:101–103) suggest that "economic necessity" is also related to the relationship between female employment and marital satisfaction. They found no difference in the marital satisfaction of the employed and unemployed wives in their Detroit sample, but when they introduced the economic necessity as a control variable they found significant differences. They did not define the phenomenon of economic necessity, and as Blood noted in his later review of this research, "'necessity' is a very slippery term in an advertising-saturated culture" (1963:284). Blood and Wolfe operationalized this variable by differentiating between those husbands making more and less than $5000 annually. Those with less than $5000 were assumed to have more economic necessity and those with more income were assumed to have less.

It seems probable that Blood and Wolfe were dealing with a conceptual phenomenon that is more abstract than the amount of income or economic necessity. They state that the "difference lies in the gains and losses from working" (1960:101). If working is "urgently desirable" for economic reasons, there is more gain (or psychological profit) to be received from it and hence there is more of a necessity. Thus the conceptual phenomenon that Blood and Wolfe were dealing with is best described by the exchange theory term of profit (as defined in Ch. 3). It is a more inclusive term than the mere economic profit received in dollars. It is the relative balance of all of the rewards and costs incurred by the wife being employed. If this term is a more exact label for the phenomenon that Blood and Wolfe were investigating, its use is more than just an improvement in the conceptualization because it also integrates their theoretical formulation with exchange theory.

It is possible that the profit from the wife's employment directly influences the relationship between the time the wife works and marital satisfaction, but it seems more defensible to argue that it has an indirect influence on this relationship. It seems reasonable that the profit variable influences the variable earlier identified as the amount the husband approved of the wife's employment, and that the latter variable influences the relationship between time employed and marital satisfaction. Both of these ideas should probably be stated, and then subsequent empirical research can determine whether the relationship exists that is identified in the first of the following two propositions.

PROPOSITION 12.23:   The profit received from the time the wife-mother spends working influences the direction of the relationship in proposition 12.21, which asserts the time the wife-mother spends working influences marital satisfaction, and this is a positive relationship.

PROPOSITION 12.24:   The profit received from the time the wife-mother spends working influences the husband's approval of the time she spends working, and this is a positive relationship.

A recent formulation about the consequences of wives' employment has asserted that one other variable is involved in the relationship between the time wives are employed and marital satisfaction. Orden and Bradburn's (1969) thesis is that variation in the freedom women have to choose whether or not to be in the employed role influences the relationship between being employed and marital satisfaction. Their independent variable is the *freedom to choose alternative life styles.* The variation they took into account in this variable was between women who were impelled into the labor force because they perceived they "needed the money" and those who entered the labor force by choice. It is doubtful, however, that this variable is totally discrete in the way it varies. It is probably more accurate to view it as a continuous variable that varies in the amount of freedom in the choice. Either way, however, the proposition they suggest is 12.25.

PROPOSITION 12.25:   The amount of freedom women have to choose whether to be in the labor market influences the direction of the relationship in proposition 12.21, which asserts that time spent employed influences marital satisfaction, and this is a positive relationship.

It is suggested by Orden and Bradburn that this is a positive relationship, and it seems reasonable that it is monotonic. Orden and Bradburn analyzed data secured in interviews with 1651 married individuals who reported that the husband was the chief wage earner. The sample was a probability sample selected by NORC. The analysis of the data found a satistically significant relationship which was present when education for stages in the life cycle and part-time versus full-time employment are controlled. Employment, when there is freedom to choose, seems to increase marital tensions only when there are preschool children in the family. (It may be worthwhile to further speculate that this presence of preschool children has a relatively indirect effect because role strain may be an intervening variable between these two. For example, this would be the case) if controlling for role strain eliminates the relationship between choosing employment and marital tensions.

Orden and Bradburn's data indicate that employment when there is low choice may influence different aspects of the marital relationship differently for husbands and wives. For example, the data show that husbands have higher tensions while the wives have lower companionate satisfactions when there is low freedom. This finding must be viewed tentatively, but it seems worth identifying in propositions so it can be more systematically tested in the future, and because it is important to try to find how employment is differentially related to different aspects of the marital relationship.

PROPOSITION 12.26:   When the wife has low freedom to choose whether to be in the labor market, the amount of time she spends in economic activity influences her satisfaction with marital companionship and this is an inverse relationship.

PROPOSITION 12.27:   When the wife has low freedom to choose whether to be in the labor market, the amount of time she spends in economic activity influences the tensions the husband experiences in the marital relationship, and this is a positive relationship.

This model of the relationship between the time the wife-mother spends working and marital satisfaction is summarized in Figure 12.2, which shows that the relationship between the time the wife-mother works is influenced by the approval of the husband. The profit received from the employment influences his approval, and it also influences the relationship between the time spent employed and satisfaction. Furthermore, the freedom to choose whether to engage in economic activity influences the relationship between amount of time spent in this activity and marital satisfaction; and it may influence the effect that the time

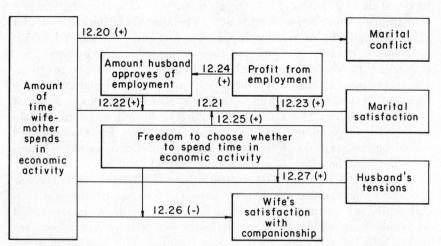

Figure 12.2   The relationship between time wives spend in economic activity and marital variables.

spent in economic activity has on wives' satisfaction with marital companionship and on husbands' marital tensions.

Employment and the Division of Labor

A number of empirical studies have attempted to find relationships between female employment and the division of labor. Hoffman (1960) made one of the most clearly stated formulations in her hypothesis that wives' employment outside the home decreases the participation of wives in household tasks relative to husbands. The reasoning behind her hypothesis was that the stress that the wife experiences by adding the employed role to her other roles makes it necessary for the husband to have greater involvement in the household tasks than he would otherwise have. It would be meaningful to postulate here a proposition to the effect that the greater the wife's activity in employment outside the home, the greater the involvement of the husband in household tasks, but another intermediate variable that is implicit in Hoffman's formulation should be identified first.

The other variable is what Hoffman terms stress, and it seems to be the same concept that Goode (1960) labels role strain. This variable was defined earlier in this book as the psychological stress that is experienced by an individual because he is not able to comply with all the role expectations in his particular life situation. It is a continuous variable that varies between having no strain to having high degrees of it. Hoffman's formulation seems to assert that women's employment outside the home increases their role strain, and that increased role strain results in a decrease in their relative task performance. These two ideas can be expressed as propositions.

PROPOSITION 12.28: The time wives spend working influences their role strain and this is a positive relationship.

PROPOSITION 12.29: The amount of role strain a woman in the wife-mother social position experiences influences her relative task performance and this is an inverse relationship.

It seems worthwhile to attempt to integrate these two propositions with another proposition that identifies a variable that apparently intervenes between employment and role strain. This other proposition is a deduction from a more general proposition that was identified in Chapter 6 as proposition 6.10.

PROPOSITION 6.10:   The amount of activity that is normatively prescribed in a person's life influences the individual's
role strain and this is a positive relationship.

The independent variable in this proposition is a continuous variable
that denotes variation between the two extremes of no activity being
prescribed to a high amount of activity. Proposition 12.30 can be deduced from this.

PROPOSITION 12.30:   The amount of activity that is normatively prescribed for a person occupying the wife-mother so-
cial position influences this person's role strain and
this is a positive relationship.

The way this proposition seems to be relevant in the present context
is that usually when a person assumes the role of employee this increases the amount of activity that is normatively prescribed in a person's life. Hence proposition 12.31 seems to follow.

PROPOSITION 12.31:   The amount of time an occupant of the wife-mother
social position spends in economic activity increases
the total amount of activity that is normatively prescribed for this individual, and this is a positive
relationship.

This entire formulation is summarized in Figure 12.3, which attempts
to show that the employment of a woman occupying the wife-mother social position positively influences the amount of activity that is normatively prescribed in her life. These prescriptions positively influence the
amount of role strain she experiences, and this inversely influences the

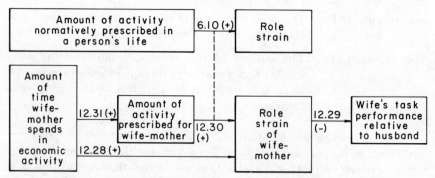

Figure 12.3   The relationship between the employment of a woman occupying the wife-mother social position and her relative task participation.

amount of her relative task performance. The logical relationship between this chain sequence and the more general proposition that asserts that prescribed activity influences role strain is identified with the dotted line.

Several comments should be made about this theoretical formulation. First, if it is true that the only way that female employment influences role strain is by the indirect manner of influencing the normative prescriptions in the woman's life, then the relationship that is identified in proposition 12.28 is an indirect relationship, and it is redundant to identify it in the same model that identifies 12.30 and 12.31. It was suggested in Chapter 6 that the relationship in proposition 6.10 is not a linear relationship but that there is probably little influence in the low range of the independent variable, and that the influence only begins to increase when there is considerable prescribed activity. It should probably be assumed here that this same relationship occurs in proposition 12.30. This would mean that when there is little activity prescribed in the wife-mother social position, the addition of the employee role would not increase the role strain sufficiently that a variation would occur in the relative task performance.

It also seems useful to introduce several ideas that may help explain the circumstances under which female employment influences role strain. There are stages of the family life cycle and certain situations (such as the number of children in the home) that probably influence the amount of activity that is demanded by the roles of the wife-mother position. For example, during the prechild and postchild stages of the marriage, the wife seems to have less activity prescribed by her familial roles; she probably has the greatest amount of activity prescribed when there are young children in the home and when there is a large number of children. These two ideas can be stated as propositions and then integrated with Hoffman's formulation about employment to develop what is hoped will be a more comprehensive and useful formulation.

PROPOSITION 12.32: The stage of the family life cycle influences the amount of activity prescribed for the wife-mother position and this is a curvilinear relationship.

PROPOSITION 12.33: The number of dependent children in the family influences the amount of activity prescribed for the wife-mother position and this is a positive relationship.

No data have been found that can serve as a basis for identifying the nature of the relationship in proposition 12.32. On a purely intuitive

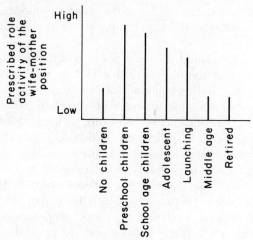

Figure 12.4   The relationship between stage of the family life cycle and role activity prescribed for the wife-mother social position.

basis, it is suggested that the relationship approximates the curve in Figure 12.4, which indicates that the amount of activity is highest when young children are in the home, and there are abrupt changes when children arrive and leave.

At the present time there are no empirical data that can be used to speculate about the nature of the relationship in proposition 12.33. It is likely to be monotonic, but it is probably not linear. The first child probably creates the greatest increment in the amount of activity prescribed in the wife-mother position.

This entire formulation is summarized in Figure 12.5, which shows the same relationships identified in Figure 12.3 and how the number of dependent children and life cycle stage influence the amount of activity that is normatively prescribed.

A More General Formulation

One of the major goals of theory building is to expand theories whenever there is a basis for enlarging them. Thus an attempt is made here to extend the formulation suggested in the preceding section by making several inductions from that model. It seems reasonable, for example, that the addition or termination of the employee role would influence the amount of prescribed activity of the occupants of other social posi-

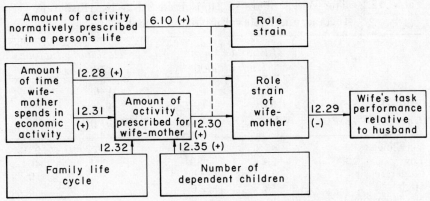

Figure 12.5 Antecedents of relative task performance of spouses.

tions in the family system, and that the amount of role strain experienced by individuals in other social positions would also frequently influence the amount they would be expected to perform household tasks. If this is the case, two additional propositions can be added to the one more general proposition (6.10) in Figure 12.5. This model is diagramed in Figure 12.6.

PROPOSITION 12.34: Occupying the employee role influences the amount of activity that is normatively prescribed in a person's life and this is a positive relationship.

PROPOSITION 12.35: The amount of role strain an individual experiences influences her task performance relative to others in a social system, and this is an inverse relationship.

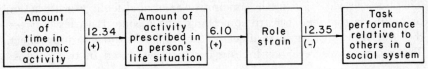

Figure 12.6 The relationship between employment and task performances in social systems.

There is some empirical evidence that is relevant for this theoretical model. Blood and Wolfe (1960:62) published data that indicate the amount of task participation is monotonically related to whether the wife is employed and with the amount of time the husband spends in his

Table 12.1   The Wife's Share of Household Tasks by Husband's Income and Wife's Employment Status

Wife's Share of Household Tasks	Husband's Income Under $5000		Husband's Income $5000 or More	
	Wife Not Working	Wife Working	Wife Not Working	Wife Working
Very low	7%	27%	7%	23%
Low	29	39	32	46
Moderate	34	20	33	19
High	18	6	23	8
Not ascertained	11	8	5	4
Total	99	100	100	100
Number of families	184	66	284	48

employment. Table 12.1 presents their data, and the fact that these data are related to the involvement of both sexes adds more evidence in support of this theory than they would if they were related to the involvement of just one of the sexes in an employee role.

Employment and Affectional Relationships

Nye (1952, 1958, 1959) has investigated the possibility that relationships exist between maternal employment and affectional patterns. His dependent variable seems to be the amount of affect that is felt toward another family member. This phenomenon of affect was defined in Chapter 3 as variation in the amount of emotional feeling of attraction or repulsion one feels toward something or someone. It varies between the low of strong negative affect to the high of strong positive affect. The relationships Nye has investigated can be stated in two propositions.

PROPOSITION 12.36:   The amount of time the wife-mother spends in economic activity is related to the affect children feel toward the mother.

PROPOSITION 12.37:   The amount of time the wife-mother spends in economic activity is related to the affect the mother feels toward the children.

Nye initially suggested, on the basis of other literature such as Bossard (1954), that there is a basis for expecting negative relationships to appear in these two propositions. His data, however, indicated a slightly curvilinear relationship that was just barely statistically significant for both propositions. He found that children of mothers who were employed part-time had slightly less hostility and more affection toward their parents than those whose mothers were employed full-time or were unemployed, and that adolescent children perceived mothers in this same category as most "accepting" of them. In view of the accumulating evidence that other variables influence the relationships that maternal employment has with many dependent variables, it is probably best to accept this evidence as supporting the propositions only tentatively.

Employment and Juvenile Delinquency

One of the most publicized relationships that has been studied is whether maternal employment is related to juvenile delinquency. It is interesting to note that the research on this particular relationship has never been integrated with any of the larger theories of deviance. Instead, it has been studied as a separate, unique relationship. Proposition 12.38 is the main proposition that has been studied.

PROPOSITION 12.38: The time mothers spend working influences the probability of juvenile delinquency of the children in the home and this is a positive relationship.

The best review of this research is in Nye and Hoffman's (1963) book, *The Employed Mother in America,* in which Hoffman summarizes data from studies such as Nye (1959), Glueck and Glueck (1957), and Gold (1961). The findings indicate the relationship may interact with socioeconomic status in a unique manner so that it holds with middle-class but not lower-class families. The data are not conclusive that this occurs, but there are enough data that it is a reasonable speculation. Nye studied a middle-class group and found a relationship between employment and delinquency. Glueck and Glueck (1957) studied a lower class group and failed to find the relationship, and Gold (1961) found the relationship appeared in his white-collar but not in his blue-collar group. This idea is summarized in the following proposition.

PROPOSITION 12.39: Socioeconomic status is related to the amount of influence in proposition 12.38, which asserts that the time mothers work influences juvenile delinquency, and this is a positive relationship.

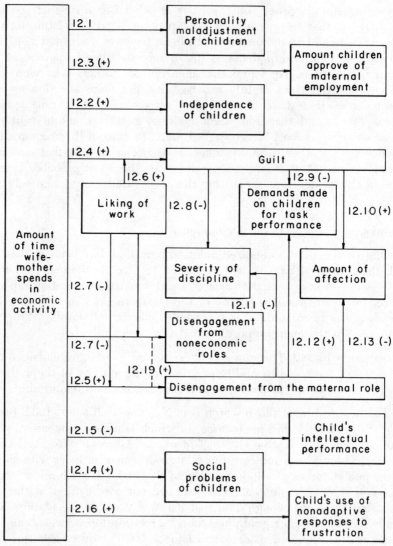

Figure 12.7 Effects of wife-mother employment.

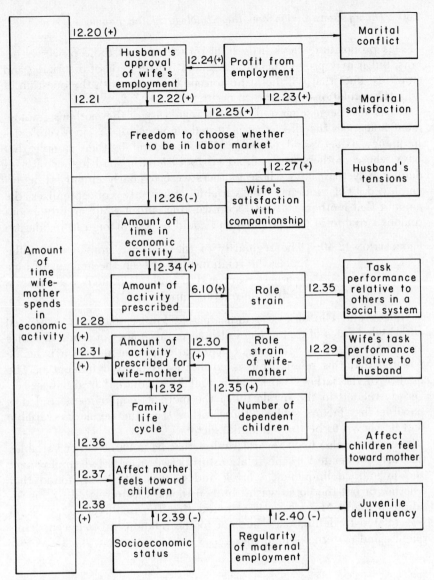

Figure 12.7 (continued).

This proposition sheds little light on why any of these processes occurs, but it may prove valuable in generating the type of theorizing and empirical data that will help this formulation cope with the question of why these relationships tend to occur.

It has also been suggested that the regularity of the mother's employment influences the effect that maternal employment has on juvenile delinquency. Glueck and Glueck (1957:335) found in their sample that boys whose mothers were employed "occasionally" had higher rates of delinquency than boys whose mothers were regularly employed or unemployed. This independent variable apparently conceptualizes the amount that mothers start and stop working, and it is apparently a continuous variable in that employment could be low or high in regularity.

PROPOSITION 12.40: The regularity of the maternal employment influences the relationship between the amount of time mothers work and juvenile delinquency and this is an inverse relationship.

Glueck and Glueck's data indicate that low regularity is associated with higher rates of delinquency. However, a number of other variables were related to the regularity of maternal employment, and it is hence possible that this relationship is covariational but not influential. The quality of the father's work habits and his emotional health were inversely related to the regularity of the mother's employment, and it is possible that factors such as these rather than the regularity variable will be shown to be the influential factors.

There have also been several studies that have found other variables that are not related to the relationship between maternal employment and juvenile delinquency. Glueck and Glueck (1957:342) found that whether or not the home was a "broken" home was unrelated to this relationship, and Maccoby (1958) found that the quality of supervision was related to delinquency but not to the relationship between delinquency and maternal employment.

Summary

Figure 12.7 is an attempt to summarize all of the propositions that have been identified in this chapter about the consequences of wife-mother employment outside the home. The ideas summarized by this model have varying degrees of clarity and proof, but it is hoped that their identification here will stimulate additional theoretical and empirical work to improve them.

CHAPTER 13

FERTILITY

Every society confines its reproductive processes to the family institution, and because of this it is important that propositions about the factors that influence fertility be included in family theory. This chapter is an attempt to identify and integrate a number of these propositions, and to stimulate additional theorizing and research in this area.

Fertility is usually conceptualized as ratios of the number of births in a given group to the population or the number of women in their childbearing years. It is a continuous variable that conceptually could vary as low as zero, and it is one of the rare social variables that is sufficiently rigorous to be a ratio (Selltiz, 1961:194–195) scale.

One of the first papers on the theoretical variables that influence fertility was published by Davis and Blake (1956) who attempted to identify what they viewed as "intermediate" variables influencing fertility. Their analysis was sufficiently comprehensive and theoretically sophisticated that it easily serves as a synthesis around which other theorizing in the area can be built. Their formulations are analyzed in the first section of this chapter, and then other propositions are integrated with it in the later sections.

The Davis-Blake Model

Davis and Blake argue that any social or cultural factors that influence the level of fertility must operate through a group of variables that they label the *intermediate variables*. They group these intermediate factors in three categories according to whether they deal with (1) sexual intercourse, (2) conception, or (3) gestation and parturition. What they essentially do is identify meaningful chain sequences by recognizing that numerous variables influence fertility indirectly by influencing the intermediate variables. They then devote their concerns to explicating, in what is a remarkably profound manner for the time they published the article, the nature of the relationships between their intermediate variables and fertility. The first 11 propositions in this chapter are their formulations. The first eight deal with factors influencing sexual

261

intercourse, the next two deal with factors influencing conceptions, and the last deals with a variable that influences the fetus during gestation.

An attempt is made here to improve the Davis-Blake propositions, and some of the resulting propositions may not conform to their intentions. This is most likely to occur in the specifications made here about the nature of the relationships in the propositions. Davis and Blake limited themselves to being concerned only with the direction of the relationships, whereas an attempt is made here to specify some of the other technical aspects of the relationships when there is a basis for doing so. If there are any differences in what is proposed here and their initial model, these can be resolved in future improvements and tests of the present model.

Age of Entry into Sexual Union

Age is an independent variable that hardly needs a definition. It is, of course, a continuous variable that varies in a ratio scale. Davis and Blake propose there is an inverse relationship between age of entry into sexual unions and fertility, since this influences the total time of sexual contact while a woman is fertile. They hasten to point out that the influence exerted by the usual range of variation (15 to 30 years of age) in this variable can be easily negated by other variables, and it is apparently negated in most societies. However, if the dependent variable were not influenced by other independent variables, the influence would still be there and this factor would influence fertility. This relationship is probably highly influential if the age of entry into sexual intercourse is delayed until 40 to 45, and if this is the case there is curvilinear relationship in this proposition, as diagramed in Figure 13.1.

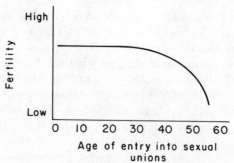

Figure 13.1 The proposed relationship between age of entry into sexual unions and fertility.

PROPOSITION 13.1:   Age of entry into sexual intercourse influences fertility and this is an inverse relationship.

Permanent Celibacy

Celibacy is variation in the amount of total sexual continence that occurs in a society. It is a continuous variable that identifies the proportion of those being continent, and Davis and Blake postulate an inverse relationship between it and fertility. It should be noted that this is also a sufficient variable, and therefore the relationship has great influence. Davis and Blake point out, however, that in the societies that have been studied there is such little variation in the independent variable that it is really inconsequential.

PROPOSITION 13.2:   The amount of celibacy influences fertility and this is an inverse, sufficient relationship.

Time in Postmarital Roles

Davis and Blake suggest that another crucial variable is the length of time during the reproductive period in postmarital roles caused by such factors as divorce, desertion, or death. This is very much like the independent variable in proposition 13.1 since it deals with variation in the amount of time during the reproductive period when sexual intercourse occurs. They suggest that variation in this independent variable is inversely related to fertility. This relationship too is probably curvilinear with the greatest influence occuring between 10 and 30 years.

PROPOSITION 13.3:   The length of time in postmarital roles during the reproductive period influences fertility and this is an inverse, curvilinear relationship.

Voluntary Abstinence

Voluntary abstinence conceptualizes variation in the amount of voluntary continence within the marital state. This is a continuous variable ranging in time from no abstinence to large amounts of it. Davis and Blake identify four different types of abstinence and suggest they have different influences on fertility. They suggest that postpartum abstinence and occasional abstinence such as during holidays have an inverse influence on fertility, and that abstinence during the gestation period and during menstruation probably has a positive influence on fertility if there is any influence. Because of these complications in their presentation it is suggested that a conceptual distinction be made be-

tween abstinence during fertile periods (which would include abstinence during what Davis and Blake label postpartum and occasional periods) and abstinence during unfertile periods such as gestation,
menstruation, and postmenarchie. It could then be proposed that variation during fertile periods would inversely influence fertility, whereas
variation during unfertile periods would positively influence fertility. It
is likely these relationships are linear, and since these are also sufficient
variables they are highly influential relationships.

PROPOSITION 13.4:   The amount of voluntary abstinence during fertile
periods influences fertility and this is an inverse relationship.

PROPOSITION 13.5:   The amount of voluntary abstinence during infertile
periods influences fertility and this is a positive relationship.

Involuntary Abstinence

The independent variable of involuntary abstinence also conceptualizes variation in the amount of sexual continence in the marital state. It
apparently is referring to variation in the amount of time involved. This
is also a detriment to fertility if it occurs during fertile periods, but if it
occurs during infertile periods, it would have either no effect or a positive influence on fertility. It is unlikely that this variable will vary
greatly in most societies, but if it were to vary, it would also be a sufficient relationship and hence highly influential.

PROPOSITION 13.6:   The amount of involuntary abstinence during fertile
periods influences fertility and this is an inverse relationship.

PROPOSITION 13.7:   The amount of involuntary abstinence during infertile periods influences fertility and this is a positive
relationship.

Frequency of Intercourse

The frequency of sexual intercourse conceptualizes a continuous variable that varies between no intercourse and a high frequency of it. It is
likely that the influence it has is highly influenced by such phenomena as
who it is that has the intercourse and the periods of time when they
have it, but such refinements of this proposition have not at present
been made. There is one basic proposition here.

PROPOSITION 13.8:   The frequency of sexual intercourse influences fertility and this is a positive relationship.

It is likely that this relationship is also linear, and during the reproductive stages of life it is probably relatively influential.

Fecundity

This variable identifies the biological capacity to propagate. It could be viewed as a dichotomous variable, but in actual fact there seem to be degrees of fecundity in that people have varying degrees of difficulty in propagating. Thus it is viewed here as a continuous variable ranging from absolute sterility to high degrees of fecundity. This is also undoubtedly a sufficient variable, and because of this the inverse relationship that is proposed is highly influential. It is also likely that this is a linear relationship. Davis and Blake differentiate between involuntary and voluntary causes of variation in fecundity. They do not, however, identify reasons that make this distinction theoretically important, so the two different types are grouped together in the proposition that is identified in this analysis.

PROPOSITION 13.9:   The amount of fecundity influences fertility and this is a positive relationship.

Use of Contraception

Contraception is defined as attempts to reduce the probability of pregnancy when sexual intercourse occurs. It varies continuously between no contraceptive being used and extensive use of them. It will probably eventually be necessary to define this variable more precisely to take into account different methods of contraception, but this is not being done here. Davis and Blake suggest the following proposition.

PROPOSITION 13.10:   The amount of contraception is used influences fertility and this is an inverse relationship.

Davis and Blake note, "Whereas the 'intercourse variables' have a negative effect on fertility only through abstinence, neither the conception nor the gestation variables require this drastic behavior by the individual or the institutionalization necessary to insure such behavior" (1956:223). It is likely then that since there is less cost in institutionalizing contraception and gestation variables, they are more readily used when efforts are made to influence fertility.

Fetal Mortality

The last major variable identified in the Davis-Blake formulation is variation in fetal mortality. They differentiate between voluntary and involuntary sources of variation in this variable, but this distinction does not seem to have theoretical significance so it is not made here. This variable conceptualizes variation in the death rate of fetuses, and it is usually expressed in terms of the number of deaths per thousand live births. Davis and Blake argue that it has an inverse influence on fertility. Apparently it is a linear relationship, and since it is another sufficient variable it is highly influential.

PROPOSITION 13.11:   The amount of fetal mortality influences fertility and this is an inverse relationship.

The Davis and Blake paper is a highly useful theoretical contribution, but there seem to be two other goals in the paper, and it is important to not view the efforts toward the attainment of these other two goals as contributions to deductive theory. One of these goals is that after they identify theoretical relationships between the intermediate variable and fertility, Davis and Blake then attempt to see how the intermediate variables are distributed in different kinds of societies. This seems to be a situation of postulating theoretical relationships and then returning to a much less sophisticated level of analysis to merely describe how the variables are distributed in various countries. They also attempt to explain why these variables are distributed the way they are in these countries, and when they do this they adopt an equilibrium-seeking type of functional analysis to provide the explanations. It should be pointed out that these explanations are specific, nongeneralizable observations and they too should not be confused with Davis and Blake's theoretical contributions.

Demographic Transition

One other theoretical formulation about factors that influence fertility has to do with the covariation of mortality and fertility (Hawley, 1950: Ch. 7). The independent variable is the *mortality rate* in a society, which varies as a continuous variable ranging from typically low rates of about 9 per 1000 population per year to relatively high rates of 50 or 60 per 1000 population. The observation that led to the theoretical proposition was that after the mortality rates were drastically reduced in various countries in the eighteenth and nineteenth centuries, there then followed a period of no change in the fertility rate for about a half century. However, after about 50 years, during which time the population grew very rapidly, the fertility rates tended to decline. This covariation was observed to occur with approximately the same time lag in different countries at different historical periods, and the combination of this pattern of covariation and the temporal priority seems to justify the following assertion.

PROPOSITION 13.12:   Variation in mortality rates influences fertility, and this is a positive relationship in which there is a time lag of about a half century.

Since this proposition was initially formulated on the basis of an empirically observed covariation rather than an understanding of the reasons the influence is exerted, and since there is such a large time period involved, it is likely that subsequent research will demonstrate this is a highly indirect influence. At present, however, little has been done to specify the role that intermediate variables play in the influential process.

Factors Influencing the Intermediate Variables

It seems that theory development in the area of fertility is in a unique historical period. There is a great deal of empirical research relating sociocultural variables to fertility, but as Freedman's (1962) review of the field demonstrates, this research has not been profitable in generating lawlike propositions about antecedents of fertility. It is merely a vast amount of conflicting empirical findings that were not guided by theory and that have not so far been used as a basis for generating new theory. It seems likely, however, that if the advances in the methodology of theorizing that have been made in the past two decades can be applied to the atheoretical data in this area, this could be one of the most profitable areas for family scholars to attempt to build theory during the 1970s.

Yaukey (1969) has made a persuasive case for one strategy in developing this theory. He suggests that one set of propositions should be developed with the intermediate variables as the dependent variables and that another set should be developed with the intermediate variables as the independent variables. He then identifies several types of variables that could be worked with as the independent variables influencing the intermediate variables. He suggests that such phenomena as norm about

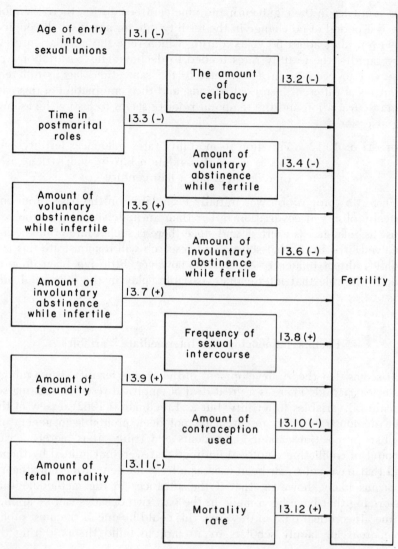

Figure 13.2 Propositions about fertility.

family size, norms about the intermediate variables, mortality rates, and social and economic structure would probably be areas where theory could be efficiently built. This type of theory building should be a major area of focus in the coming years.

Summary

This chapter has analyzed several propositions about factors that influence fertility. The intermediate variables suggested by Davis and Blake (1956) were reviewed, and an analysis was made of one strategy of using the atheoretical literature in this area to generate new theoretical formulations. The propositions are summarized in Figure 13.2 This chapter, probably more than any of the others in this book, is a beginning of the process of systematizing the theory in the area. There is a vast amount of literature that needs to be analyzed to expand the present model and determine how adequately it has been tested. It is hoped that this expansion will be undertaken in the near future.

CHAPTER 14

NOTES ON FUTURE THEORIZING AND RESEARCH

The success of this book will be measured more by the conceptual, theoretical, and empirical work that it stimulates than by what it says about the current status of theory. This being the case, it seems useful to use whatever perspective has gained by writing this book to make a few observations about such things as the current status of family theory, the directions it perhaps ought to be going in the immediate future, and the relative efficiency of stategies for moving in these directions. Hopefully these very subjective comments will be useful to others who are working at theory building. The first section of the chapter addresses these issues by making several comments about the current status of family theory. The second section identifies a number of needs that require fulfillment in the immediate future, and the last section consists of some of this author's opinions about the strategies for meeting these needs.

The Present Status of Family Theory

Scientific theorizing about family variables was begun several decades ago, but such factors as the complexity of the subject matter, lack of methodological tools, scarcity of resources, lack of systematic theory in basic disciplines such as sociology and psychology, and sensitivity of many of the substantive areas have made progress very slow. The result is that theorizing about family variables is not yet beyond its neonatal stage of development. This observation is not made to depreciate any previous work. It has taken decades of work by extremely able scholars to make the progress that has been made. The point here is that the job that remains is *very very* large.

Even though only modest progress has been made in building theories about family processes, there is evidence that increasing attention is being paid to systematizing the theoretical ideas in the field and then empirically testing these propositions. Books like Reiss' (1967) analysis of premarital sexual attitudes and behavior and papers like Christensen's (1969) normative theory and Bartz and Nye's (1970) anaylsis of factors influencing age at marriage are examples of this type of activity. In addition, there has been an active movement in professional organizations such as the National Council on Family Relations to increase the amount of attention that is given to theory construction.

Two books that should give more impetus to theory development in the field are Goode, Hopkins, and McClure's (1971) propositional inventory, and the present volume. The Goode et al. book amasses a vast number of propositions that will probably be useful in generating new theory and research. It gives little information about the propositions such as how the terms are defined, how they vary, and what the characteristics of the relationships are, but just the fact that such a comprehensive array of ideas are assembled in one place should be a valuable resource for those who work on theory building.

The present book performs a different function from the Goode et al. inventory, but it is not an attempt to be a definitive statement of family theory. This volume is more of a "progress report" that identifies a group of theoretical models that are at a certain stage of development. It would be a mistake to assume that any of the theoretical models in the individual chapters are comprehensive statements of theory in that area, or that in the mind of the author they have arrived at a point of closure. They are tentative statements that are written only to be revised, expanded, and modified by further improvements in theorizing and additional empirical data. There are large bodies of literature in each of these areas that are not incorporated into the chapters, and it is hoped that a large group of scholars will become involved in the process of further developing these models.

One other aspect of the current status of theorizing about family variables is that the theories are sufficiently ambiguous, premature, and untested that they are of relatively limited value to practitioners—family life educators, marriage and family counselors, and community action workers. The professionals in these areas will have to continue for the near future to rely primarily on information acquired by personal experience, cultural traditions, and philosophical essays. This is not to argue that contemporary theories are of no value, because some of them do have practical implications, but there is at present so little systematic theory that practitioners will have very little to do if their intervention systems are based primarily on systematic theory.

Immediate Theoretical and Research Needs

Conceptual Refinement

One of the biggest obstacles to the scientific study of the family is conceptual ambiguity, and hopefully considerable effort will be devoted in the near future to improving the concepts that are used. One of the main goals of this book was to try to find or invent rational definitions of the variables that were used, but *much* more refinement is needed. Such conceptual refinement could very soon produce a nucleus of terms that will be clearly defined and widely used. This is an open encouragement of conceptual essays such as Rodgers' (1964) attempt to develop a taxonomy and Lively's (1969) critique of a group of concepts. Lively's paper would have been more useful if he had developed some alternative system of conceptualization, but the critique alone does have value.

Two things that would probably improve conceptualizations would be to have (*a*) an explicit, rational definition of variables whenever they are used in a theoretical paper or research report and (*b*) a statement identifying how each of the variables varies. Two other things are desirable but more difficult to acquire. One is to identify several points on the range of variation of variables, and the other is to identify several different ways to empirically measure variables. The process of identifying the points in the variation of variables can be illustrated by proposition 7.15.

PROPOSITION 7.15: Societal complexity influences the extendedness of the kinship structure and this is a curvilinear relationship.

Both the societal complexity variable and the extendedness of the kinship system are continuous variables, and both have three points identified in their range of variation. The extendedness variable has a low and high point, and Goode (1963) has suggested there is an intermediate point, which he labeled a conjugal system. Winch and Blumberg (1968) pointed out that the societal complexity variable also has low, medium, and high levels of complexity. This identification of three points in the range of these two variables permits a much more complex statement about the nature of the relationship than if only two points were identified. This unique curvilinear relationship is diagramed in Figure 7.8. Since most of the variables that are dealt with in studying families are ordinal rather than interval variables, it seems less important to be concerned with the size of the intervals between the points than it does to identify the points.

There are unfortunately several issues that seem to distract scholars when they focus on the nature of concepts. They frequently become concerned with how the variables are distributed in different populations rather than with the nature of the concepts themselves or the theoretical ideas that use the concepts. An example of this diverted concern is the debate about whether the family system in the United States is an isolated nuclear family, a modified extended system, or some other type of system. This debate is a descriptive rather than a theoretical issue, and it is unfortunate that so much ink has been wasted about it. The issue to the original writers in this area was trying to identify how various factors influence the kinship system, and with the exception of research by Winch and his colleagues (1967, 1968), this issue has almost become lost in the debate over whether the family system is primarily one type or another.

A second area where distraction has occurred is in identifying, refining, and differentiating between conceptual "frameworks." Hill and Hansen (1960) pointed out there are different conceptual frameworks that are used in studying the family, and this was a valuable contribution that should have helped scholars be more precise in their theorizing. Knowing that there are different conceptual taxonomies sensitizes the theorist to the fact that some concepts are incompatible with other concepts, and this is useful. This seems, however, to be the only reason to pay attention to conceptual frameworks as *frameworks,* and scholars have already been adequately sensitized to this problem. The conclusion that emerges from this is that spending additional time on such things as the identification, differentiation, and refinement of the assumptions, histories, unique characteristics, and so on, of conceptual *frameworks* does not seem to be an efficient way to spend time. However, spending time on such activities as the refinement, clarification, interdefining, and operationalization of *concepts* does seem to be a productive use of research time and energy.

Acceleration of Theory Building

It is not impossible that the next few years will eventually be known in family sociology (and perhaps even in the larger disciplines of the behavioral sciences) as an "era of theory building." There are three events that have coalesced in recent years that might bring this about. One is that there has been a marked improvement in the *methodology of theorizing.* This culminated in books such as those by Zetterberg (1965),

Stinchcombe (1968), Dubin (1969), Blalock (1969, 1971), Mullins (1971), Reynolds (1971), and Hage (1972).

The second event is that before these recent advances were made in the methodology of theorizing, although theories were developed, most of them were written in a style that made it very difficult to know precisely what was being asserted. Many of these verbose essays buried the ideas in obscure rhetoric. This means that many theoretical ideas are even now so unclearly and ambiguously written that they are not valuable parts of the discipline. Two other deficincies in the way that theories are stated are that (1) even when relationships were asserted, the concepts are frequently poorly defined and (2) usually very imprecise statements are made about the nature of the relationships.

The third phenomenon is that vast amounts of descriptive data have been gathered in the last several decades, and most of this research was neither guided by nor explicitly related to theory. It merely interrelated large numbers of variables. The findings, however, were published and it is hence still possible to use many of the findings as a basis for theory building. Materials such as the KWIC classified bibliography (Aldous and Hill, 1967) of the Minnesota Family Study Center and the annotated bibliographies of the committee on Family Research of the International Sociological Association published in *Current Sociology* in 1958 and 1970 as well as Goode et al.'s recent inventory can be useful aids to the scholar in locating these somewhat disparate research findings.

These three events have created a situation in which most of the ideas that social scientists use are obscurely written, and there is great difficulty in getting large groups of them to agree on the basic theoretical ideas in the disciplines. At the same time, the social scientists who have kept up with the recent advances in the methodology of theorizing now have the tools to dissect earlier theoretical ideas and systematize the theories in them. Moreover, there are large bodies of previously atheoretical data that can now be used as the basis for generating new theoretical ideas and testing the reworked theories. *It thus seems likely that the next few years may be a period in which great resources can be profitably devoted to the systematization of theoretical ideas.* It is a timely activity that is desperately needed, and it will lay groundwork for two other types of activity—empirical research to further test the validity of these theories and the development of social action programs that can be based on scientific social theories.

Several scholars have been working at this type of theory building. Papers as old as the essay by Katz and Hill (1958) and as recent as the paper by Bartz and Nye (1970), and monographs such as that of Goode et al. (1971) and the present volume illustrate this type of activity. It is important, however, that more scholars become involved in this type of activity and that it be done more efficiently. One way to help attain these two goals would be for organizations such as the Family Section of the American Sociological Association and the National Council on Family Relations to take the initiative to do such things as publicize the need for this type of scholarly activity, aid in securing funding for it, provide situations where researchers involved in theory building can react to each other's work, and provide mechanisms for sharing working papers more quickly than is done by the cumbersome and slow process of publication in journals.

Another program that would help attain these two goals would be for a team of theorists at different universities to collaborate in the near future in a project to systematically rework and extend theories about family processes. Each theorist could identify theoretical areas in which he would work and then head a team of colleagues and/or graduate students at their university in gradually formulating a comprehensive statement of the current status of theory in that substantive area. They could identify the substantive areas that are included in this book and a number of other areas such as the effects of variables like power and support (Strauss, 1964), the effects of spacing and number of children, the effects of the various innovative marriage and family systems, and the effects of different types of social networks. Hopefully funding for the time to undertake this type of theoretical systematization and to have the theorists be in frequent contact with each other to provide critiques and reactions of the work of each team will not be too difficult to find. The products of such a program could be published in a series of books that would then be available for guiding and inspiring further empirical research and social action.

The Use of Carefully Explicated Theory to Guide Research

There are several different types of research, and some of them do not attempt to build a scientific discipline. For example, program evaluation research and descriptive research (Simon, 1969:52–54) only at best make indirect contributions to science. On the other hand, the primary objective in verificational research (Zetterberg, 1965: Ch. 7) is to test the validity of theoretical ideas. It is to be hoped that an increasing amount of this latter type of research will be undertaken in the immediate future, and whenever it is done there will be very *clear* statements of (*a*) the theoretical ideas that are being tested and (*b*) the logical connection between the empirically testable hypotheses and the more abstract theoretical ideas.

These verificational studies might be very useful in assessing the validity of theories, even if they are done with small, atypical samples. There are so many sources of invalidity in research other than the unrepresentativeness of samples that it is important to replicate verificational research with different samples, different measurement techniques, different historical periods, different cultures, and different research teams. This means that even if a highly expensive, random sample is acquired, it is still important to replicate the research. In many ways it may be more defensible to use the same economic, temporal, and personnel resources to do several small studies with unique, atypical, economical samples than to do one large study with a quantitatively adequate sample.

The Use of New Empirical Data as a Basis for Extending and / or Modifying Theory

The various editions of Merton's (1968) monograph on *Social Theory and Social Structure* have discussed the interplay between theory and research, and Merton has emphasized that there is more to this interplay than theory guiding research and research testing the theoretical ideas. He points out that empirical data should also be used to modify and/or extend the theoretical ideas. If research reports in the future heed his advice, the authors will not only explicitly state the theoretical ideas that are being tested and make inferences from the data about the validity of these ideas but also attempt to extend and/or modify in a post hoc manner the theory with which they started.

Translation of Theory into Information Usable by Practitioners

There is some evidence that most practitioners in related fields such as family life education and marriage and family counseling find it difficult to apply theories about family processes in their professions. For example, few bona fide theories are included in functional marriage texts. These texts tend to be almost entirely reports of descriptive research and normative exhortations. There are numerous factors that could be contributing to this. It could be that the obscure way that theories have been stated in the past has not made the theories clear enough to use. This is probably not the only reason, though, because the theories that have been well stated also tend not to be used. Another possibility is that many of the theories deal with issues that are not useful to practitioners in these areas.

Another of the possible reasons is that when theories are stated in highly abstract, general terms, it is too large a jump to apply the abstract theory to the specific type of situation that the educator and counselor encounter in the classroom and clinic. If this is the case, then as the theories in the social sciences become more sophisticated and concomitantly more useful to the practitioners, it may become necessary to have a group of professionals play a middle-man role by translating the theories into the kind of information that can be used by the practitioners. It is difficult to know just what form this will take because so little of it is done now, but it may need to be done in the near future. It may take the form of journals that popularize the technical and abstract literature or it may be that as the theories become more clearly stated and useful, the text writers will incorporate them into texts in ways that will be useful to the practitioners.

Strategies for Theory Building

The primary objective in this section is to evaluate the advantages and disadvantages of the various strategies of theory building. Before this evaluative analysis can be undertaken, however, it seems necessary to first identify the strategies that are available. Aldous' (1970) list of five strategies is an effective beginning point, but there are several reasons that this earlier taxonomy no longer seems adequate. The dialogue about her strategies by Nye (1970) and Sprey (1970) and Hill's (1971) later analysis of strategies plus the value of distinguishing between inductive and deductive strategies seem to justify a reworking of Aldous' taxonomy. This is done in the next section, and then an analysis is made of the relative advantages and disadvantages of the strategies.

A Taxonomy of Strategies of Theory Building

It is possible to view theory building with varying degrees of breadth. When it is viewed in a very narrow sense it has several specific goals such as (*a*) inventing new theories, (*b*) extending existing theories, (*c*) integrating theories that have not been previously combined, and (*d*) modifying existing theories by reworking them in the light of new information. These four goals are fairly exhaustive if activities such as borrowing theories from different disciplines and translating highly abstract theories into the kind of specific information practitioners can use are included within the goal of extending existing theories.

When theory building is viewed in a more broad sense it also includes such activities as conceptual development, gathering empirical data to generate, test, and/or modify theory, improving data retrieval systems, improving measurement instruments. There are multiple strategies for each of these activities, and when theory building is viewed in its more inclusive sense all of these strategies are genuine methods of theory building. It is beyond the scope of this chapter, however, to comment on this large list of strategies, so only activities that create, extend, integrate, or modify theories are included in the following taxonomy. This excludes several activities that are closely related to theory building. For example, attempts to refine conceptualization and activities that gather empirical data to use as the basis for theory building are not included. This exclusion should not in any way be interpreted as a judgment that these related activities are less important or less valuable. They are indispensable parts of the scientific enterprise, and it would be impossible to build theory without them.

I.   INDUCTIVE STRATEGIES OF THEORY BUILDING

Inductive strategies are activities that use ideas that are *relatively* specific and concrete to generate *new* ideas of a more general, less specific, and more abstract nature. Four inductive strategies have been identified.

A.   Grounded Strategy

This strategy was developed by Glazer and Strauss (1967) and discussed by Aldous (1970). It is the process of the theorist immersing himself in the data of a research project to attempt to generate new theoretical insights. Glazer and Strauss emphasize that two important parts of this method are to avoid preconceptions of what is being looked for and not be limited to the variables that were initially thought to be important in the research. They also prefer to use this method with qualitative rather than quantitative data.

B.   Codification

Merton (1968:154–55) describes codification as the process of systematizing available empirical generalizations in such a way that findings that are *apparently* different are used as the basis for inducing new theoretical propositions. This strategy was used by Bartz and Nye (1970) and in Chapters 5 and 7 of this book. Merton (1968:69–72) also argues that an efficient way to lay groundwork for the codification process is to develop what he refers to as "paradigms" for sociological analysis. These paradigms are summaries of such phenomena as the assumptions, concepts, logic of procedure, and relationships that are frequently obscure in the sociological literature. It is important to make a clear differentiation between the process of codification and the process of making paradigms. The inventorying process involved in making paradigms lays groundwork for theory building, but it does not actually build; it abstracts. Merton was not only aware of this difference, but he was also aware of some of the dangers of paradigm building or inventorying theories. He commented that paradigms should be used as "a tentative point of departure" in the theory-building process rather than as absolutized blinders or ends themselves.

C.   Axiomatic Method with Definitional Reduction

Zetterberg (1965:94–100) identifies two ways to use inductive strategies to develop what he refers to as axiomatic theory. One is his definitional reduction method, which is done by collapsing several different variables into a single variable or redefining variables so one of the variables includes several previously separate variables. This results in a new theoretical formulation that is more general than any of the original ideas.

D.   Axiomatic Method with Propositional Reduction

The other inductive method Zetterberg (1965:94–100) identifies is proposition reduction. This strategy is to select some of the original propositions as general postulates and then logically derive the others from these more general propositions. This is inductively building theory because some propositions are identified as being more general than others. This strategy can also lead to expanding the theory by then deducing new specific propositions that were not known, but this is not what he terms propositional reduction; it is a deductive rather than inductive strategy.

II.   DEDUCTIVE STRATEGIES OF THEORY BUILDING

Deductive strategies of theory building are the processes of identifying *relatively* abstract, general propositions, and then building *new* theory by the logical process of deducing from these general ideas new propositions that have not previously been identified. It seems useful to differentiate between two deductive strategies at the present stage of family theory development. Probably as the field matures this distinction will seem less useful. These two types are borrowed theory and deduction within one substantive area.

A. Borrowed Theory

This strategy was initially identified by Aldous (1970) and is the process of taking propositions that were generated in a different substantive area and applying them to a new substantive area. When the initial propositions are sufficiently general that it is possible to make deductions about phenomena in the new substantive area, this is a deductive strategy of building theory. It should probably be noted that merely borrowing *concepts* from a different discipline does not build theory. It merely increases the size of a conceptual taxonomy. It might facilitate theory building because the new concept might lead indirectly to new theoretical insights, but merely borrowing concepts is very different from borrowing theoretical propositions, and it is not by itself theory building.

B. Deduction within a Substantive Area

This strategy is the process of building *new* theory by deductively extending a theory within a substantive area of inquiry. This method was not discussed by Aldous (1970) or by Hill (1971) in their lists of strategies, nor was it identified as a separate strategy by Zetterberg in his monograph, although he gives examples of deductively expanding theories (1965:98–99). This is also the strategy that Costner and Leik respond to in their attempt to specify some of the rules of deduction in their paper "Deductions from Axiomatic Theory" (1964).

It is probably important to briefly discuss how this strategy is related to different types of theories such as general theories, middle-range theories, and partial theories. General theories are apparently theories that have great scope and high informative value, and they are not specifically tied to any social context. They are believed to be made up of universal principles. The distinction between general and middle-range theories is not clear in the literature, but it is apparently that middle-range theories are less context free and less generalizable. They are apparently smaller and less complex. The distinction between middle-range theories and partial theories is still less clear, but apparently partial theories are more fragmented or still in the process of being refined. The distinctions between these different types of theories are not important in the present context, because the process of deductively extending any of them is exactly the same as the process of deductively extending the others. No special procedures, qualifications, or risks are unique to any of the types.

III. RETRODUCTIVE STRATEGY

This strategy is the process of combining the deductive and inductive methods to expand theory (Hanson, 1958). One way of doing it is to identify several relatively specific propositions and induce a more general proposition from these propositions. This builds new theory, but it is only half of the process of retroduction. The other half is then deducing new, relatively specific propositions from the more general propositions.

IV. FACTOR STRATEGY

Aldous (1970) refers to a method identified by Gibson (1960:140–144) as a factor method. This is generating new theoretical insights by learning how various independent variables interact with each other. It is different from Zetterberg's inventory of determinants, since the inventory of determinants is just a list of known propositions. The factor method of theory building is generating new knowledge by learning how independent variables interact or may be contingent on one another in influencing one or more common dependent variables.

V. THEORY REWORKING

This strategy is the process of modifying or remodeling a theory to improve it. It is defensible when such things as new methodological tools, new conceptualization, new logical insights, or new empirical data provide a basis for modifying existing theory. It may not build theory in the sense of increasing the amount of theory, but it can build theory in the sense of improving such things as the clarity, testability, communicability, parsimony, and heuristic value. A summary of these strategies of theory building is presented in Table 14.1.

Table 14.1 A Taxonomy of Theory-Building Strategies

  I.   Inductive strategies
       A.   Grounded strategy
       B.   Codification
       C.   Definitional reduction
       D.   Propositional reduction
 II.   Deductive strategies
       A.   Borrowing theory
       B.   Deduction within one substantive area
III.   Retroductive strategy
 IV.   Factor strategy
  V.   Theory reworking

An Evaluation of the Strategies of Theory Building

Theory Reworking: This strategy was found to be very useful in the present theory-building program and there are several factors that can be identified that probably contributed to this usefulness. These same factors seem to argue that this will probably be an efficient strategy in the immediate future. The reasons are that there have been recent advances in the methodology of theorizing and there are vast amounts of theory that, in the light of this methodology, must be defined as poorly written. It is possible, however, that this strategy will be more useful during the next several years than it will be in 10 to 20 years. If a relatively large and concentrated effort is made to rework theories in the next few years, this may systematize the theory in the field enough that there will be less of a need to continue to rework theories and more of a need to use other strategies to build and test theory.

Thus far relatively few professionals have seemed motivated to intensely work at this strategy. This seems unfortunate to the present author because this method seems so timely and it also seems to be a relatively efficient strategy in that rather sizable improvements can be made in theories with relatively few resources.

Borrowing Theory: There are large amounts of theoretical literature in related disciplines that have not been brought to bear on family processes, yet the methodological tools (primarily logic) are available to do so. This means that the strategy of borrowing theory could be an efficient and productive strategy in the immediate future. In the long run borrowing and reworking will probably make less of a contribution than the codification method, but they seem especially timely in the present historical period. Nye (1970) has accurately cautioned that theorists should not *assume* that theories in other substantive areas apply in family situations, but this caution should probably not discourage such activity. It should only sensitize theorists that there may be variables in the familial system or other social contexts that make the principles operate differently in those situations.

Much less has been written about the methodology of this strategy than of the reworking and codification strategies, and there are several comments about this strategy that may be useful. It seems indefensible, for example, to transplant to familial situations theoretical propositions that were generated in unique social situations. It seems more defensible to use a retroductive strategy to do the borrowing. This would entail examining the original theoretical proposition in the context in which it was generated and then attempting to generate a more general theoretical proposition that would be less bound to the specific social context where the idea was discovered. It may be necessary to have several levels of generality before it is possible to begin the process of deducing from the general idea to the familial situation. This method is more complicated than just transplanting a proposition, but it is likely to prove more useful in the long run.

Another issue in the methodology of the borrowing strategy has to do with the skepticism that some theorists in the family area have about adopting propositions from other substantive areas such as the "small groups" research, because the family system is different from the ad hoc laboratory groups used in small groups research. Just the fact that the groups differ seems to be an insufficient reason to hesitate in borrowing theoretical ideas from this literature. The important issue seems to be that there are probably variables in the family system operating as contingencies that influence the operation of propositions which are discovered in small ad hoc groups when these propositions are applied to family processes. Hill (1971) has identified some of these possible variables and suggested that a more detailed analysis of them would be useful. Actually this is a situation that is potentially very valuable for the scholars in both areas rather than a situation in which the family researchers should be overcautious about borrowing. The family theorists can begin the process of specifying the circumstances under which the relationships do and do not operate in the family system, and this seems to be a most efficient way to study families. At the same time the small groups theorists should be interested in seeing if the contingencies discovered in the family system influence the operation of the principles in the types of ad hoc groups they are studying.

The Codification Strategy: This strategy has had and will probably continue to have great value. It tends to be efficient in that it seems to make substantial contributions to theory with moderate amounts of time and effort *when data are available,* and the methodological tools to generate this type of theory are well developed. This strategy seems at the present time to be of less value than it will be in the future because most of the existing data in the field were gathered to describe variables rather than to test existing theory and generate new theory. However, a greater proportion of future data probably will be designed to be used as bases for developing theory.

There are several resources that have been made available in recent years that may facilitate the use of this strategy. The *International Bibliography of Research in Marriage and the Family, 1900–1964* (Aldous and Hill, 1967) provides an extensive bibliography that arranges references according to key words in titles. The Goode et al. (1971) propositional inventory identifies a large number of covariational statements, and its greatest utility to the field will probably be in helping identify empirical generalizations that can be used as the basis for generating more abstract propositions. The idea developed by Merton (1968:69–72) of using sociological paradigms may also be useful in organizing the ideas in literature in such a way that codification can be performed.

Other Strategies: Each of the other strategies of theory building were tried while writing the present volume, but they seemed to be less productive than the strategies discussed previously. This may be because of personal inclinations of the author, or it may be because of other reasons. For example, these other strategies may be more useful at different historical periods, or it *may* be that they are inherently less efficient approaches than the reworking, borrowing, and codification strategies. The real test of the utility of these other strategies will be to see how useful they are in producing theory in the future.

Criticism and Creativity

At the present neophyte stage of theory development, it is easy to find fault with theories. Virtually every theoretical model can be faulted for such things as conceptual ambiguity, the meager amount of data used to develop the theory, the quality of the data, conflicting findings when the ideas are tested, and the fact that there are always other variables that are not taken into account. It is important in the scientific method to be critical, and no attempt is being made here to eliminate criticism. However, an observation is being made here that when criticism is not accompanied by an analysis of ways to improve the deficiencies or problems in a theory it is much less valuable than if creative suggestions are also made about how to correct the faults. *Criticism alone is seldom appreciated, but a dialogue about problems and possible solutions is one of the most rewarding and productive aspects of the scientific profession.* In the current stage of theory development, when so much creative work is needed, this author certainly hopes that criticism will always be accompanied with positive suggestions.

Nonstatistical Bases for Deductions

Zetterberg's (1954) exposition on theory created a new era in sociology as it led to a number of attempts to develop axiomatic or deductive theories. Later, however, the critical comments by Duncan (1963) and the methodological paper by Costner and Leik (1964) seemed to have a depressing effect on the use of deductive theories because they pointed out that the type of deductions that were being made demanded either extremely high covariation or an almost formidable set of assumptions such as one-way causality (asymmetry) as well as independence of all of the error terms. It is argued here that the rules for deduction developed by Costner and Leik (1964) are appropriate under the set of assumptions they made, but it is possible to identify a different set of assumptions that leads to a different set of rules for deduction. It seems important to identify this other set of assumptions and rules, because they will probably stimulate deductive theorizing.

One of the assumptions that is made in the Costner and Leik approach is that it is the strength of the covariation between the variables that provides the basis for making new deductions from theoretical propositions. The different assumption is that the nature of the assertion that is made in the proposition provides the basis for deducing the statistical covariation between the variables. When this is assumed and propositions assert that the variation in some variables tends to bring about variation in other variables, then it is the theorized existence of this causal connection between the variables that provides the basis for deductions. If all of the contingencies were known that affect when this influence occurs, and if it were possible to operationalize all of the variables in these propositions, it would be possible to get statistical covariation that would then approach unity. However, very little is known about contingencies in the modern social sciences and it is presently impossible to measure empirically the abstract variables used in theories. The result is that the relationships proposed in social theories can be thought to have characteristics that cannot be described adequately with correlation coefficients.

The way these differences in assumptions have relevance for theory building is that when the statistical relationship is used as the sole basis for making deductions, the expansion of deductive theories will be very slow, and the theories will have relatively little abstraction. These theories will, however, be highly testable because they will be tied closely with empirical referents. On the other hand, when the assertions made in the theoretical statements are used as the basis for making deductions, this permits relatively rapid expansion of theoretical ideas, and the theories will undoubtedly be larger and more complex. There will undoubtedly be more predictions to divergent social phenomena and broader applications of theories to social situations.

These apparently desirable results of the second method of deducing should be tempered, however, with several of the limitations of this method. The theories that are developed with this method will be more indirectly tied to the empirical data from which they were generated and should hence be viewed with an appropriate tentativeness. They also will be more difficult to corroborate or refute, and the assessment of their validity by the scientific community will be more subjective than the assessment of the validity of the more empirically oriented theories. Another disadvantage is that some of the rules of making deductions have been identified with the Costner and Leik argument, but the only guidelines available for the alternative system discussed here are the rules of logic. There is nothing written about the criteria for judging the "level of proof" of the abstract theoretical ideas when the basis for asserting these ideas is free from statistical covariation.

Even with these limitations, it is suggested here that the method that uses the assertions in theoretical ideas as the basis for deducing is a useful strategy. The ideas in modern theories will probably be usable in the applied professions more quickly, and the expansion of theoretical ideas will provide a broad range of social situations where theoretical ideas can be tested.

Summary

This author's assessment of where the field is and where it is going is that some high-quality theoretical development has occurred, but it is only a very small beginning when compared to the amount that needs to be developed. There has been an increasing amount of it in recent years, and the prospects look excellent for a rapid expansion in the immediate future. This expansion must, of course, proceed in connection with conceptual and empirical developments, but there seems to be a more appropriate balance between these three components of the scientific method at the present time than at any period in the recent past.

REFERENCES

Adams, Bert N.
    1967   "Occupational position, mobility and the kin of orientation." *American Sociological Review* 32 (No. 3):364.
Adams, Bert N.
    1968   *Kinship in an Urban Setting*. Chicago: Markham.
Aldous, Joan
    1970   "Strategies for developing family theory." *Journal of Marriage and the Family* 32:250–257.
Aldous, Joan and Reuben Hill
    1967   *International Bibliography of Research Marriage and the Family 1900–1964*. Minneapolis: University of Minnesota Press.
Allport, G. W.
    1960   "The open system in personality theory." *Journal of Abnormal Social Psychology* 3:301–310.
Angell, R. C.
    1963   The Family Encounters the Depression. New York: Scribner.
Axelson, Leland J.
    1963   "The marital adjustment and marital role definitions of husbands of working and non-working wives." *Marriage and Family Living* 25 (No. 2):189–195.
Baber, Ray E.
    1937   "A study of 325 mixed marriages." *American Sociological Review* 2:705–716.
Baber, Ray E.
    1953   *Marriage and the Family*. Second Edition. New York: McGraw-Hill Book Company, Inc.
Barnett, Larry E.
    1963   "Interracial marriage in California." *Marriage and Family Living* 25 (No. 4):424–427.
Barnett, Larry E.
    1963a "Research on international and interracial marriages." *Marriage and Family Living* 25:105–107.
Bartz, Karen Winch and F. Ivan Nye
    1970   "Early marriage: a propositional formulation." *Journal of Marriage and the Family* 32:258–268.
Bell, Howard M.
    1938   "Youth tell their story." Washington, D.C.: American Council on Education.
Bell, Robert R. and Jack V. Buerkle
    1961   "Mother and daughter attitudes to premarital sexual behavior." *Marriage and Family Living* 23 (No. 4):390–392.

Bell, Robert R. and Jay B. Chaskes
    1970   "Premarital sexual experience among coeds, 1958 and 1968." *Journal of Marriage and the Family 32* (No. 1):81–84.
Bell, W. and M. D. Boat
    1957   "Urban neighborhoods and social participation." *American Journal of Sociology 62:391–398*.
Benson, Purnell
    1955   "The common interests myth in marriage." *Social Problems* 3:27–34.
Bernard, Jessie
    1934   "Factors in the distribution of success in marriage." *American Journal of Sociology* XL:49–60.
Bernard, Jessie
    1966   "Marital stability and patterns of status variables." *Journal of Marriage and the Family* 28:421–439.
Biddle, B. J. and E. J. Thomas
    1966   *Role Theory: Concepts and Research*. New York: John Wiley and Sons.
Blalock, Hubert M., Jr.
    1964   *Causal Inferences in Non-Experimental Research*. Chapel Hill: University of North Carolina Press.
Blalock, Hubert M., Jr.
    1969   *Theory Construction*. Englewood Cliffs, N. J.: Prentice-Hall.
Blalock, Hubert M., Jr.
    1971   *Causal Models in the Social Sciences*. Chicago: Aldine-Atherton.
Blau, Peter M.
    1960   "Structural effects." *American Sociological Review 25:178–193*.
Blau, Peter M.
    1970   "A formal theory of differentiation in organizations." *American Sociological Review 35* (No. 2):201–218.
Blood, Robert O., Jr.
    1952   "Romance and premarital intercourse—incompatibles?" *Marriage and Family Living 14:105–108*.
Blood, Robert O., Jr.
    1963   "The husband and wife relationship." *The Employed Mother in America*. Chicago: Rand McNally Sociology Series: 282–345.
Blood, Robert O., Jr.
    1965   "Long range causes and consequences of the employment of married women." *Journal of Marriage and the Family 27:43–47*.
Blood, Robert O., Jr., and Robert L. Hamblin
    1958   "The effect of the wife's employment on the family power structure." *Social Forces 36* (May):347–352.
Blood, Robert O. and Donald M. Wolfe
    1960   *Husbands and Wives: The Dynamics of Married Living*. Glencoe, Ill.: Free Press.
Blum, Alan F.
    1966   "Social structure, social class, and participation in primary relationships." In William J. Goode (Ed.), *The Dynamics of Modern Society*. New York: Atherton Press, p. 77–86.

Blumer, Herbert
  1956   "Sociological analysis and the variable." *American Sociological Review* XXI (December):683–690.
Bolton, Charles D.
  1961   "Mate selection as the development of a relationship." *Marriage and Family Living 23* (No. 3):234–240.
Bolton, Charles D.
  1963   "Is sociology a behavior science?" *Pacific Sociological Review* VI (Spring):3–9.
Bossard, James H. S. and Eleanor S. Boll
  1954   *Sociology of Child Development.* New York: Harper and Brothers.
Bossard, James H. S. and H. C. Letts
  1956   "Mixed marriages involving Lutherans." *Marriage and Family Living 18:*308–310.
Bott, Elizabeth
  1957   *Family and Social Network.* London: Tavistock Publications, Ltd.
Bowerman, Charles E.
  1956   "Age relationships at marriage, by marital status and age at marriage." *Marriage and Family Living 18* (No. 3):231–233.
Bowerman, Charles E.
  1964   "Prediction studies." In Harold T. Christensen (Ed.), *Handbook of Marriage and the Family.* Chicago: Rand McNally, p. 215–246.
Bowerman, Charles E. and Barbara R. Day
  1956   "A test of the theory of complementary needs as applied to couples during courtship." *American Sociological Review 21:*602–605.
Bradburn, N. M.
  1963   "In pursuit of happiness." National Opinion Research, University of Chicago (May):53, Report No. 92.
Braithwaite, R. B.
  1953   *Scientific Explanation.* London: Cambridge University Press.
Bridgman, P. W.
  1927   *The Logic of Modern Physics.* New York: Macmillan.
Brim, Orville G.
  1959   *Education for Child Rearing.* New York: Russell Sage Foundation.
Brown, Robert
  1963   *Explanation for Social Science.* Chicago: Aldine Publishing Company.
Buck, John L.
  1930   *Chinese Farm Economy.* Chicago: University of Chicago Press.
Buckley, Walter
  1967   *Sociology and Modern Systems Theory.* Englewood Cliffs, N. J.: Prentice-Hall.
Buerkle, J. V. and T. R. Anderson
  1961   "Altruism, role conflict, and marital adjustment: a factor analysis of marital interaction." *Marriage and Family Living 1:*2–26.
Buerkle, J. V. and F. R. Badgley
  1959   "Couple role-taking: the Yale marital interaction battery." *Marriage and Family Living 21:*53–58.

Burchinal, Lee G.
  1957   "Marital satisfaction and religious behavior." *American Sociological Review* 22:306–310.
Burchinal, Lee G.
  1961   "Maternal employment, family relations and selected personality, school-related and social-development characteristics of children." Bulletin 497 (October). Ames: Iowa State University Agricultural and Home Economics Experiment Station.
Burchinal, Lee G.
  1964   "The premarital dyad and love involvement." In Harold T. Christensen (Ed.), *Handbook of Marriage and the Family*. Chicago: Rand McNally, p. 623–674.
Burchinal, Lee G. and Elmer W. Bock
  1959   "Religious behavior, premarital pregnancy, and early maturity." *Alpha Kappa Deltan 29* (No. 2):39–44.
Burchinal, Lee G. and Loren Chancellor
  1962   "Survival rates among religiously homogamous and heterogamous marriages." Research Bulletin 512 (December). Ames: Iowa State University Agricultural and Home Economics Experiment Station.
Burchinal, Lee G. and Loren Chancellor
  1963   "Survival rates among religiously homogamous and interreligious marriages." *Social Forces 41* (No. 4):353–362.
Burchinal, Lee G. and William F. Kenkel
  1962   "Ages at marriage, occupations of grooms and interreligious marriage rates." *Social Forces 40* (No. 4):348–354.
Burchinal, Lee G. and Jack Rossman
  1961   "Personality characteristics of children." *Marriage and Family Living* XXIII (November):334–340.
Burgess, Ernest W. and Leonard S. Cottrell, Jr.
  1936   "The prediction of adjustment in marriage." *American Sociological Review 1*:737–751.
Burgess, Ernest W. and Leonard S. Cottrell, Jr.
  1939   *Predicting Success or Failure in Marriage*. Englewood Cliffs, N. J.: Prentice-Hall.
Burgess, Ernest, Harvey J. Locke, and Mary Margaret Thomas
  1963   *The Family*. Third Edition. New York: American Book Company.
Burgess, Ernest W. and Paul Wallin
  1953   *Engagement and Marriage*. Philadelphia: J. B. Lippincott Company.
Burma, John H.
  1952   "Research note on the measurement of interracial marriage." *American Journal of Sociology* 57 (No. 6):587–589.
Burma, John H.
  1963   "Interethnic marriage in Los Angeles, 1948–1959." *Social Forces* 42:156–165.
Burr, Wesley R.
  1967   "Marital satisfaction: a conceptual reformulation; theory and partial test of the theory." Unpublished Ph.D. dissertation, University of Minnesota.
Burr, Wesley R.

1971 "An expansion and test of a role theory of marital satisfaction." *Journal of Marriage and the Family 33:*368–372.

Campbell, D. A. and J. Stanley
1963 *Experimental and Quasi-Experimental Designs for Research.* Chicago: Rand McNally.

Campbell, E. Q. and T. F. Pettigrew
1959 "Racial and moral crisis: the role of Little Rock ministers." *American Journal of Sociology 64:*509–516.

Catton, William R., Jr., and R. J. Smirich
1964 "A comparison of mathematical models for the effect of residential propinquity on mate selection." *American Sociological Review 29:*522–529.

Cavan, Ruth Shonle
1962 "Self and role in adjustment during old age." In Arnold M. Rose (Ed.), *Human Behavior and Social Processes.* Boston: Houghton Mifflin.

Cavan, Ruth Shonle
1969 *The American Family.* Third Edition. New York: Thomas Y. Crowell.

Cavan, Ruth Shonle and Katherine H. Ranck
1938 *The Family and the Depression.* Chicago: University of Chicago Press.

Chancellor, Loren E. and Thomas P. Monahan
1955 "Religious preference and interreligious mixtures in marriages and divorces in Iowa." *American Journal of Sociology 41:*233–239.

Cheng, C. K. and Douglas S. Yamamura
1957 "Interracial marriage and divorce in Hawaii." *Social Forces 36* (No. 1):77–84.

Christensen, Harold T.
1960 "Cultural relativism and premarital sex norms." *American Sociological Review 25:*31–39.

Christensen, Harold T.
1962 "A cross-cultural comparison of attitudes toward marital infidelity." *International Journal of Comparative Sociology 3:*124–137.

Christensen, Harold T.
1963 "Child spacing analysis via record linkage: new data plus summing up from earlier reports." *Marriage and Family Living 25:*272–280.

Christensen, Harold T.
1969 "Normative theory derived from cross-cultural family research." *Journal of Marriage and the Family 31* (May):209–222.

Christensen, Harold T. and Kenneth E. Barber
1967 "Interfaith versus intrafaith marriage in Indiana." *Journal of Marriage and the Family 29:*461–469.

Christensen, Harold T. and George Carpenter
1962 "Timing patterns in premarital sexual intimacy: an attitudinal report on three modern western societies." *Marriage and Family Living 24* (No. 1):30–35.

Christensen, Harold T. and Christina F. Gregg
1970 "Changing sex norms in America and Scandinavia." *Journal of Marriage and the Family 32* (No. 4):616–627.

Christensen, Harold T. and Hanna H. Meissner
    1953   "Studies in child spacing: III—premarital pregnancy as a factor in
            divorce." *American Sociological Review 18* (No. 6):641–644.
Clarke, Alfred C.
    1952   "An examination of the operation of residential propinquity as a
            factor in mate selection." *American Sociological Review 17*:17–22.
Cohen, M. and E. Nagel
    1934   *An Introduction to Logic and Scientific Method.* New York: Har-
            court.
Coombs, Robert H.
    1962   "Reinforcement of values in the parental home as a factor in mate
            selection." *Marriage and Family Living 24* (No. 2):155–157.
Corsini, Raymond J.
    1956   "Multiple predictors of marital happiness." *Marriage and Family
            Living 18:*240–242.
Corsini, Raymond J.
    1956a   "Understanding and similarity in marriage." *Journal of Abnormal
            and Social Psychology 52*(No. 3):326–332.
Costner, Herbert L.
    1969   "Theory, deduction, and rules of correspondence." *American Jour-
            nal of Sociology 75*(No. 2):245–263.
Costner, Herbert L. and Robert K. Leik
    1964   "Deductions from 'Axiomatic Theory.'" *American Sociological Re-
            view 29* (December):819–835.
Cottrell, L. S., Jr.
    1933   "Roles and marital adjustment." *American Sociological Society,*
            University of Chicago Press (May):108–115.
Cottrell, L. S., Jr.
    1942   "The adjustment of the individual to his age and sex roles." *Ameri-
            can Sociological Review 7*(October):617–620.
Cumming, Elaine, et al.
    1960   "Disengagement—a tentative theory of aging." *Sociometry XXIII*
            (March):23–25.
Davis, Katherine B.
    1929   *Factors in the Sex Life of Twenty-Two Hundred Women.* New
            York: Harper and Brothers.
Davis, Kingsley
    1940   "Extreme social isolation of a child." *American Journal of Sociol-
            ogy XLV* (January):554–565.
Davis, Kingsley
    1947   "Final note on a case of extreme isolation." *The American Journal
            of Sociology 52* (No. 5):432–437.
Davis, Kingsley
    1949   *Human Society.* New York: Macmillan.
Davis, Kingsley
    1962   "The role of class mobility in economic development." *Population
            Review 6*(July):67–73.
Davis, K. and J. Blake
    1956   "Social structure and fertility: an analytical framework." *Economic
            Development and Cultural Change 4* (April):211–235.

Day, Barbara R.
  1961 "A comparison of personality needs of courtship couples and same sex friendships." *Sociology and Social Research* 45 (No. 4):435–440.
Dean, Dwight G.
  1961 "Romanticism and emotional maturity: a preliminary study." *Marriage and Family Living 23* (February):44–45.
Dean, Dwight G.
  1964 "Romanticism and emotional maturity: a further exploration." *Social Forces 42:*298–303.
DeBurger, J. E.
  1961 "Selected factors in premarital experience related to marital adjustment." Master's thesis, Indiana University.
Deutscher, Irwin
  1959 *Married Life in the Middle Years.* Kansas City, Mo.: Community Studies.
Deutscher, Irwin
  1962 "Socialization for post-parental life." In Arnold M. Rose (Ed.), *Human Behavior and Social Processes.* Boston: Houghton Mifflin, pp. 506–525.
Doby, J. T.
  1967 *An Introduction to Social Research.* New York: Appleton-Century-Crofts.
Douvan, Elizabeth
  1963 "Employment and the adolescent." *The Employed Mother in America.* Chicago: Rand McNally.
Dubin, Robert
  1969 *Theory Building.* Glencoe, Ill.: Free Press.
Duncan, Otis Dudley
  1963 "Axioms or correlations?" *American Sociological Review 28* (June):452.
Duvall, Evelyn
  1945 "Loneliness and the serviceman's wife." *Marriage and Family Living* (August):77–82.
Duvall, Evelyn
  1967 *Family Development.* Philadelphia: Lippincott.
Dyer, Everett D.
  1963 "Parenthood as crisis: a re-study." *Marriage and Family Living 25* (May):196–201.
Dyer, William G. and Dick Urban
  1958 "The institutionalization of equalitarian family norms." *Marriage and Family Living 20:*53–58.
Dymond, Rosalind
  1953 "The relation of accuracy of perception of the spouse and marital happiness." *American Psychologists* VIII:344.
Ehrmann, Winston W.
  1959 *Premarital Dating Behavior.* New York: Henry Holt and Co.
Elder, Gen, Jr.
  1962 "Structural variations in the child-rearing relationships." *Sociometry 25:*241–262.

Ellis, Robert A. and Clayton W. Lane
  1967   "Social mobility and social isolation: a test of Sorokin's dissociative hypothesis." *American Sociological Review 32* (April):237–253.
Essig, May and D. H. Morgan
  1945   "Adjustment of adolescent daughters of employed mothers to family life." *Journal of Educational Psychology* XXXVII (April):219–233.
Farber, Bernard
  1957   "An index of marital integration." *Sociometry 20*(June):117–134.
Foote, Nelson and L. B. Cottrell
  1955   *Identity and Interpersonal Competence.* Chicago: University of Chicago Press.
Francis, R. G.
  1967   *Some Elementary Logic: An Introduction to Social Research.* New York: Appleton-Century-Crofts.
Freedman, R.
  1962   "The sociology of human fertility: a trend report and bibliograph." *Current Sociology 11:*35–121.
French, John R. P. and Bertram Raven
  1960   "The bases of social power." In D. Cartwright and A. Zander, Group Dynamics Research and Theory. Second Edition. New York: Row, Peterson, and Company, p. 607–622.
Gianopulos, Artie and Howard E. Mitchell
  1957   "Marital disagreement in working wife marriage as a function of husband's attitude toward wife's employment." *Marriage and Family Living 19*(November):373–378.
Gibson, Q.
  1960   *The Logic of Social Enquiry.* New York: Humanities Press.
Glazer, B. G. and A. L. Strauss
  1967   *The Discovery of Grounded Theory: Strategies for Qualitative Research.* Chicago: Aldine Press.
Glick, Paul C.
  1957   *American Families.* New York: John Wiley and Sons.
Glueck, S. and E. Glueck
  1957   "Working   mothers   and   delinquency."   *Mental   Hygiene 41:*327–352.
Goffman, Erving
  1959   *The Presentation of Self in Everyday Life.* New York: Doubleday-Anchor.
Gold, M. A.
  1961   *A Social-Psychology of Delinquent Boys.* Ann Arbor, Mich.: Institute for Social Research.
Golden, Joseph
  1954   "Patterns of Negro-white intermarriage." *American Sociological Review 19* (No. 20):144–147.
Goode, William J.
  1956   *After Divorce.* Glencoe, Ill.: Free Press.
Goode, William J.
  1960   "A Theory of role strain." *American Sociological Review 25* (August):488–496.

Goode, William J.
  1961   "Illegitimacy, anomie, and cultural penetration." *American Socio-
        logical Review 26* (No. 6):910–925.
Goode, William J.
  1963   "Norm commitment and conformity to role status obligations."
        *American Journal of Sociology 66:*253.
Goode, William J.
  1963a *World Revolution and Family Patterns.* New York: Free Press of
        Glencoe.
Goode, William J., Elizabeth Hopkins, and Helen McClure
  1971   *Social Systems and Family Patterns: A Propositional Inventory.*
        New York: Bobbs-Merrill.
Gross, N., et al.
  1957   *Explorations in Role Analysis: Studies of the School Superinten-
        dency Role.* New York: John Wiley and Sons.
Guilford, J. P.
  1954   *Psychometric Methods.* Second Edition. New York: McGraw-Hill.
Hage, Jerald
  1972   *Techniques and Problems of Theory Construction in Sociology.*
        New York: Wiley-Interscience.
Hamblin, Robert L. and Robert O. Blood, Jr.
  1956   "Premarital experience and the wife's sexual adjustment." *Social
        Problems 3:*122–130.
Hamilton, Gilbert V.
  1929   *A Research in Marriage.* New York: A and C Boni.
Hansen, Donald A.
  1965   "Personal and positional influence in formal groups: propositions
        and theory for research on family vulnerability to stress." *Social
        Forces 44:*202–210.
Hansen, Donald A. and Reuben Hill
  1964   "Families under stress." In Harold T. Christensen (Ed.), *Handbook
        of Marriage and the Family.* Chicago: Rand McNally.
Hanson, Norwood R.
  1958   *Patterns of Discovery.* London: Cambridge University Press.
Hanson, Norwood R.
  1958a "The logic of discovery." *Journal of Philosophy* 25(De-
        cember):1073–1089.
Hanson, Norwood R.
  1960   "More on 'The logic of discovery.'" *Journal of Philosophy 57·*
        (January):182–188.
Hardy, Kenneth
  1964   "An appetitional theory of sexual motivation." *Psychological Re-
        view 71:*1–18.
Hartley, Ruth E.
  1960   "Some implications of current changes in sex role patterns." *Mer-
        rill Palmer Quarterly 6* (No. 3) (April):1953–164.
Hawkins, James L. and Kathryn Johnsen
  1969   "Perception of behavioral conformity, imputation of consensus,
        and marital satisfaction." *Journal of Marriage and the Family 31*
        (No. 3):507–511.

Hawley, Amos H.
  1950 *Human Ecology.* New York: Ronald Press.
Hays, W. L.
  1963 *Statistics for Psychologists.* New York: Holt, Rinehart, and Winston.
Heer, David M.
  1958 "Dominance and the working wife." In R. I. Nye and Lois W. Hoffman, *The Employed Mother in America.* Chicago: Rand McNally, p. 341–347.
Heer, David M.
  1963 "The measurement and bases of family power: an overview." *Marriage and Family Living* 25 (May):133–139.
Heer, David M.
  1963a "Reply." *Marriage and Family Living* 25 (November):477–478.
Heer, David M.
  1966 "Negro-white marriage in the United States." *Journal of Marriage and the Family* 28(August) (No. 3):262–273.
Heider, F.
  1958 *The Psychology of Interpersonal Relations.* New York: John Wiley and Sons.
Heiss, Jerold S.
  1960 "Premarital characteristics of the religiously intermarried in an urban area." *American Sociological Review* 25:47–55.
Heiss, Jerold S.
  1961 "Interfaith marriage and marital outcomes." *Marriage and Family Living* 23:228–233.
Heiss, Jerold S.
  1962 "Degree of intimacy and male-female interaction." *Sociometry* 25:196–208.
Heltsley, Mary E. and Carlfred B. Broderick
  1969 "Religiosity and premarital sexual permissiveness: reexamination of Reiss's traditionalism proposition." *Journal of Marriage and the Family* 31 (No. 3):441–443.
Henry, A. F.
  1957 "Sibling structure and perception of the disciplinary roles of parents." *Sociometry* 20:67–74.
Herbst, P. G.
  1953 "Analysis and measurement of a situation: the child in the family." *Human Relations:* 113–140.
Herzog, Elizabeth
  1960 "Children of working mothers." Children's Bureau Publication. U.S. Department of Health, Education, and Welfare. Social Security Administration.
Hill, Reuben
  1949 *Families under Stress.* New York: Harper.
Hill, Reuben
  1958 "Sociology of marriage and family behavior, 1945–56: a trend report and bibliography." *Current Sociology* 7:1–98.
Hill, Reuben
  1965 "Decision making and the family life cycle." In Ethel Shanas and Gordon F. Streib, *Social Structure and the Family,* Englewood Cliffs: Prentice Hall, Inc., pp. 113–139.

Hill, Reuben
    1966   "Contemporary developments in family theory." *Journal of Marriage and the Family* 28:10–25.
Hill, Reuben
    1971   "Payoffs and limitations of contemporary strategies for family theory systematization." Paper presented at NCFR Meetings in Estes Park, Colorado, August 1971.
Hill, Reuben and Donald A. Hansen
    1960   "The identification of conceptual frameworks utilized in family study." *Marriage and Family Living* 22:299–311.
Hill, Reuben and D. A. Hansen
    1962   "The family in disaster." In G. Baker and D. Chapman (Eds.), *Man and Society in Disaster.* New York: Basic Books.
Hill, Reuben, Alvin M. Katz, and Richard L. Simpson
    1957   "An inventory of research in marriage and family behavior: a statement of objectives and progress." *Marriage and Family Living* 19 (February):89–92.
Hill, Reuben and R. H. Rodgers
    1964   "The developmental approach." *Handbook of Marriage and the Family.* Chicago: Rand McNally, pp. 171–211.
Hillman, Karen G.
    1962   "Marital instability and its relation to education, income, and occupation: an analysis based on census data." In R. F. Winch, R. McGinnis, and H. R. Barringer (Eds.), *Selected Studies in Marriage and the Family.* (Revised Edition.) New York: Holt, Rinehart, and Winston.
Himes, Joseph S.
    1952   "Value consensus in mate selection among Negroes." *Marriage and Family Living* 14:317–321.
Himes, Joseph S.
    1960   "The interrelation of occupational and spousal roles in a middle class Negro neighborhood." *Journal of Marriage and the Family* (No. 22):362–363.
Hobart, Charles and William Clausner
    1959   "Some social interactional correlates of marital role disagreement and marital adjustment." *Marriage and Family Living* 21:256–263.
Hobart, Charles W. and Lauralee Lindholm
    1963   "The theory of complementary needs: a re-examination." *Pacific Sociological Review* 6 (No. 2):73–79.
Hobbs, Daniel F., Jr.
    1965   "Parenthood as crisis: a third study." *Journal of Marriage and the Family* 27 (August):367–372.
Hobbs, Daniel F., Jr.
    1968   "Transition to parenthood: a replication and an extension." *Journal of Marriage and the Family* 30 (August):413–417.
Hodge, Robert W., et al.
    1964   "Occupational prestige in the United States, 1925–1963." *American Journal of Sociology* 70 (November):286–302.
Hoffman, Lois W.
    1960   "Parental coerciveness, child autonomy and child's role at school." *Sociometry* 23:15–22.

Hoffman, Lois W.
  1961   "Effects of the employment of mothers on parental power relations and the division of household tasks." *Marriage and Family Living* 22 (No. 1):27–35.
Hoffman, Lois W.
  1961a "Effects of maternal employment on the child." *Child Development* 32:187–197.
Hoffman, Lois W.
  1963   "Mother's employment of work and effects on the child." In F. I. Nye and L. W. Hoffman, *The Employed Mother in America*. Chicago: Rand McNally, p. 95–105.
Hollingshead, August B.
  1949   *Elmtown's Youth*. New York: John Wiley and Sons.
Hollingshead, August B.
  1950   "Cultural factors in the selection of marriage mates." *American Sociological Review* 15:619–627.
Homans, George C.
  1950   *The Human Group*. New York: Harcourt Brace.
Homans, George C.
  1958   "Social behavior as exchange." *American Journal of Sociology* 63:597–606.
Homans, George C.
  1961   *Social Behavior: Its Elementary Forms*. New York: Harcourt, Brace and World.
Homans, George C.
  1964   "Contemporary theory in sociology." In R. E. L. Faris (Ed.), *Handbook of Modern Sociology*. Chicago: Rand McNally.
Homans, George C.
  1964a "Bringing men back in." *American Sociological Review* 29 (December):809–818.
Huntington, Robert M.
  1958   "The personality-interaction approach to study of the marital relationship." *Marriage and Family Living* 20:43–46.
Ikeda, Yoshisuke, and Eiji Sasaki
  1957   "The circle of intermarriage in the contemporary huge urban society." *Japanese Sociological Review* 7 (No. 2):52–58.
Jackson, Jay M.
  1966   "Structural characteristics of norms." In B. J. Biddle and E. J. Thomas. *Role Theory: Concepts and Research*. New York: John Wiley and Sons, p. 113–125.
Jacobson, Alver H.
  1952   "Conflict of attitudes toward the roles of the husband and wife in marriage." *American Sociological Review* 17:146–150.
Jacobson, Paul Harold
  1959   *American Marriage and Divorce*. New York: Rinehart and Company.
Kanin, Eugene J. and David H. Howard
  1958   "Postmarital consequences of premarital sex adjustments." *American Sociological Review* 23 (No. 5):556–562.
Katz, Alvin M. and Reuben Hill

1958 "Residential propinquity and marital selection: a review of theory, method, and fact." *Journal of Marriage and the Family* 20:27–35.

Kaplan, Abraham
1964 *The Conduct of Inquiry*. San Francisco: Chandler.

Karlsson, Georg
1951 *Adaptability and Communication in Marriage: A Swedish Predictive Study of Marital Satisfaction*. Uppsala: Almqvist and Wiksells Boktryckeri.

Karlsson, Georg
1963 *Adaptability and Communication in Marriage*. Totowa, N.J.: The Bedminister Press.

Katz, Alvin and Reuben Hill
1958 "Residential propinquity and marital selection," *Marriage and Family Living* 20:27–35.

Kelley, E. Lowell
1939 "Concerning the validity of Terman's weights for predicting marital happiness." *Psychological Bulletin* XXXVI (March): 202–203.

Kelley, E. Lowell
1955 "Consistency of the adult personality." *American Psychologist* X:659–681.

Kennedy, Ruby and Joe Reeves
1944 "Single or teiple melting pot? Intermarriage trends in New Haven 1870–1940." *American Journal of Sociology* 39:331–339.

Kent, Donald P.
1951 "Subjective factors in mate selection: an exploratory study." *Sociology and Social Research* 35:391–398.

Kephart, William M.
1954 "The duration of marriage." *American Sociological Review* XIX (June):287–295.

Kephart, William M.
1961 *The Family, Society and the Individual*. Boston: Houghton Mifflin.

Kerckhoff, A. C.
1956 "Notes and comments on the meaning of residential propinquity as a factor in mate selection." *Social Forces* 35 (No. 3):207–213.

Kerckhoff, A. C. and K. E. Davis
1962 "Value consensus and need complementarity in mate selection." *American Sociological Review* 27 (No. 3):295–303.

Kerlinger, Fred N.
1964 *Foundations of Behavioral Research*. New York: Holt, Rinehart, and Winston.

Kernodle, W.
1959 "Some implications of the homogamy-complementary needs theories of mate selection for sociological research." *Social Forces* 38:145–152.

Kimura, Yukiko
1957 "War brides in Hawaii and their in-laws." *American Journal of Sociology* 63:70–76.

King, Charles E.
1951 A research technique of marital adjustment applied to a southern

urban minority population group. From Factors Making for Success or Failure in Marriage Among 466 Negro Couples in a Southern City. Ph.D. thesis, University of Chicago.

Kinsey, Alfred C., et al.
  1953   *Sexual Behavior in the Human Female*. Philadelphia: W. B. Saunders Company.

Kirkendall, Lester A.
  1961   *Premarital Intercourse and Interpersonal Relations*. New York: Julian Press.

Kirkpatrick, Clifford and Charles Hobart
  1964   "Disagreement, disagreement estimate and non-empathetic imputation for intimacy groups varying from favorite date to be married." *American Sociological Review 19* (No. 1):10–19.

Kligler, Deborah H.
  1954   "The effects of the employment of married women on husband and wife roles." Unpublished PhD. dissertation, Yale University.

Kogan, Kate L. and Joan K. Jackson
  1964   "Perceptions of self and spouse: some contaminating factors." *Journal of Marriage and the Family 26*:60–64.

Koller, Marvin R.
  1948   "Residential propinquity of white mates at marriage in relation to age and occupation of males." *American Sociological Review 13* (October):613–616.

Komarovsky, Mirra
  1940   *The Unemployed Man and His Family*. New York: Dryden Press.

Komarovsky, Mirra
  1962   *Blue-Collar Marriage*. New York: Random House.

Koos, E. L.
  1946   *Families in Trouble*. New York: King's Crown Press.

Koos, E. L.
  1953   *Marriage*. New York: Henry Holt and Company.

Kotlar, Sally L.
  1961   "Middle class roles . . . ideal and perceived in relation to adjustment in marriage." Unpublished doctoral dissertation, University of Southern California, Los Angeles, California.

Kotlar, Sally L.
  1962   "Instrumental and expressive marital roles." *Sociology and Social Research 2*:46.

Lajewski, Henry C.
  1959   "Child care arrangements of full time working mothers." U.S. Department of Health, Education, and Welfare, Children's Bureau Publication.

Landis, Judson T.
  1949   "Marriages of mixed and non-mixed religious faith." *American Sociological Review 14*:401–407.

Landis, Judson T.
  1956   "The pattern of divorce in three generations." *Social Forces 34* (No. 3):201–207.

Landis, Judson T.
  1960   Religiousness, family relationships, and family values in Prot-

estant, Catholic, and Jewish families." *Marriage and Family Living* 22 (No. 4):341–347.

Landis, Judson T.
1962 "A comparison of children from divorced and non-divorced unhappy marriages." *The Family Life Coordinator 11* (No. 3):61–65.

Landis, Judson T.
1963 "Social correlates of divorce or non-divorce among the unhappy married." *Marriage and the Family Living 25* (May):178–180.

Landis, Paul H.
1950 "Sequential marriage." *Journal of Home Economics 42*:625–627.

Lansing, J. B. and L. Kish
1957 "Family life cycle as an independent variable." *American Sociological Review 22*:512–519.

Lazarsfeld, Paul F.
1955 "Interpretation of statistical relations as a research operation." In Paul F. Lazarsfeld and Morris Rosenberg (Eds.), *The Language of Social Research.* New York: Free Press.

LeMasters, E. E.
1957 "Parenthood as crisis." *Marriage and Family Living 19*:352–355.

Lenski, G.
1954 "Status crystallization: a nonvertical dimension of social status." *American Sociological Review 19*:405–413.

Lerner, D.
1965 *Cause and Effect.* New York: Free Press.

Leslie, Gerald R.
1967 *The Family in Social Context.* New York: Oxford University Press.

Leslie, Gerald R. and Arthur H. Richardson
1956 "Family versus campus influences in relation to mate selection." *Social Problems 55* (No. 2):117–121.

Lewis, Oscar
1958 *Village Life in Northern India.* Urbana: University of Illinois Press, p. 17.

Levinger, George
1964 "Note on need complementarity in marriage." *Psychological Bulletin 61*:153–157.

Linton, Ralph
1936 *The Study of Man.* New York: Appleton-Century, p. 348–355.

Linton, Ralph
1959 "The natural history of the family." In Ruth Nanda Anshen, *The Family: Its Function and Destiny.* New York: Harper and Brothers, p. 30–52.

Litwak, Eugene
1960 "Occupational mobility and extended family cohesion." *American Sociological Review 25* (February):9–21.

Litwak, Eugene
1960a "Geographic mobility and extended family cohesion." *American Sociological Review 25* (June):385–394.

Lively, Edwin
1969 "Toward concept clarification: the case of marital interaction." *Journal of Marriage and the Family 31* (February):108–114.

Livingstone, Frank B.
    1959   "A formal analysis of prescriptive marriage systems among the
           Australian Aborigines." *Southwestern Journal of Anthropology 15*
           (No. 4):261–372.
Locke, Harvey J.
    1951   *Predicting Adjustment in Marriage: A Comparison of a Divorced
           and a Happily Married Group.* New York: Henry Holt and Com-
           pany.
Locke, Harvey J.
    1956   "Correlates of primary communication and empathy." *Research
           Studies of the State College of Washington 24*:116–124.
Locke, Harvey J. and William Klausner
    1948   "Prediction of marital adjustment of divorced persons in subse-
           quent marriages." *Research Studies of the State College of Wash-
           ington 16*:30–33.
Locke, Harvey J. and Muriel Mackenprang
    1949   "Marital adjustment and the employed wife." *American Journal of
           Sociology 18*:536–538.
Locke, Harvey J. and Karl M. Wallace
    1959   "Short marital adjustment and prediction tests: their reliability and
           validity." *Marriage and Family Living 21* (August):250–255.
Locke, Harvey J., et al.
    1957   "Interfaith marriages." *Social Problems 4* (No. 4):329–333.
Locke, Harvey J., et al.
    1963   *The Family.* New York: American Book Company.
Luckey, Eleanore B.
    1960   "Marital satisfaction and its association with congruence of percep-
           tion." *Marriage and Family Living 22*:49–54.
Luckey, Eleanore B.
    1961   "Perceptual congruence of self and family concepts as related to
           marital interaction." *Sociometry 24*:234–250.
Lundy, Richard M.
    1958   "Self-perceptions regarding masculinity-feminity and descriptions
           of same and opposite sex sociometric choices." *Sociometry
           21*:231–246.
Maccoby, Eleanor
    1958   "Children and working mothers." *The Child 3* (No. 3)
           (May–June):83–89.
Maccoby, Eleanor
    1958a "Effects upon children of their mother's outside employment."
           Work in the Lives of Married Women. New York: Columbia Uni-
           versity Press, p. 150–172.
Mangus, A. R.
    1957   "Role theory and marriage counseling." *Social Forces 35*
           (March):202–209.
Manheim, Henry L.
    1961   "A socially unacceptable method of mate selection." *Sociology and
           Social Research 45* (No. 2):182–187.
Marshall, Alfred
    1961   *Principles of Economics.* Ninth Edition. New York: Macmillan.

Martinson, Floyd M.
  1959   "Ego deficiency as a factor in marriage: a male sample." *Marriage and Family Living 21*:48–52.
Marx, Melvin H. (Ed.)
  1963   *Theories in Contemporary Psychology.* New York: Macmillan.
McGinnis, Robert
  1958   "Campus values in mate selection: a repeat study." *Social Forces 36* (No. 4):368–373.
Mead, George
  1934   *Mind, Self, and Society.* Chicago: The University of Chicago Press.
Mead, Margaret
  1935   *Sex and Temperament in Three Primitive Societies.* New York: Morrow.
Mering, Fay Higier von
  1955   "Professional and non-professional women as mothers." *Journal of Social Psychology XLII* (August):21–34.
Merton, R. K.
  1963   "The ambivalence of scientists." *Bulletin of the Johns Hopkins Hospital 112* (February):77–97.
Merton, Robert K.
  1968   *Social Theory and Social Structure.* Enlarged Edition. Glencoe, Ill.: Free Press.
Meyerowitz, Joseph H. and Harold Feldman
  1966   "Transition to parenthood." *Psychiatric Research Reports 20*:78–84.
Michel, Andree
  1967   "Comparative data concerning the interaction in French and American families." *Journal of Marriage and the Family 29* (May):337–344.
Middleton, Russell and Snell Putney
  1960   "Dominance in decisions in the family: race and class differences." *American Journal of Sociology LXV* (May):605–609.
Mitchell, Howard E., et al.
  1962   "Areas of marital conflict in successfully and unsuccessfully functioning families." *Journal of Health and Human Behavior 3*:88–93.
Monahan, Thomas P. and William M. Kephart
  1954   "Divorce and desertion by religious and mixed-religious groups." *American Journal of Sociology 59*:454–465.
Morris, Richard R.
  1956   "A typology of norms." *American Sociological Review* (October):610–613.
Mullins, Nicholas C.
  1971   *The Art of Theory: Construction and Use.* New York: Harper & Row.
Murdock, George P.
  1949   *Social Structure.* New York: Macmillan.
Murdock, George P.
  1950   "Family stability in non-European cultures." *Annals 272*:195–201.
Murdock, George P.

1957   "World enthnographic sample." *American Anthropologist* XX (No. 4)(August):664:687.

Murray, H. A.
1938   *Explorations in Personality*. New York: Oxford.

Murstein, Bernard I.
1961   "The complementary need hypothesis in newlyweds and middle-aged married couples." *Journal of Abnormal and Social Psychology* 63 (No. 1):194–197.

Murstein, Bernard I.
1967   "Empirical tests of role, complementary needs, and homogamy theories of marital choice." *Journal of Marriage and the Family* 29 (November):689–696.

Nagel, E.
1961   *The Structure of Science*. New York: Harcourt, Brace and World.

National Office of Vital Statistics
1957   *Special Reports*. Vol. 46, No. 4.

Newcomb, Theodore M.
1956   "The prediction of interpersonal attraction." *American Psychologist* 11:575–586.

Newcomb, Theodore M.
1961   *The Acquaintance Process*. New York: Holt, Rinehart, and Winston.

Nimkoff, M. F. and Russell Middleton
1960   "Types of family and types of economy." *American Journal of Sociology* 66:215–225.

Nye, F. Ivan
1952   "Adolescent-parent adjustment: age, sex, sibling number, broken homes, and employed mothers as variables." *Marriage and Family Living* XIV (November):327–332.

Nye, F. Ivan
1957   "Child adjustment in broken and in unhappy unbroken homes." *Marriage and Family Living* 17:356–361.

Nye, F. Ivan
1958   *Family Relationships and Delinquent Behavior*. New York: John Wiley and Sons.

Nye, F. Ivan
1959   "Employment status of mothers and adjustment of adolescent children." *Marriage and Family Living* 20:240–244.

Nye, F. Ivan
1967   "Values, family and a changing society." *Journal of Marriage and the Family* 29 (May):241.

Nye, F. Ivan
1970   "Comments on Aldous' 'Strategies for Developing Family Theory.'" *Journal of Marriage and the Family* 32 (No. 3):338–339.

Nye, F. Ivan and A. E. Bayer
1963   "Some recent trends in family research." *Social Forces* 41:290–301.

Nye, F. Ivan and Felix M. Berardo (Eds.)

1966   *Emerging Conceptual Frameworks in Family Analysis.* New York: Macmillan.

Nye, F. Ivan and Lois Hoffman
1963   *The Employed Mother in America.* Chicago: Rand McNally.

Nye, F. Ivan, et al.
1963   "Anxiety and anti-social behavior in pre-school children." In F. Ivan Nye and L. Hoffman, *The Employed Mother in America.* Chicago: Rand McNally.

Orden, Susan R. and Norman M. Bradburn
1968   "Dimensions of marriage happiness." *American Journal of Sociology 73* (May):715–731.

Orden, Susan R. and Norman M. Bradburn
1969   "Working wives and marriage happiness." *American Journal of Sociology 74* (No. 4) (January):392–407.

Ort, Robert S.
1950   "A study of role conflicts as related to happiness in marriage." *Journal of Abnormal and Social Psychology 45* (October):691–699.

Parsons, Talcott
1943   "The kinship system of the contemporary United States." *American Anthropologist 45* (January–March):22–38.

Parsons, Talcott
1951   *The Social System.* Glencoe, Ill.: Free Press.

Pavela, Todd H.
1964   "An exploratory study of Negro-white intermarriage in Indiana." *Journal of Marriage and the Family 26*:209–211.

Perry, Joseph B., Jr.
1961   "The mother substitute of employed mothers: an exploratory inquiry." *Marriage and Family Living 23* (No. 4):362–367.

Peterson, Evan T.
1958   "The impact of maternal employment on the mother-daughter relationship and on the daughter's role orientation." Unpublished Ph.D. dissertation, University of Michigan.

Peterson, Evan T.
1961   "The impact of maternal employment on the mother-daughter relationship." *Marriage and Family Living 23* (No. 4):353–361.

Phillips, Bernard S.
1966   *Social Research Strategy and Tactics.* New York: Macmillan.

Pineo, Peter C.
1961   "Disenchantment in later years of marriage." *Marriage and Family Living 23*:3–11.

Popenoe, Paul
1938   "A study of 738 elopements." *American Sociological Review 3*:1–4.

Popenoe, Paul
1940   *Modern Marriage.* New York: Macmillan.

Popper, Karl R.
1959   *The Logic of Scientific Discovery.* London: Hutchison & Company, Ltd.

Powell, Kathryn Summers
    1961   "Maternal employment in relation to family life." *Marriage and Family Living* 23 (No. 4):340–349.
Ramsøy, Natalie Rogoff
    1966   "Assortative mating and the structure of cities." *American Sociological Review* 31 (December):773–785.
Rapoport, Robert and Rhonda Rapoport
    1965   "Work and family in contemporary society." *American Sociological Review* 30:384.
Reevy, William R.
    1959   "Premarital petting behavior and marital happiness prediction." *Marriage and Living* 21(November):349–355.
Reiss, Ira L.
    1957   "The treatment of premarital coitus in 'marriage and the family' texts." *Social Problems* 4(No. 4):334–338.
Reiss, Ira L.
    1960   *Premarital Sexual Standard in America*. New York: Free Press of Glencoe.
Reiss, Ira L.
    1961   "Sexual codes in teenage culture." *Annals of the American Academy of Political and Social Science* 338:53–62.
Reiss, Ira L.
    1964   "The scaling of premarital sexual permissiveness." *Journal of Marriage and the Family* 26 (May):188–198.
Reiss, Ira L.
    1965   "Social class and premarital sexual permissiveness: a re-examination." *American Sociological Review* 30:747–756.
Reiss, Ira L.
    1967   *The Social Context of Premarital Sexual Permissiveness*. New York: Holt, Rinehart, and Winston.
Reiss, Paul J.
    1962   "The extended kinship system: correlates of and attitudes on frequency of interaction." *Marriage and Family Living* 24 (November):333–339.
Reynolds, Paul Davidson
    1971   *A Primer in Theory Construction*. New York: Bobbs-Merrill.
Rodman, Hyman
    1961   "Marital relationships in a Trinidad village." *Marriage and Family Living* 23 (No. 2):166–170.
Rodman, Hyman
    1967   "Marital power in France, Greece, Yugoslavia, and the United States: a cross-national discussion." *Journal of Marriage and the Family* 29 (May):320–324.
Rodgers, R. H.
    1962   *Improvements in the Construction and Analysis of Family Life Cycle Categories*. Kalamazoo: Western Michigan University.
Rodgers, Roy H.
    1964   "Toward a theory of family development." *Journal of Marriage and the Family* 26 (No. 3):262–270.
Rogers, Everett M. and Hans Sebald

1962   "Familism, family integration and kinship orientation." *Marriage and Family Living* 24 (No. 1):25–29.

Rose, Arnold M.
1954   *Theory and Method in the Social Sciences.* Minneapolis: Lund Press.

Rose, Arnold M.
1955   "Factors associated with the life satisfaction of middle class, middle-aged persons." *Marriage and Family Living 17* (February):15–19.

Rose, Arnold M.
1962   *Human Behavior and Social Processes.*

Rosenthall, R.
1967   "Covert communication in the psychological experiment." *Psychological Bulletin 67:*356–367.

Rosow, Irving
1957   "Issues in the concept of need-complementarity." *Sociometry 20:*216–233.

Roth, Julius and Robert F. Peck
1951   "Social class and social mobility factors related to marital adjustment." *American Sociological Review 16:*478–487.

Roy, Prodipto
1961   "Maternal employment and adolescent roles: urban differentials." *Marriage and Family Living 23* (No. 4):340–349.

Safilios-Rothschild, Constantina
1970   "The study of family power structure: a review 1960–1969." *Journal of Marriage and the Family 32* (No. 4):539–549.

Scanzoni, John
1965   "Resolution of occupational conjugal role conflict in clergy marriages." *Journal of Marriage and the Family 27:*398.

Schellenberg, J. A. and L. S. Bee
1960   "A re-examination of the theory of complementary needs in mate selection." *Marriage and Family Living 22:*227–232.

Schnepp, Gerald J. and Mary Margaret Johnson
1952   "Do religious background factors have predictive value?" *Marriage and Family Living* XIV (November):301–304.

Schroeder, Clarence W.
1939   "Divorce in a city of 100,000 population." Ph.D. Thesis, University of Chicago, 1938, Private Edition; distributed by Bradley Polytechnic Institution Library, Peoria, Ill.

Selltiz, Claire, et al.
1961   *Research Methods in Social Relations.* Revised Edition. New York: Henry Holt and Company.

Shibutani, Tomotsu
1961   *Society and Personality.* Englewood Cliffs, N.J.: Prentice-Hall.

Siegel, A. E., et al.
1959   "Dependence and independence in the children of working mothers." *Child Development 30:*533;546.

Silverman, William and Reuben Hill
1967   "Task allocation in marriage in the United States and Belgium." *Marriage and the Family 29* (No. 2):353–359.

Simenson, William and Gilbert Geis
    1956   "Courtship patterns of Norwegian and American university stu-
            dents." *Marriage and Family Living 18:*334–338.
Simon, H. A.
    1951   *Models of Men.* New York: John Wiley and Sons.
Simon, Julian L.
    1969   *Basic Research Methods in Social Science.* New York: Random
            House
Simpson, George
    1965   "A Durkheim fragment." *American Journal of Sociology* LXX (No.
            5):527–536.
Sorokin, P. A., et al.
    1931   *A Systematic Sourcebook in Rural Sociology,* Vol. 2. Minneapolis:
            University of Minnesota Press.
Sprey, Jetse
    1970   "On Aldous' 'Strategies for developing family theory'" *Journal of
            Marriage and the Family 32* (No. 4): 496–497.
Stewart, C. M.
    1957   "Future trends in the employment of married women." *British
            Journal of Sociology 12* (No. 4):1–11.
Stinchcombe, Arthur L.
    1968   *Constructing Social Theories.* New York: Harcourt, Brace and
            World.
Stolz, Lois Meek
    1960   "Effects of maternal employment on children: evidence from re-
            search." *Child Devlopment* XXXI (December):749–482.
Stone, Gregory P.
    1962   "Appearance and the self." In Arnold M. Rose, *Human Behavior
            and Social Processes.* Boston: Houghton Mifflin.
Straus, Murray
    1964   "Measuring families." In Harold Christensen's (Ed.), *Handbook of
            Marriage and the Family.* Chicago: Rand McNally.
Straus, Murray
    1964a   "Power and support structure of the family in relation to socializa-
            tion." *Journal of Marriage and the Family* XXVI (Au-
            gust):318–326.
Strauss, Anselm
    1946   "The ideal and chosen mate." *American Journal of Sociology*
            51:204–208.
Strauss, Anselm
    1956   *The Social Psychology of George Herbert Mead.* Chicago: Univer-
            sity of Chicago Press.
Stryker, Sheldon
    1957   "Role-taking accuracy and adjustment." *Sociometry 20:*286–296.
Stryker, Sheldon
    1959   "Symbolic interaction as an approach to family research." *Marriage
            and Family Living 21:*111–119.
Stryker, Sheldon
    1964   "The interactional and situational approaches." In Harold Chris-

tensen (Ed.). *Handbook of Marriage and the Family.* Chicago: Rand McNally.

Stuart, Irving R.
1962 "Complementary vs. homogeneous needs in mate selection: a television program situation." *Journal of Social Psychology* 56:291–300.

Struckert, Robert P.
1963 "Role perception and marital satisfaction—a configurational approach." *Marriage and Family Living* 25 (November):415–419.

Sumner, W. G.
1906 *Folkways: A Study of the Sociological Importance of Usages, Manners, Customs, Mores, and Morals.* New York: Dover Publications, Inc.

Sundal, A. P. and T. C. McCormich
1951 "Age at marriage and mate selection: Madison, Wisconsin 1937–1943." *American Sociological Review 16* (February):37–48.

Sussman, Marvin B.
1961 "Needed research on the employed mother." *Marriage and Family Living 23* (November):368–373.

Sussman, Marvin B. and Lee Burchinal
1962 "Kin family network: unheralded structure in current conceptualizations." *Marriage and Family Living 24* (August): 231–240.

Terman, Lewis M. and Melita H. Oden
1947 *The Gifted Child Grows Up: Twenty-Five Years Follow-up of a Superior Group.* Stanford, Calif.: Stanford University Press.

Terman, Lewis M., et al.
1938 *Psychological Factors in Marital Happiness.* New York: McGraw-Hill.

Tharp, Roland G.
1963 "Psychological patterning in marriage." *Psychological Bulletin 60:*97–117.

Thibaut, J. W. and H. H. Kelley
1959 *The Social Psychology of Groups.* New York: John Wiley and Sons.

Thomas, John L.
1951 "The factor of religion in the selection of marriage mates." *American Sociological Review 16:*487–491.

Udry, J. Richard
1963 "Complementarity in mate selection: a perceptual approach." *Marriage and Family Living 25* (August):281–288.

Udry, J. Richard
1966 *The Social Context of Marriage.* Philadelphia: Lippincott, p. 393–398.

Udry, J. Richard
1968 "Marital instability by race, sex, education, occupation and income, using 1960 census data." In Robert Winch et al., *Selected Studies in Marriage and the Family.* Third Edition. New York: Holt, Rinehart, and Winston.

Vernon, Glenn M.

1960   "Bias in professional publications concerning interfaith marriage." *Religious Education* 55:261–264.

Vernon, Glenn M. and Robert L. Stewart
1957   "Empathy as a process in the dating situation." *American Sociological Review* 22 (No. 1):48–52.

Vincent, Clark E.
1962   *Unmarried Mothers.* New York: Free Press of Glencoe.

Vital Statistics Bulletin
1969   "Divorce statistics analysis: United States, 1964 and 1965." Series 21 (No. 17), Public Health Service, U.S. Department of Health, Education, and Welfare.

Wallen, J. L.
1957   "Mutual value-prediction of husbands and wives." Unpublished Ph.D. Dissertation, Ohio State University.

Waller, Willard
1937   "The rating and dating complex." *American Sociological Review* 2:727–734.

Waller, Willard and R. L. Hill
1951   *The Family: A Dynamic Interpretation.* Revised Edition. New York: Dryden.

Wallin, Paul
1957   "Religiosity, sexual gratification, and marital satisfaction." *American Sociological Review* 22:300–305.

Wallin, Paul and Alexander Clark
1958   "Marital satisfaction and husbands' and wives' perception of similarity in their preferred frequency of coitus." *Journal of Abnormal and Social Psychology* 57:370–373.

Wallin, Paul and Alexander Clark
1963   "A study of orgasm as a condition of women's enjoyment of coitus in the middle years of marriage." *Human Biology* 35:131–139.

Wallin, Paul and Alexander Clark
1964   "Religiosity, sexual gratification and marital satisfaction in the middle years of marriage." *Social Forces* 42:303–309.

Warner, W. Lloyd and Paul S. Lunt
1941   *The Social Life of a Modern Community.* New Haven: Yale University Press.

Weber, M.
1947   *The Theory of Social and Economic Organization.* Glencoe, Ill.: Free Press.

Weeks, H. Ashley
1943   "Differential divorce rates by occupation." *Social Forces* 21:336.

Willer, David and Murray Webster, Jr.
1970   "Theoretical concepts and observables." *American Sociological Review* 35 (August):748–757.

Wilson, Thomas P.
1970   "Conceptions of interaction and forms of sociological explanation." *American Sociological Review* 35 (August):697–707.

Winch, Robert F.
1949   "Courtship in college women." *American Journal of Sociology* 55:269–278.

Winch, Robert F.
 1955 "The theory of complementary needs in mate selection: final re-
    sults on the test of the general hypothesis." *American Sociological
    Review* 20:552–555.
Winch, Robert F.
 1958 *Mate Selection: A Study of Complementary Needs.* New York:
    Harper and Brothers.
Winch, Robert F.
 1963 *The Modern Family.* Revised Edition. New York: Holt, Rinehart,
    and Winston.
Winch, Robert F. and Rae Lesser Blumberg
 1968 "Societal complexity and familial organization. In R. F. Winch and
    L. W. Goodman (Eds.), *Selected Studies in Marriage and the
    Family.* New York: Holt, Rinehart, and Winston.
Winch, Robert F. and Scott Greer
 1968 "Urbanism, ethnicity, and extended familism." *Journal of Marriage
    and the Family* 30:40–45.
Winch, Robert F., Scott Greer, and Rae Lesser Blumberg
 1954 "The theory of complementary needs in mate selection: an analytic
    and descriptive study." *American Sociological Review* 19 (No. 3):
    241–249.
Winch, Robert, et al.
 1967 "Ethnicity and extended familism in an upper-middle-class sub-
    urb" *American Sociological Review* 32 (April):265–272.
Wirth, Louis
 1938 "Urbanism as a way of life." *American Journal of Sociology 44*
    (July):1–24.
Wirth, Louis and Herbert Goldhamer
 1944 "Negro-white marriage in recent times." In Otto Klineberg (Ed.),
    Characteristics of the American Negro. New York: Harper and
    Brothers.
Yarrow, Marian Radke
 1961 "Changes in family functioning as intermediary effects of maternal
    employment." In Alberta Engvall Siegel (Ed.), Research Issues
    Related to the Effects of Maternal Employment on Children. Uni-
    versity Park, Penn.: Social Science Research Center, 14–24.
Yaukey, David
 1969 "On theorizing about fertility." *The American Sociologist 4*
    (May):100–105.
Young, Michael and Peter Willmott
 1957 *Kinship and Family in East London.* Glencoe, Ill.: Free Press.
Zelditch, Morris
 1955 "Role differentiation in the nuclear family." In Talcott Parsons and
    Robert F. Bales (Eds.), *Family, Socialization, and Interaction Pro-
    cess.* Glencoe, Ill.: Free Press.
Zetterberg, Hans L.
 1954 *On Theory and Verification in Sociology.* Almquist and Wiksell.
Zetterberg, Hans L.
 1963 *On Theory and Verification in Sociology.* Second Edition. Totawa,
    N.J.: Bedminster Press.

Zetterberg, Hans L.
  1965   *On Theory and Verification in Sociology.* Third Edition. Totawa, N.J.: Bedminister Press.
Zimmerman, Carle E. and Lucius F. Cervantes
  1960   *Successful American Families.* New York: Pageant.

AUTHOR INDEX

313

TOPIC INDEX